European Governmentality

This book contributes to the literature on the change of governance in the context of its European multilevel organization. The integration of Europe is a process of fundamental social change: a process of constructing a European society and of deconstructing the national societies.

Münch demonstrates that there is a movement away from republican and representative features of a democracy and towards liberal and pluralistic features. The book illustrates this change in the nature of European political regulation, European jurisdiction and the intellectual debates in France, Germany and Britain on legitimizing the emerging system of multilevel governance. He discusses how far the new European regime of liberal governmentality converges with the American type of constitutional liberalism. Following a sociological approach, the book focuses on identifying the causes, features and consequences of the fundamental social change taking place in the process of European integration.

This book will be of interest to scholars and graduate students from political science, sociology, law and philosophy interested in political theory, comparative politics, international relations and political communication, as well as practitioners of policy-making in governments, administration, parties, associations and the media.

Richard Münch is Professor of Sociology at Bamberg University, Germany. He is Associate Editor of the journal *Sociological Theory*. His most recent publications include *Nation and Citizenship in the Global Age* and *The Ethics of Modernity*.

Routledge / UACES Contemporary European Studies
Edited by Federica Bicchi, *London School of Economics and Political Science*, Tanja Börzel, *Free University of Berlin*, and Roger Scully, *University of Wales*, Aberystwyth, on behalf of the *University Association for Contemporary European Studies*

The primary objective of the new Contemporary European Studies series is to provide a research outlet for scholars of European Studies from all disciplines. The series publishes important scholarly works and aims to forge for itself an international reputation.

European Governmentality
The Liberal drift of
multilevel governance

Richard Münch

Routledge
Taylor & Francis Group

LONDON AND NEW YORK

First published 2010
by Routledge
2 Park Square, Milton Park, Abingdon, Oxon, OX14 4RN

Simultaneously published in the USA and Canada
by Routledge
270 Madison Avenue, New York, NY 10016

Routledge is an imprint of the Taylor & Francis Group, an informa business

© 2010 Richard Münch

Typeset in Sabon by Swales & Willis Ltd, Exeter, Devon
Printed and bound in Great Britain by MPG Books Group, UK

British Library Cataloguing in Publication Data
A catalogue record for this book is available
from the British Library

Library of Congress Cataloging in Publication Data
Münch, Richard, 1945-
    European governmentality: the liberal drift of multilevel gover-
    nance / Richard Münch.
    p. cm.—(Routledge/UACES contemporary European studies ; 14)
    Includes bibliographical references and index.
    1. Federal government—European Union countries. 2.
    Liberalism—European Union countries. 3. Law—European Union
    countries. 4. European Union. 5. European Union countries—
    Politics and government. I. Title.
    JN30.M866 2010
    320.44'049—dc22
    2009049407

ISBN: 978–0–415–48581–4 (hbk)
ISBN: 978–0–203–85048–0 (ebk)

Contents

Acknowledgements

This book is based on my more extensive study *Die Konstruktion der europäischen Gesellschaft*, which appeared in German in fall 2008. A shorter version of Chapter 2 was published under the title 'Constructing a European Society by Jurisdiction' in the *European Law Journal* 14 (5), 2008: 519{-}41. When writing the book I profited from collaborating with a number of helpful people. The doctoral program Markets and Social Systems in Europe is mainly an interdisciplinary setting at the University of Bamberg, Germany. The program covers sociology, political science, law, economics and management science and is funded by the German Research Foundation. I am grateful to all the colleagues and students involved in this program for providing such an excellent environment for my research. For their assistance in carrying out this study, I would like to thank especially Céline Morin, Sven Weber and Viola Geberzahn, who contributed reports on the intellectual debates on Europe in France, Germany and Britain, which formed the basis of the chapters on the French, German and British dilemmas of constructing Europe. Brigitte Münzel and Benjamin Wilson helped to translate the chapters from German into English. Brigitte Münzel, Margrit Seuling and Andrea Gehring assisted in the technical production of the book. Many thanks to all of them.

Bamberg, June 2009
Richard Münch

Introduction

The future of democracy within the European Union's system of multilevel governance is a much-debated problem. There is still no solution in sight. While the intellectual debate is searching for a democracy in the multilevel system, which is strongly built along the lines of national representative government, a form of multilevel governance that features strong elements of liberalism is actually evolving. The latter increasingly gets the upper hand of the republican and representative traditions of national government. This is what can be identified as European governmentality in the sense outlined by Foucault (2007, 2008) in his studies on the history of governmentality. Instead of engaging in wishful thinking, a realistic sociological analysis must aim to grasp the main features of that kind of liberal governance, to understand its meaning, to explain why this kind of governance is emerging in Europe and to point out the conflicts that come about with the turn from national representative government to European liberal governance. Within this framework, there is a drift towards the type of liberal democracy.

What is liberal democracy? A few words shall clarify what it means. It lays particular emphasis on checks and balances in order to prevent the uncontrolled exercise of power, including the power of the majority over the minority, and provides strong protection against discrimination. There is less emphasis on representing the common good or Rousseau's *volonté générale* as against the *volonté de tous* in political decision making. Therefore, democratic decision making in the liberal sense does not search for procedures that help to generate and implement the general will of republican citizens or the will of the majority, but it does search for procedures that allow the greatest variety of interest to be articulated in a never-ending process of trial and error. In this perspective, any political decision is but a snapshot of endless bargaining and always entails errors that need to be corrected in further decision making.

Understanding democracy in this way generates a preference for diversity over homogeneity as creative potential for the governance of society, a precedence of civil rights over political and social rights and the private citizen over the public citizen. In institutional terms, the protection of civil rights needs a strong judiciary up to the constitutional court. While a strong representative government intervenes in society on behalf of a better life for the citizens who are unable to do that by themselves, a strong judiciary intervenes in society in order to protect the individual rights, whatever the exercising of these rights might produce in its effects.

Representative republican government tries to coordinate the rights of individuals by law, while liberal government leaves this coordination to litigation in court. Liberalism assumes that the law constrains the private citizens and cannot find out a really optimal harmonization of rights in advance. Therefore, it is more effective for liberal thought to rely on the accordation of rights from day-to-day court litigation. In the republican perspective, society needs a strong government to be productive for the citizens. In the liberal view, society is more productive if it is founded on the activities of free citizens, their voluntary association and self-organization. It is republican to see civil society only arising from a strong republican spirit, which might even need governmental sponsoring and licensing in order to flourish and to be helpful for the citizens. In liberal thinking, civil society is a spontaneous creation of free and private citizens. This is the comparison of liberal democracy to representative republican democracy which we will apply throughout this study. It is the democratic part of liberal governance. Both of them embody the standards of liberal governmentality. The latter is precisely that art of governance which finds the optimal point of coordinating as much individual freedom of action as possible and of allocating as many scarce resources to articulated preferences as possible, according to the economic laws. Liberal governmentality is particularly called for when governance reaches beyond national monopoly of power, territorial rule and disciplinary power over the individual, which is characteristic of multilevel governance beyond the nation state (Foucault 2007, 2008).

In the context of European multilevel governance, the nation state representative democracy will be transformed in the framework of a more varied system of arenas of political decision making (Münch 1998: 363–414). The dominating discourse about the European Union's democracy deficit obstructs, however, a clear assessment of the new realities. It is far too concerned with the transfer of the nation state model of representative democracy onto the European level. A European *demos* (from the Greek term meaning the people who share a common life and form a common political will) is looked for alongside a European public and a European system of associations and parties. Moreover, the establishment of a European government is demanded. It should report both to a parliament endowed with all imaginable rights and to a second chamber issuing from the Council of Ministers (Lepsius 1991; Eriksen and Fossum 2000; Rosamond 2000; Hooghe and Marks 2001; Bache and Flinders 2004).

Nevertheless, national representative democracy has become fictional not only due to the transfer of an ever-increasing amount of competence to Brussels, but also due to structural features at the national level. Even within national representative democracy, political decision making is not focused on one single act of public opinion formation and one single act of legislation by the parliament resulting from public opinion formation. It is only marginally the formation of public welfare that is concerned, especially as there is no homogeneous *demos* (people) that might cover such public welfare. Instead, it is important to include a wide variety of values and interests from a plurality of groupings, depending on the situation, and to convert them into binding decisions. A multistage procedure in a variety of arenas is best suited to accomplish this task, where coalitions and compromises can be worked out in line with the situation. As a matter of fact, the legitimation of such decisions does not result from their realization of a type of public welfare that cannot be defined anyway, but rather from the openness of the procedure and from the fact that all interests, which have not been taken into account, rely on the chances of revising decisions. Confidence in decision making can be maintained if the detailed elaboration of the law is not concentrated on parliamentary decisions and if parliament only sets a frame, which will then be worked out further on in additional procedures through regulation agencies, administrations and courts in open procedures which offer further chances for participation in a great number of single, specified decisions. Moreover, the parliamentary procedure itself can be made more open by going through various committees and subcommittees. This multistage differentiation of a plurality of arenas is most strongly marked in the American governmental system of checks and balances (Jauß 1999; Münch et al. 2001, Chapters V and VI,4).

We also have to recognize that multilevel decision making extends chances of participating and articulating interests beyond the boundaries of national politics. Making use of EU legislation and jurisdiction breaks up limitations of national decision making and establishes new arenas in which political actors can realize interests so far prohibited on the national level because of long-established and hitherto unquestioned traditions and narrow-mindedness. National law is the outcome of a long historical process influenced by well-organized interests. It is supported by vested interests. The transfer of decision making to the European level opens up a new game in which new political actors have chances to exert influence thus far blocked by national coalitions. In this sense, the emerging European multilevel polity has to be understood as an extension of opportunities for political participation and not simply as a limitation of such opportunities when compared to national polities. The multistage character and differentiation of decision-making procedures also involves a disaggregation of interests so that larger conflicts are split up into a variety of smaller conflicts, which are therefore easier to deal with. In doing so, conflicts are removed from ideological debates on principles and are being made accessible to a type of solution which is deliberative in character and oriented to the technical matter in question. There are, therefore, two converging motives that promote the acceptance of decisions: on the one hand, the confidence in the openness of the procedures and the revisability of decisions and on the other hand, the splitting up of conflicts into individual technical questions and decisions, as well as the resulting insight into the technical correctness of solutions. Since, however, not everybody can take part in this procedure and only the advocates of the given range of interests are admitted, the additional trust of those citizens who are not included in the representative participants in these procedures is essential. This not only covers members of the government and members of parliament, but also experts and advocates of the most different types of interest. The participating actors have to rely on a double sort of confidence: first, on the confidence of those interested parties whom they represent, and second, on the confidence of the others in that they carry out their job in recognition of other interests and with a view to the integration of the different interests to form a coherent pattern.

This trend of decision-making processes has increased along with the formation of the level of European decision making. The European Union's noteworthy ability to solve problems relies to a large extent on the multistage character and pluralization of the arenas and the related avoidance of big ideologized conflicts and their splitting into a variety of smaller conflicts with disaggregated interests and a corresponding turn to technical solutions. This can, above all, be observed in the fields of environmental protection, industrial health and safety standards and product safety (Eichener 1996; Joerges and Neyer 1997; Gehring 1998, 2002; Gehring and Krapohl 2007).

A continuation of this trend is the rising significance of subnational units within this process, along with the increasing multistage character and plurality of decision-making processes. Such procedures may solve many little problems, while big problems and conflicts are cut out. As a result, on the one hand, political regulation will lose depth but, on the other hand, it will extend its ability to solve problems in many small, individual steps. Seen from a normative yardstick that is strongly oriented towards the national welfare state, the results of such a regulation practice do not comply with the Pareto optimum and can be attributed to a political entanglement which is far too strong. The results include imprisonment in games involving, out of necessity, a disadvantageous outcome for all actors (Scharpf 1999). One should point out, however, that this yardstick must be called into question in view of the structural prerequisites (Jachtenfuchs 2001).

The matter in question cannot be about a representative democracy of the European Union. Compared to the nation state representative democracy, it will suffer from substantial democratic deficits for an indefinite period. The consequence that has frequently been drawn from this situation, namely the even stricter holding on to national democracy, has to avoid European and, beyond that, global economic entanglements. A national democracy in transnational markets no longer possesses the necessary power of decision making to act on the basis of democratic formation of will. Therefore, there is no other way than promotion of transnational integration and the related transfer of competence to the supranational level. Nevertheless, the structural conditions of the new political unit do not allow for shifting the model of national representative democracy to this unit. It is, therefore, even more essential to attain a realistic assessment of possible forms of democratization of the European decision-making processes. They should in no way be equated with the actual processes. Since decision-making processes are handled more than on the national level individually according to functions and sectors, the formation of public welfare beyond functions and sectors is pushed even further to the background than in the nation-states as against the mere summing up of particular decisions. The preparation and implementation of decisions of committees include experts only and are closed to the public. Moreover, there is frequently a one-sided selection of experts from industry and the established large scientific organizations (comitology). In a representative democracy, it is first and foremost the task of the parliament to counter such trends of functional and sectoral splitting and the rule of experts. Yet, the national parliaments, too, succeed to a very limited degree in playing this role effectively. The representative formation of public welfare, which is thought to be a matter of the parliament, is frequently nothing but a glossed-over padding of a certain constellation of interests and power.

Of course, we should not conclude from the parliament's insufficient fulfilment of its function that we can completely do without such an organ. A badly functioning parliament is better than none at all. When forming democratic decision-making processes, however, we cannot rely exclusively on the parliament's representative function; it can only be one body in a system of multiple controls, as can be found most strikingly in the United States. Therefore, a democratization of decision-making processes prior to and after parliamentary deliberation has dealt with them is even more important, which means that they should be made accessible to a wider range of interests and expert views. The less structural heterogeneity allows to determine public welfare, the more important criteria such as the openness of procedures, their multistage character, their transparency, the revisability of decisions, the subsidiarity of levels of decision making and the wealth of arenas and partial publics will be. This even goes for the parliament, which will consequently have to work more actively than before in a variety of competing committees and subcommittees – as has been achieved most markedly in the United States – so that the plenum loses some of its integrative power. We may certainly opt for a strengthening of the plenum, yet this cannot be more than a counterweight to the unavoidable differentiation of committee work (Axford and Huggins 1999).

A strengthening of the European Parliament, and above all of the plenary debates, might also be most desirable for the European decision-making processes. Yet, this can be but one element within a complex process that can no longer be reduced to the one single function of the representative formation of opinion and will with a European system of parties and associations and a European public. Similarly, the strategy of a stronger participation of national parliaments in EU decisions is not sufficient either. It is likewise restricted and but a minor element within the complex process. If it gained too much significance, either the governments' latitude of action would be limited so much that nothing would be decided on a European level anymore or the national parliaments and/or their representatives in consultations would lose their independence from the governments and would be reduced to mere instruments of legitimation procurement. It is therefore better to limit the role of national parliaments to public discussion of major European questions.

In this context, we have to take into account the structural change of social integration, which is occurring in the process of Europeanization. By Europeanization, we mean first and foremost a process of changing solidarity fuelled by the logic of single market integration, which pushes back national solidarities and makes transnational solidarities inch forward. This process can be regarded as creative destruction in Schumpeter's sense. It is being advanced by the modernization elites, which form transnational networks and, at the same time, work towards loosening national bonds. The positive side of this development is attaining much farther-reaching integration. Its negative side is the dissolution of national welfare coalitions that have to give way to a stronger differentiation of solidarity relationships. For a transitional period at least, anomic conditions, social conflicts and nationalistic counter-movements will grow. The new structure of farther-reaching, more widely branched and more differentiated solidarity relationships means a new boost to the formation of network solidarity and a weakening of mechanical solidarity accompanied by a notion of justice in the sense of equal standards of living. Exclusive unity and the justice of equal standards of living in the national collective are being replaced with open networks of individual relationships and justice as fairness. The stepping back of the state's regulation of society through legislation will then require compensation by the legal protection of individual rights and an active civil society. Neither its transfer to the European level nor a stronger link between the European decision-making processes and the national parliaments can compensate for the loss of nation state representative democracy. What is needed instead is the greater weight of elements from liberal competition democracy on several levels. This type of democracy cannot be measured by the yardstick of representative definition of 'public welfare' that has long become a fiction, but rather by the yardstick of openness, transparency, revisability and the multistage character and subsidiarity of decision-making processes.

The process of Europeanization is part of a far more comprehensive, farther-reaching process of globalization. On the one hand, it has an opening effect which is similar to globalization with regard to national collective solidarities but, on the other hand, it has a closing effect by setting certain limits to transnational entanglement. This means that network solidarity is embedded into a more differentiated and weaker mechanical and organic solidarity. The network solidarity resulting from the transnational division of labour beyond the boundaries of Europe sets limits to European collective solidarity in the long run. A strong social integration of Europe, similar to that of the

European welfare states, would be an obstacle on the way towards a more comprehensive social integration of the world society.

The debate about European integration leaves no doubt about the fact that this is, above all, a process dominated by the establishment of the single market and the granting of free competition within this market. Wondering how market integration can be complemented with political and legal integration, we have to expect that this integration cannot follow the pattern of the European welfare states' nation state integration due to the completely different structural prerequisites. Welfare state integration and a comprehensive guarantee of equal standards of living for all depend on a level of structural homogeneity and 'mechanical solidarity' (Durkheim 1964) that cannot be accomplished on a supranational, European level in the foreseeable future. Both the extent and depth of intervention in the regulation of society on the part of the European Union cannot attain the level of the highly developed European welfare states. To the degree politics restrains itself from the regulation of society through legislation, the citizens are given a wider range of opportunities for their autonomous formation of life. This autonomy finds them more frequently involved in conflicts about the reach of their rights, and not all can exploit their rights in the same way. Accordingly, as compared to legislation, the courts play a more important role in social integration through conflict settlement and the guaranteeing of legal equality, equal opportunities and fairness.

The transfer of social integration from legislation to jurisdiction can be excellently observed with the example of the United States. There, the courts contribute an essential part to social integration through jurisdiction, which is carried out by legislation and corresponding interventions in society in the European welfare states. Social integration through jurisdiction without a comprehensive system of social welfare law aims at the coordination of subjective rights guaranteed by the constitution. This means, above all, struggle against discrimination. The most striking example is the contribution made by the courts – and ultimately the Supreme Court – in the United States to reducing discrimination of, first of all, Black Americans, and, subsequently, a number of other minorities and women. In the United States, integration through jurisdiction means, above all, reducing obstacles and corresponding unequal opportunities to carry out individual rights. If we look at the situation of the European Union, we will witness a similar development. With the turn of integration policies from complete legal harmonization to the principle of mutual acknowledgement of product standards, the European Court of Justice (ECJ) has been given an even stronger role in the integration process (Dehousse 1998; Maduro 1998; Weiler 1999). The logic of this integration achievement goes towards the dismantling of barriers which hinder market access through discriminating national regulations. As a result of the European Union's comparatively low activity in social policy, the ECJ also plays a major role in this field of politics. Of course, the corresponding integration service of the ECJ cannot consist in granting collective security, but it is exclusively focused on protecting individual rights against discrimination. Consequently, the decisions of the ECJ in the field of social security lead, for instance, towards reducing discriminatory obstacles to the mobility of workforce by granting them – through court ruling – the claims to insurance payments outside their home country and giving them access to insurance payments in their country of residence.

The formation of a 'court democracy', which Tocqueville already observed in the United States, of course has positive and negative aspects (Tocqueville 1945, vol. 1: 48). A positive side is granting citizens a wider range of freedom to act. Conflicts regarding the carrying out of their rights are settled afresh over and over again in each case so that a comparatively flexible type of social integration will result. A negative side is that only those interests which are supported by wealthy backgrounds and by good lawyers are taken into account. We cannot claim, however, that social integration granted by the European welfare state's general legislation has a more inclusive character in any case. The neocorporatist arrangement of the preparation of legislation leads to privileging majority interests over minority interests, such as those of immigrants, unemployed people and environmentalists. In contrast, the United States' powerful legal system is an important tool for protecting minorities against the majority. Of course, the courts can never bear the full load of social integration. To the extent that the state restrains from the regulation of society, they become, however, more important in completing this job. Yet, they can only carry out this task in their own way, namely by ensuring legal equality, procedural justice and fairness.

In Europe, a new shape of democracy appears in the context of the emerging system of multilevel governance of the European Union. This system of multilevel governance weakens the traditional actors that have dominated the national policy fields thus far: parliaments, parties and associations. It strengthens new actors that have already begun to dominate the transnational policy fields: the EU administration, regulatory committees, the ECJ, lawyers, scientific experts and lobbyists. This transformation of governance has an enormous impact on the shape of democracy: it changes from representation to liberal pluralism and it is increasingly captured by the laws of scientific governance, lobbyism and media communication. We will study this transformation of democracy throughout this book. Chapter 1 will deal with the growth, nature and legitimacy of European political regulation and its trend towards the American adversarial model. Chapter 2 will focus on the construction of a liberal society of empowered individuals by the jurisdiction of the ECJ. Chapters 3, 4 and 5 will look into the conflict between national traditions of understanding democracy and law and the emergence of a European regime of liberal democracy. We will consider the French dilemma of a European Union undermining the institutions of political republicanism while promoting economic liberalism, the German dilemma of a European Union searching in vain for constitutional patriotism while disrespecting the sovereignty of the people and the British dilemma of a European Union establishing supranational power while abolishing national parliamentary sovereignty. The conclusion will discuss the question of how far the emerging European regime of liberal democracy is approaching the model of constitutional liberalism as it is paradigmatically represented by the United States of America.

We will deal with fundamental dilemmas of multilevel governance that trouble the construction of Europe throughout the Union, not only in France, Germany and Britain. Also, the dilemmas identified as French, German and British are of a general nature and are equally relevant in the other countries, that is the French one in Germany and Britain, the German one in France and Britain and the British one in France and Germany. They are, however, rooted in intellectual tradtions that are particularly strong in the countries to which they have been ascribed. This is why we identify specific dilemmas in the French, German and British intellectual debates on Europe, though they are of a general and ubiquitous nature. Focusing on the intellectual debate on Europe means that we try to uncover the semantics of constructing a legitimate order of the emerging European multilevel society. As we will see, the intellectual traditions in France, Germany and Britain have created specific semantics for dealing with constructing a legitimate order of society. In France it is the semantics of republicanism, in Germany it is the semantics of legalism and in Britain it is the semantics of conventional liberalism. Each of them regards state, government and society in a unique way and each poses specific problems when it comes to constructing a legitimate order of the European Union. A semantics of this kind entails a vocabulary and mode of looking at and speaking about the social world. Practising such a semantics means that we see the world in a certain way, discover problems and find solutions. Certainly, the semantics itself is continuously reconstructed in this practice so that the vocabulary changes more or less comprehensively and deeply. Thus, debating about Europe contributes itself to recreating the semantics of republicanism, legalism and conventional liberalism, raising them beyond their original national context.

In the conclusion we will look at the semantics of constitutional liberalism as it originated in the United States. The crucial question of this section is whether or not the semantics of constitutional liberalism complies better with the structural conditions of the emerging multilevel society in Europe than the other semantics. The question is also whether or not it is promoted by these conditions to establish itself as the semantics that is increasingly being used when the legitimacy of European governance is at stake. Speaking of constitutional liberalism, we again refer to an intellectual tradition that has emerged and has been embodied in the institutions of governance in one country – the United States – in an exemplary way, though the intellectual tradition and its institutional embodiment is of a universal nature and in some respects present in every modern society. Referring to the United States, however, helps to understand the features of this tradition and its institutional embodiment better than when referring to any other country.

Carrying out this program, this book will aim to understand and explain European integration in its basic causes, features and consequences from a sociological perspective. This perspective conceives of European integration as a broad and deep transformation of society on the way from a system of national societies towards a multilevel society with multiple solidarities, multiple identities, multiple arenas of governance and multiple reference points of legitimizing the emerging order of society. Unlike intergovernmentalism, we are not only interested in the forces driving European integration, for example the interests of national governments, their relative power and the outcome of their negotiations (Moravcsik 1998). Unlike neofunctionalism not only in the functional dynamics of cross-border trade and its spillover to legal and political integration (Haas 1958; Stone Sweet 2004). Unlike constructivism not only in the construction of European institutions as an outcome of intellectual struggles (Delanty 1995; Jachtenfuchs 2002). Our focus reaches beyond these more technical questions which dominate political science research on European integration. Going beyond these more technical questions, our interest is focused on the transformative power of European integration in deconstructing the old system of national societies and constructing a new multilevel society with a new structure of governance, solidarity and identity, which are closely linked with each other. With this focus on the transformative power of European integration in the broad sense of constructing a new society, we join the growing attempts to let sociology contribute to the broad field of research on the integration and transformation of Europe (see e.g. Therborn 1995; Crouch 1999; Beck and Grande 2004; Delanty and Rumford 2005; Gerhards 2005; Trenz 2005; Vobruba 2005; Bach 2008; Fligstein 2008; Haller 2008; Outhwaite 2008). We continue in this attempt along the lines set in earlier works (Münch 1993b, 2001b).

1 European regulation
Towards an adversarial process

In this chapter we explore the features of political regulation as political decision making transcends national boundaries and is carried out on different interrelated levels and in a multiplicity of arenas (Kohler-Koch 1998, 2000; Majone 2005). The first section deals with the growth of EU regulation against the background of national models of regulation. The second section explains this change with the example of regulatory politics and includes an assessment of three accounts dealing with the problem of legitimacy: Majone's (1996) fiduciary legitimacy, Joerges's and Neyer's (1997) deliberative legitimacy and Gehring's (2002) two-step legitimacy of consent under the veil of ignorance on the level of politics and consent on the best argument on the level of norm setting.

The growth of European regulation

The more demanding European harmonization efforts have become in the standardization of all trade restricting regulations in the member countries, the more difficult the merely systematic work of adjusting the standardization catalogues of the individual countries has proved to be in areas of food law, consumer protection, environmental protection, workplace health and safety standards or product safety. Therefore, in its White Book on the accomplishment of the single market, the EU Commission initiated a turn in its harmonization policy from the continuous standardization of legal regulations towards the mutual acknowledgement of regulations which apply in a product's country of origin. The standards of a product's country of origin have to be acknowledged in all other EU member states so that there will be no limits to free goods flow arising from different norms (European Commission 1985). A regulation on a union-wide level should only be made in as far as it is required by the protection of health, environment and other important legally protected rights. The EU regulation may restrict itself to setting basic requirements and leave the purely technical standardization procedures to the European standardization committees – the European Committee for Standardization (CEN) and the European Committee for Electro-Technical Standards (CENELEC) – in the framework of EU

procedural guidelines, to the various member states and their national standardization bodies in the framework of EU minimum requirements or to the
various manufacturers in the framework of their product liability. As an
example of the limitation of European regulation policy to the formulation of
fundamental requirements, we might take the directive on simple pressure
containers. It only outlines fundamental safety requirements, such as, for
example, the maximum pressure the containers have to withstand, and
ascribes the conversion of the directive on European product norms to the
European standardization organizations.

The way towards liberalization and decentralization of norm setting
according to the principle of country of origin had been shown by the ECJ's
judgements in the *Dassonville* (C-8/74) and *Cassis de Dijon* (C-120/78) cases
in 1974 and 1979 according to Articles 28 and 30 of the EC Treaty (ECJ
1974, 1979). In line with the *Cassis de Dijon* judgement referring to the sale
of French blackcurrant liqueur in Germany, only those statutory orders that
correspond to urgent requirements are allowed to restrict the free goods flow
as guaranteed in Art. 28 ECT. In addition to this, it is ruled that no positive
harmonization is required. The subsequent judgements on beer purity regulations in 1987 (ECJ 1987), the quality of flour used in the production of
pasta in 1988 (ECJ 1988) and meat products in 1989 (ECJ 1989) continued
that way. So far, German brewers have instituted proceedings aiming to use
their purity regulations from 1516, which stipulate that only barley malt,
hops, yeast and water are allowed to be used for the brewing of beer, to ban
the import of other types of beer produced, for instance, with rice or corn
starch, in vain. Italian pasta manufacturers did not succeed in preventing the
import of German pasta, which is not produced from semolina according to
the Italian formula, but rather from wheat flour, into Italy. In both cases, the
ECJ assumed that the differing recipes would present no danger to the health
of consumers, so preference should be given to the free goods flow. The court
ruled that an appropriate labelling of the products to make the consumers
aware and enable them to make a free choice from the goods being supplied
would suffice. From an economic viewpoint, this policy of regulative competition is welcomed as a means to promote product competition and arrive at
more sovereignty on the part of the consumers. The assessment of product
safety is then shifted some way to the consumer's side (Joerges 1991:
253–55).

The goal of accelerating the single market's integration has been achieved
with the new harmonization policy. EU harmonization has advanced more
successfully. Yet, the new harmonization policy has also less positive side
effects. Along with the growing mobilization of environmental and consumer
protection organizations, regulative competition in the framework of the
European single market tightens conflicts on appropriate regulatory measures in the individual states. It arouses the interest of national industries being
subjected to the same obligations everywhere to stand up in competition with
foreign rivals. As a result of this policy, a competition for the lowest possible

national obligations could be fostered (Scharpf 1990: 34–38). German industry, for instance, struggled aggressively against the stranglehold in terms of environmental and safety policies.

Individual states may gain locational advantages from establishing weaker obligations, but as soon as this competition produces risks of being put on the agenda of public discussion by alarmed consumer and environmental protection organizations, a need to raise minimum standards on the EU level or to establish new standards will arise. In that case, specific national industrial interests will collide on the EU level. The admission of all national standards to meet minimum norms was therefore an elegant and quickly achievable solution at short notice. However, it only postponed conflicts between the industry's interests and consumer or environmental protection, as well as conflicts between specific national industrial interests. Following the population's increased scepticism of the further development of a European Political Union, politicians are readily castigating the Eurocrats' regulatory obsession by promising less centralism, more subsidiarity, less bureaucratic regulation and more closeness to the citizens in order to make the ailing EU train roll again. Whether or not this promise can be fulfilled and irrespective of its consequences, one problem remains unsolved: It is not exactly determined in how far the single market requires European regulation, social, product safety and environmental policies so as to allow for a well arranged economic flow and keep the latter's external negative effects under tight control. Referring to the permissible curvature of cucumbers as an example of EU regulation, one has not yet disproved that the market dynamics, which grow tremendously along with the single market, will require similarly growing political control so that the regulatory requirements on the EU level will increase in spite of all promises of politicians looking for popular support. The democratization of European politics, in the interest of bridging the gap to the citizens, will increase regulatory needs in view of the number of articulated interests growing along with it. If subsidiarity meant competition of norm systems, there would be unlimited deregulation of the market. This would leave us unprotected from enormously growing strains, risks and impairments of unhindered economic growth. The call for EU controls has therefore become louder and has involved a wave of regulations.

The new harmonization policy has initiated comprehensive norm-setting activities on the level of the European Union. In fact, the European Union has demonstrated surprising activities in regulating the single market (Eichener 1996, 1997) under the leadership of the energetic EU Commission as a political entrepreneur since the mid-1980s, despite prevailing scepticism. In this context, the Commission could rely upon the obligation to a high protective level, which has been stipulated in the EC Treaty with the Single European Act. Its biggest success has been the passing of a common directive on workplace health and safety standards, which goes, according to experts, beyond the level so far given in all member states. This achievement can be explained by the Commission's determined leadership, the application of qualified majority decision, the greater influence of technical experts from the highly developed countries and the majority of technical experts in the consulting bodies. Ministers from the same sector are among themselves in the Council of Ministers and do not have to struggle with ministers from other departments; this procedure helps to raise the Council's decision-making power. Another positive contribution is made by the permanent raising of technical standards through scientific, technical innovations and moral discourses, pushing any new norm setting to a higher level than before. Furthermore, the historic limited relevance of EU legislation to public discussion allows for concentration on technical solutions without being subjected to vanities, constraints of self-presentation, self-blockades through public statements and mobilization of voters (Eichener 1997). Nevertheless, along with the growing success in norm setting, the problems are transferred to the level of norm implementation, as we will see later.

The Commission's Green Book of 1990 set the ambitious goal for the EU to achieve a transfer of the norm-setting procedures to the European level in the interest of single market integration and a European certification system for the admission of products. The members of the standardization commission are requested to turn away from national interests and adopt a European viewpoint. By way of precise directives covering detailed regulations on the issuing of certificates, the issuing practice, which is decentralized and shifted to the member states, is expected to produce uniform results (Joerges 1991: 246–47).

The legal regulation of the transnational space established by the European Union has expanded steadily, and even enormously, since the establishment of the European Single Act in 1986. This growth of European law has provoked new explanations of European integration. They draw on Ernst B. Haas's (1958) neofunctionalist approach, which explains legal and political integration as a functionally necessitated spillover effect from international trade to transnational legal regulation and political decision making promoted by transnational actors and supranational organizations. Stone Sweet, Sandholtz, Caporaso, Fligstein and others (Sandholtz and Stone Sweet 1998) have launched a renewal of neofunctionalist thought against the approach of intergovernmentalism as it is represented most powerfully by Moravcsik (1993). Intergovernmentalism explains advances in and the direction of European integration exclusively by the interests of bargaining national governments and the power they can exert in the bargaining process. Stone Sweet, Sandholtz, Caporaso, Fligstein and others do not completely deny the existence of intergovernmental bargaining, but they argue that it has become increasingly embedded in a framework constituted by three components: (1) supranational organizations, (2) supranational rules and (3) transnational society. Within this framework European politics varies between the two extremes of intergovernmental politics and supranational politics. Supranational organizations, supranational rules and transnational society grow in closely linked relation with each other and spillover effects transfer from one component to another. According to a study carried out by Stone Sweet and Caporaso (1998) growing intra-EU trade precipitated increasing references of national courts to the ECJ to obtain preliminary decisions on the application of European law according to Art. 234 [177] of the Treaty of Rome. Individual citizens or companies have increasingly taken advantage of rights established by European law, which they believe are violated by national regulations. Most important was the early establishment of the principle of primacy of EU law over national law by the ECJ in its *Costa* (C-6/64) and *Simmenthal* (C-106/77) decisions, and of the principle of direct effect, which immediately confers legal rights on individuals to be respected by any public authority in the *Van Gend en Loos* (C-26/62) decision. Additionally, the *Dassonville* (C-8/74) and *Cassis de Dijon* (C-120/78) cases were of great importance for the removal of national barriers to intra-EU trade.

There are strong and significant correlations between the number of references issued by the courts of a single country and that country's share in interstate trade, between the growth of references to the ECJ and between intra-EU trade growth and EU-legislation growth (Stone Sweet and Caporaso 1998). Similar accounts exist for the correlation between trade growth and the extension of EU activities in terms of budget, personnel and areas of regulation (Fligstein and McNichol 1998), as well as EU legislation (Fligstein and Stone Sweet 2002). According to the neofunctionalist explanation, the Treaty of Rome paved the way for increasing transnational trade and established supranational organizations, which took up responsibility for removing barriers to transnational trade and served as agents addressed by individual citizens, companies and lobbying groups seeking the realization of rights and interests by transnational law. Being addressed as responsible supranational organizations, the ECJ and the Commission, in particular, advanced EU jurisdiction and legislation, even against the resistance of individual member states. Increasing jurisdiction and legislation contributed to the further growth of intra-EU trade from which, again, further demands for EU jurisdiction and legislation resulted. In this process, trade and legal regulation push each other towards steady growth. The process has its own dynamic and has overcome member state resistance quite often. This supports the neofunctionalist account and contradicts the basic assumption of the purely intergovernmentalist perspective (see Figures 1.1 and 1.2).

For a deeper understanding and explanation of the political and legal transformation taking place in the evolution of a new multilevel society it is, however, insufficient to only give an account of the quantitative growth of EU jurisdiction and legislation. We also have to assess the structure of decision making and the character of legal regulation, which emerge in this process. The question arises as to what kind of democracy and what kind of legitimacy of EU law is going to be established. Various ideas compete with each other in this respect. We therefore have to examine their viability (Joerges and Vos 1999; Pollack 2003; Héritier 2003; Wiener and Diez 2004).

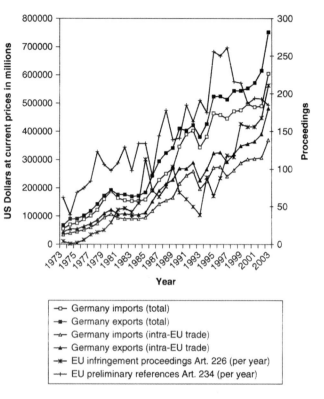

Figure 1.1 Imports/exports and number of proceedings per year

The nature and legitimacy of European regulation

The EU's regulatory activity, which is first and foremost a standardization process, is handled by a wealth of committees. Experts from the administrations of the individual states, the industrial associations and the technical standardization bodies cooperate with the EU's administrative experts. So far, a sort of sectoral EU corporatism has developed (Joerges 1991: 256–57). It has long been dominated by technical experts from industrial associations and technical standardization bodies. This situation has changed somewhat, as associations for the protection of the environment and consumers have become more active on the EU level (Lahusen and Jauß 2001). The European Commission itself has recognized that pluralizing the standardization procedures became urgent in the early 1990s: 'Other interested groups such as consumers, users and workforce must likewise be prepared to be better organized in order to be able to participate in the European standardization process.' (European Commission 1990: 33; quoted in Joerges 1991: 257; see also Eichener 1997; Joerges and Vos 1999; Héritier 2003).

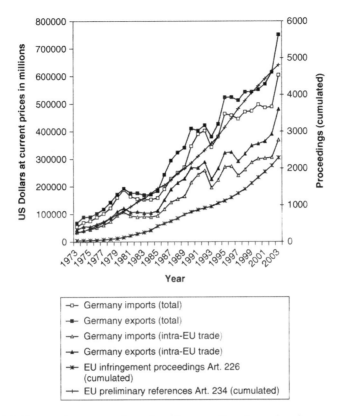

Figure 1.2 Imports/exports and number of proceedings (cumulated)

Source imports/exports: Germany = until 1990 without GDR; United Nations Conference on Trade and Development (UNCTAD), Statistical databases online, UNCTAD Handbook of Statistics 2008. http://stats.unctad.org/Handbook/ReportFolders/reportFolders.aspx

Source infringement proceedings: Integrated Project on New Modes of Governance (coordinated by the European University Institute and its Robert Schumann Centre for Advanced Studies), Legal Task Force Team II – Litigating EU-Law, Alec Stone Sweet and Thomas L. Brunell, The European Court and Enforcement Actions: Data Set on Infringement Proceedings (Art. 226), 1958–2005.

Source preliminary reference procedures: Integrated Project on New Modes of Governance (coordinated by the European University Institute and its Robert Schumann Centre for Advanced Studies), Legal Task Force Team II – Litigating EU-Law, Alec Stone Sweet and Thomas L. Brunell, The European Court and National Courts: Data Set on Preliminary References in EC Law (Art. 234), 1961–2006.

The establishment of European regulatory agencies, such as the European Medicines Agency (EMEA) and the European Food Safety Agency (AFSA), favours the pluralization of the norm-setting process if these agencies are not regarded as authorities that administer the consensus of experts, but follow the US model (Kelemen 2003; Kotzian 2003; Gehring and Krapohl 2007; Ansell and Vogel 2006; Krapohl 2004, 2007). According to this model, the EU has to establish agencies charged with setting technical norms for certain areas of product safety or environmental protection and deciding on the admission of products according to such norms, while taking interest groups affected into account. In the United States, extremely controversial risk assessments face each other in the regulatory activities of such agencies. Experts from industry, organizations protecting consumers and environment, experts from various national research institutions and the agencies themselves tackle negotiations with very different goals and risk definitions in mind (Jauß 1999; Münch et al. 2001). In this pluralistic system, technical norm setting does not result from the consensus of experts fed by objective truth, but rather from a conflict-laden process of bargaining. The process of product admission follows the same path. The controversial bargaining of norm setting and certificates often does not end with the agencies' decisions; it is pursued in just as controversially-led court proceedings since the defeated parties frequently appeal to the courts in order to have the tables turned a little bit in their own favour.

The norm-setting and certification agencies on the part of the EU do not directly mirror this pluralistic and controversial form of norm setting; a different scientific culture which has not yet fully abandoned its belief in the objective judgement of experts prevails. Consequently, the European authorities only act as consultants and coordinators (Joerges 1993: 25). Technical norm setting is considered a matter of experts, who will consent on objectively correct judgements based on scientific evidence (Wolf 1991). The more, however, participants representing a plurality of groups enter expert commissions, the more this belief will crumble in the course of discussions on threshold values and risk assessment. They lose all splendour of objectivity and are trapped in political conflicts, which are settled by the mobilization of power and not by invoking arguments. As we see, the stipulation of threshold values on people's resilience and the assessment of risks depend on the priority given to the need for protection and safety or to the economic need for growth. The stipulation of threshold values and the assessment of risks vary strongly, depending on the attention given to these goals in the wake of controversial opinions discussed in public.

The idea that norm-setting agencies carry out their tasks as a purely scientific, technical job more or less on behalf of the legitimate political organs (i.e. parliament or government, the EU and the Council of Ministers) as put forward by Giandomenico Majone (1996, 2001) has to be questioned in the light of arguments, which point to the inherent political nature of norm setting. The gap between scientific evidence on some causal relations and the decision on thresholds beyond which some substance would negatively affect a human being's health cannot be closed by logical inference from that causal relationship; it needs additional balancing of affected preferences, mostly cost versus health. In as much as engineers decide about a technique according to the principle of the best available technical means without excessive costs, they presume to be arbiters weighing two conflicting preferences. The resolution of such a conflict is, however, inherently political in nature because politics is exactly about collectively resolving collective conflicts. Whenever such decisions are taken by technical experts behind closed doors there is the danger of a hidden bias in decision making; this might provoke general mistrust in as much as such a (mostly pro-industry) bias is revealed after some time. Hidden decision making of this kind provokes basic criticism of its non-constitutional character and calls for attempts at controlling uncontrolled bodies of technical decision making (Bach 1992, 1999; Eberlein and Grande 2005).

According to Majone, EU decision making is of a largely technical and regulative nature and of a much less distributive nature. It is therefore much easier to leave this type of regulative decision making to scientists and technical experts. The legitimacy of their decisions is of a fiduciary character in Majone's eyes. In a fiduciary relationship a trustor hands responsibility with regard to a specific problem area (e.g. health, environmental protection, product safety, etc.) over to a trustee who has better knowledge than the trustor. The trustee then decides on behalf of the trustor. For Majone, such a fiduciary model would help to solve a major problem in modern politics, namely the conflict between long-term and short-term interests, and the corresponding time inconsistency between long-term interests and democratic politics inclined to serve primarily short-term interests, because political representatives have to win a majority of votes within the relatively short time period from one election to the next election. With growing complexity of problems and divergence of interests, policy making is in danger of slipping from here to there and back to here without any ability of long-term orientation. The fiduciary responsibility of scientists and technical experts would implant such an ability of long-term orientation in the polity (Majone 2001).

Majone's fiduciary model represents classical conservative criticism of democracy, as was launched by Edmund Burke (1790/1993) in his critique of the French Revolution or by Alexis de Tocqueville (1945) in his *Democracy in America*. Objecting to Majone's model, we have to point to the political nature of seemingly 'technical' norm setting, which is underestimated by Majone. Correspondingly, he overestimates the ability of technical experts to define what should be in the long-term interest of the people. Because of the political nature of norm setting, such assessments are heavily dependent on the political climate. It is therefore very common that substances or procedures are defined as too risky in a political climate of risk aversion, but they have not been assessed in such a way since before the change of the political climate. This obvious dependence of risk assessment on political climate undermines the functioning of Majone's fiduciary model. It simply cannot provide the legitimacy expected from such a procedure. It rather implies upheavals of protest from time to time when some bias and too little protection against risks are being criticized in cases of extraordinary failing in damage prevention. In such cases, a lack of transparent technical decision making is repeatedly criticized. It would therefore be more realistic to acknowledge technical norm setting as an area of political dispute to make hidden subpolitics an open forum of politics (Beck 1986). A realistic answer to the question of control is therefore the pluralization of decision-making procedures through the inclusion of participants from all affected groups. According to the American understanding, it is itself a form of mutual control of experts (cf. Schneider 1985; Brickmann, Jasanoff and Ilgen 1985: 174–80, 187–217; Jauß 1999). In addition to this, control is guaranteed by the experts obliged to report to and held responsible by Congress. Both forms of control result in the conversion of the norm-setting procedures from an objectively valid consensus of experts to a scientific controversy between experts and to a political controversy between interested parties. As Martin Shapiro (2001) has demonstrated, EU regulation has indeed come closer to the American adversarial model, requiring greater transparency and participation of affected interest groups. This change has been promoted by judgements of the Court of First Instance (CFI) and the ECJ.

The increasing number of infringement proceedings proves that the Union's increasing regulatory activities have also implied growing conflicts. Since the end of the 1970s, the EU has been confronted with a tremendous increase in infringement proceedings, according to Community law (see Figures 1.1 and 1.2). Without a doubt, a more active policy of implementation on the part of the EU Commission has led to the more frequent application of infringement proceedings. In addition to this, a steady increase in the number of regulations, directives and decisions has contributed to increasing the number of infringement proceedings. It would, however, be wrong to infer a more efficient accomplishment of EU law from this increase in infringements. In reality, the number of noncompliance cases seems to reflect only a small part of the actual deficit in implementation. The number of non-compliance cases indicated and/or established by the Commission alone is, in some years, twice as high as the number of proceedings formally instituted in the form of a letter of request (sent by the Commission to the member state in question and asking for a statement on the indicated case of noncompliance). The southern European countries, in particular, frequently lack the administrative staff and technical prerequisites necessary to guarantee a strict implementation and application of EU law. However, countries which are better equipped in this context often tend to believe that their own law and administrative practice offers an appropriate conversion of EU law or is even better than EU law.

According to a study by Padoa-Schioppa et al., on the one hand, the practice of mutual acknowledgement of standards and the establishment of a first court at the ECJ has helped to tone down the situation. On the other hand, the expansion of legislation and the increasing application of the majority principle has involved a further aggravation of the matter. Successful legislation is counteracted by substantial implementation deficits:

On the other hand, solely the number of legislative measures required by the White Paper will inevitably enhance the problem of compliance. The more frequent application of the majority decision is certainly an unavoidable step towards facilitating the legislative process, but – to a certain extent – might involve even greater problems in those countries that have been overruled in the Council. According to the judgement of some experts on the Community's legal system, the institutional problems are much more related with abiding by the law than with legislation itself.

Padoa-Schioppa et al. 1988: 67–68.

Referring to the previous practice of consensual decision making in the EU, this phenomenon has been described as a paradox of compliance with the law (Krislov, Ehlermann and Weiler 1985: 59–88). The individual states tend to meet their obligations to implement and apply the law upon which they had agreed in legislation increasingly less. One main reason for this phenomenon is the growing frustration in regards to consensus formation and the practice of accepting compromises without national interests having enjoyed sufficient consideration. Denmark, for instance, is considered a tough negotiator in the game, but it is said to be reliable in obeying the law. Italy, in contrast, is seen as generous in negotiations, but it cannot be relied upon when it comes to abiding by the law. In Denmark, the national parliament and the national authorities are more strongly involved in EU negotiations than in other countries. On the one hand, their influence makes sure that national interests are taken into account in EU legislation. On the other hand, it guarantees a reliable implementation of EU laws in their own country. This experience favours a stronger inclusion of national parliaments and authorities in EU negotiations. Certainly, consensus formation is being slowed down by their participation, yet they ensure a smoother implementation of EU law without too great a devaluation taking place in the form of delays, deviations, blurs and resistance.

The implementation of EU law in the different member states is made even more difficult by the fact that the EU does not have its own executive power. The EU depends on the cooperation of the individual states and their administration (Snyder 1993). Therefore, EU law may easily fail as a consequence of open or hidden resistance in the individual states or it may get stuck in the jungle of national legal and administrative traditions and administrative policies (Falkner et al. 2005). EU guidelines are then delayed, blurred and adjusted to national traditions beyond recognition; they are incorporated into national law and are applied in a way that was not intended originally. Whereas individual countries showing a particular interest in one or another guideline may convert the law in an exemplary manner, others, which adopted them only reluctantly, may rob them of their meaning beyond recognition. This is demonstrated, for instance, by the conversion of the EU guideline on environmental compatibility of 27 June 1985. The Netherlands, for example, tried to transfer the guideline as precisely as possible by passing a new law. Nevertheless, they set their application level so high that the agricultural sector, including mass livestock farming, is generally exempted from this measure. Italy, Spain, Portugal and Greece formulated relatively sophisticated laws that attribute an important role to the ministers in charge of environmental matters. Doubts arose, however, in regards to their application and control since the necessary staff skilled in such matters is lacking. According to the position taken by France, Denmark, the UK and Ireland, their established laws conforms to the guideline's requirements so that hardly anything needed to be changed in the existing legal and administrative practice. They move along the fluid borderline between meeting minimum standards and undermining the requirements (cf. Coenen and Jörissen 1989). In this way, EU law is not only devaluated by noncompliance, but also by sluggish, undermining or even distorting conversion and insufficient implementation as a result of a lack of effective control.

Another trend to devaluate EU law may result when the individual states increasingly make use of their right to undertake a solo national effort. They may do so in the case of urgent requirements according to Art. 30. Highly ranked public goods such as the working environment, the natural environment and health or consumer safety may justify such national solo efforts. With increasing EU legislation and because of the heterogeneous interests and different mentalities of the individual states, there are growing reasons for attempts to undertake such solo efforts. In this case, EU law is being devaluated by deviating national law.

The expansion of EU legislation might reach beyond the boundaries within which a reliable consensus and a readiness to comply can be expected. However, the Community depends heavily on the cooperation and support of the individual member states, both in legislation and implementation of the law. The more the critical limit of cooperation and support is exceeded, the more EU law will become mere paperwork that is not being put into practice. The growing disproportion between the proposals of the Commission and the laws passed will then mirror a corresponding devaluation of EU power, whereas the growing disproportion between the laws passed and compliance with the law will reflect a devaluation of EU law (cf. Münch 1992).

As far as norm setting is concerned, a decentralized institutional structure which aims for the cooperation of the norm-setting bodies might be suited to the complexity of requirements. Such a model has been drafted by Christian Joerges (1991: 260–61). According to this model, the EU would have to present the guidelines for norm setting and product certification in the individual states on the basis of its legislation, which is supported by pluralistic expert committees with a European responsibility, and on the basis of European agencies. These guidelines would then be transferred to the legislation of the individual states and their agencies by respecting the particular situation of each country. This model differs from mere regulatory competition in that the EU is not released from its responsibility of setting guidelines and the prerequisites for the formation of a European responsibility have to be created and the norm-setting and certification bodies of the different states have to cooperate with the EU level. Nevertheless, even with this model in mind, norm setting will not be easy and will have to struggle with all the problems related to 'policy entanglement'. Yet, it will better live up to the intention of an entanglement of unity and variety. Unity will be guaranteed by the strengthened drafting of European guidelines, while variety will be ensured by the decentralized conversion of the guidelines; their linkage will be promoted through cooperation between the bodies of the EU and the individual member states.

So far we have argued for a pluralistic understanding of EU decision making approaching the liberal type of democracy as exemplified by the United States. This does, however, not imply that such a movement towards liberal democracy will not have to face problems. It will be a type of democracy that takes place on a greater number of levels in a greater number of arenas. It is a polity full of veto players (Tsebelis 2002). It is easy for such a system to slip into competition about regulation with the effect of no regulation because of inflationary waves. Nevertheless, this interpretation of the trend of EU decision making seems to be more realistic than attempts at establishing a kind of representative democracy on the European level, an interpretation in terms of a Habermasian discourse ethics as proposed by Thomas Gehring (2002) or a Habermasian deliberative democracy (Habermas 1992) as envisioned by Christian Joerges and Jürgen Neyer (1997).

According to an analysis by Gehring (2002), EU legislation has achieved regulations with high standards after introducing a division of labour between passing abstract directives on the level of the Council of Ministers and defining their substance more concretely in norm-setting committees of experts. Because of the abstract nature of the directive, the ministers decide under a Rawlsian veil of ignorance. They do not exactly know which of their country's interests are affected in which way. Therefore, they are inclined to consent to abstract guidelines recommended by experts. In the norm-setting committees, decision making does not follow the tracks of unrelenting interest bargaining, but the tracks of arguing under the condition of a Habermasian ideal speech situation in which consensus is formed according to the technically best solution to a problem. Because interests are kept away here, it is easier to reach a consensus among experts.

Joerges and Neyer (1997, 2006) have gone even farther in finding the site of a unique 'deliberative democracy' in the elaborated EU committee decision making called 'comitology' because it is not interests which are mutually adjusted here but, arguments which are discussed while looking for the common good. The committee members are engaged in reasoning, which reaches well beyond simple interest representation. They carry out a kind of reflection approaching the quality of deliberative democracy.

Gehring and Joerges and Neyer argue for a realistic view on democracy on the EU level. They object to the prevailing complaints about the European democracy deficit. The complaints are focused on the European Parliament's lack of power and the lack of opinion formation, as well as interest representation on the supranational level. For Gehring, such claims go much too far. However, if we look more closely at EU decision making, we see at least processes, which demonstrate that outputs are approaching the common good made possible, as he says. According to a distinction explained by Fritz Scharpf (1998), this kind of decision making is producing 'output-legitimacy' in contrast to the 'input-legitimacy' resulting from participatory and representative decision making. Joerges and Neyer go even farther in claiming the quality of deliberative democracy for comitology decision making, which compensates for lacking democracy in terms of public debate and representative decision making by the European parliament.

Gehring and Joerges and Neyer are right in their realistic assessment of the chances for a European representative democracy and in turning their attention to comitology decision making. However, their framing of this kind of decision making in terms of a Rawlsian veil of ignorance (Rawls 1972; Gehring 2002) and a Habermasian deliberative democracy (Joerges and Neyer 1997) goes too far. They underestimate the political and arbitrary nature of norm setting because a technical standard cannot be derived from scientific knowledge. It has to be set according to priorities for lower or higher protection and under inclusion of a broader set of interests (e.g. those of producers, consumers, scientists, technicians, bureaucrats, etc.). Thus every technical norm is based on a political decision. What Joerges and Neyer have to play down is the absence of public debate in comitology decision making, which is the very essence of a Habermasian deliberative democracy.

In contrast to such deliberative interpretations of comitology decision making, an interpretation which draws on Niklas Luhmann's (1983) concept of legitimation by procedure seems to be more appropriate. According to this concept, legitimation of decisions does not come about because of some kind of true representation of the people's will (i.e. input-legitimacy) or some kind of production of best solutions to problems or of the common good (i.e. output-legitimacy), but because interests and potential conflict are being absorbed by the decision-making process in such a way that every interest and every potential protest and resistance is made a resource of the operations of the decision-making system so that decisions are accepted and resistance is channelled in forms, which again can be made a resource for further decisions or revisions of decisions. According to this interpretation, EU decision making works for several reasons. It is rather an extension than a limitation of political participation. The European Union is a further arena of politics, which can be particularly used for interests that have been blocked in the national arena, by national governments as well as parties and interest groups. The major quality keeping this multilevel and multiarena system working is not its ability to provide a place for arguing and deliberation, but its open character. This open character gives every single interest a chance of articulation so that the relevant political actors continue to play the game and do not apply illegitimate means of resistance. For comitology decision making, it seems to be much more important to be open to a greater variety of interest groups, particularly public interest groups and different scientific and technical paradigms, than to carry out arguing and deliberation behind closed doors. It might be more realistic to meet the requirements of a liberal democracy of the US type with greater emphasis on accessibility, transparency, accountability and revisability of decision making than to look for a discursive or deliberative legitimacy, which cannot be more than a disguised rule of experts.

The European multilevel system is conceived in such a way that Art. 28 ECT attributes clear priority to market creation on the European level. Art. 95 ECT entitles the Council of Ministers to seize measures serving the establishment and operation of the single market. According to Art. 308 ECT, the Council of Ministers may intervene in order to achieve the Community's goals in the framework of the single market. On this basis, the community has in fact ensured regulations in the field of environmental protection, health protection at work and equality of genders, both as regards legislation and jurisdiction. These regulations go far beyond the regulations passed by the member states. Nevertheless, a large part of market regulation is left up to the member states in line with Art. 30 ECT, though only insofar as corresponding restrictions of the free goods flow are justifiable in the interest of the protection of public morals, safety and health. The ECJ has to decide on such measures. This regulation can be considered an unclear, mixed situation of competences between the Union and its member states, resulting in ineffective solutions (Gehring 1997) and a trap of political entanglement of uncoordinated decisions on both the European and the national level, involving uncontrolled interdependences and unintended effects and lacking output legitimacy (Scharpf 1999).

In turn, the conclusion may be drawn that a clearer delimitation of competences and, possibly, a shift of competences on to the European level might involve more effective solutions. We may, however, object to this line of argument that politics has to cope with conflicts between ends instead of factual problems by definition and that the transfer of decisions into the field of expert commissions – optimally on the European level – merely glosses over conflicts between ends. The mixed situation of European and national competences mirrors simply the existing conflicts between ends: (1) the European goal of an integrated single market (market creation); (2) the European goal of nondiscriminating market regulation; and (3) completely different national goals of market regulation, depending on national interests. The intersection of European and national competences is not simply an obstacle to effective solutions, but an expression of the existing conflicts between ends that have to be fought over and over again. To do so, a system of checks and balances appears better suited than a system of clearly attributed competences. The consequence of this system is, however, that the European project prefers negative integration to positive integration, has a deregulating effect on the way of interfering into the member states and paves the way for a regime of liberalism. This dialectic of transnational integration and national disintegration is an unavoidable side effect of the European project. It is hard to mend through a clarification of competences in the multilevel system since the prerequisites for this clarification, namely nonconflicting goals between the Union and the member states on the one hand, and the member states themselves, on the other hand, are lacking.

A double structure of governance emerges. The transnational field of politics superimposes itself on the national field. In the national field, the political elites and administrative elites, governments, parliaments, parties and associations have the upper hand, while the knowledge elite of experts and the economic elite of managers and business consultants is in a subordinate position. This is the classical form of democratic rule in the nation state, where science is a servant and the media play the role of informant. In the now superimposed field of transnational politics, the knowledge elite and the economic elite join forces in taking a dominant role, whereas the political elite, the administrative elite, governments, parliaments, administrations and associations find themselves in an inferior position. Science leaves its subservient position to become the ruler of politics. The mass media inform less about politics than they construct political reality. The legitimate structure of democratic rule in the nation state is dominated by the nonlegitimate structure of scientifically and economically controlled governance. On the x axis, the centre of rule moves from the political capital of parties and associations to the scientific and economic capital of the knowledge and the economic elites. On the y axis, the symbolic capital of transnational expert networks and institutions grows along with their dominant position in multilevel governance. In contrast, the symbolic capital of parties and associations decreases on the transnational level. The transnational field assumes the superior position and the national field assumes the inferior one (see Fig 1.3).

Concluding remarks

The outlined structural change of governance is justified in social science with theoretical models that focus on the legitimation of regulative politics through the trusteeship of experts. In paradigmatic terms, it is represented by Giandomenico Majone's (1996) contribution, which covers the replacement of old 'distributive' politics in the national welfare state with new 'regulative' politics at the level of the European Union. While the legitimacy of distributive politics can only emerge from the compromise between the affected groups organized in associations, regulative politics is based on expert knowledge. This expert knowledge represents the authority of science. Accordingly, decisions taken by regulative politics do not result from bargaining, but rather from discursive arguing. The results of such procedures should stand out by helping 'general interest' to assert itself and by restraining

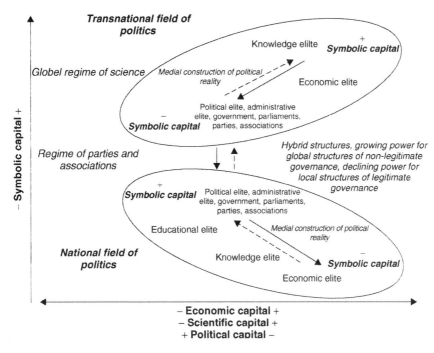

Figure 1.3 The double structure of governance in the national and transnational fields of politics

the particular interests of national governments and individual societal groups (Joerges and Neyer 1997; Gehring 2002).

In this way, the regime of scientific experts obtains the quality seal of legitimacy from social science. Nevertheless, it must be recognized in this context that any real discourse is closed by power structures, especially since no binding result could otherwise be achieved. Closure occurs by certain groups of experts making their way in the field and exercising essential definitional power. If, however, power cannot be kept out of the process, legitimacy cannot arise from an artificial separation of technical problem solving from politics, but only from a sufficient level of checks and balances, which keeps power under control. This is why multilevel governance moves towards an adversarial process of regulation, which is a central feature of the liberal, pluralistic type of democracy.

2 European law

Constructing a liberal society by jurisdiction

Research on European integration is largely in the hands of political science and legal scholarship (Mattli 1999; Rosamond 2000). Sociology still has to find its proper place in this research field. What makes the difference of a genuinely sociological approach to European integration is its focus on the deeper structural changes resulting from this process. Of central interest is the change of the structure of solidarity and justice that is taking place. To find an answer to this question is the task addressed in this chapter (cf. Frerichs 2008).

From a sociological point of view, European integration is specifically a process of transforming deeper structures of solidarity, legal order and justice away from the segmentally differentiated European family of nations and towards an emerging European society. This transformation is the subject matter that is to be explained (*explanandum*) by a set of mutually supporting explanatory factors (*explanans*) with the example of jurisdiction by the ECJ: (1) establishing the formal legitimate power of European jurisdiction in order to complement and form the driving force of international labour division (i.e. preliminary reference, supremacy and direct effect of European law); (2) establishing a substantial conception of control in the field of legal discourse (i.e. free movement and nondiscrimination); (3) enforcing a genuinely European legal order against national varieties of law by establishing a dominant European legal community; and (4) making transnational sense of legal change by legitimizing Europeanized law in terms of advancing justice as equality of opportunity across and within nations, as opposed to equality of results within nations accompanied by inequality of opportunity across nations.

The transformative power of European legal integration

In the long term, the course of European integration is being advanced by the functional developmental dynamics as explained by Ernst Haas (1958). Stone Sweet and Caporaso (1998), as well as Fligstein and Stone Sweet (2002), have proven these functional developmental dynamics in quantitative empirical studies demonstrating the mutual building up of cross-border trade and

European jurisdiction and legislation (see also Stone Sweet et al. 2001; Stone Sweet 2004; de Búrca 2005). Burley and Mattli (1993) have shown how the EU's legal integration has been advanced by the convergence of interests and the interaction of the ECJ, national judges and private plaintiffs in the framework of the preliminary reference procedure according to Article 234 (ex 177) EC.

Nevertheless, the functional developmental dynamics do not explain the concrete form of the European Union's progressing legal integration. To this end, we have to look at the specific developmental path (Pierson 1996) and the specific social construction of Europe by the essential driving forces behind the EU's legal integration (Checkel 1999; Christiansen, Jørgensen and Wiener 1999). We have to work out the basis upon which the ECJ's strong position rests. We have to explain why its decisions are accepted by the member states even against their situationally contrasting interests and upon what their legitimacy is based. Weiler (1999) has brought this aspect of explanation to the fore. It also depends on which judicial tools allowed the ECJ to make legal integration precede political integration (i.e. preliminary rulings, direct effect, supremacy, constitutionalization and market integration as the given objectives). Dehousse (1998) has underlined this aspect in particular. Another important element is the kind of order the ECJ judges construct according to their juridical logic. Here the European philosophy of market liberalization through the dismantling of barriers to market access (negative integration) is set against the nation state philosophy of market regulation (positive integration). Maduro (1998) has made an essential contribution to this subject matter. This aspect covers the specific judicial construction of Europe in the sense of a social constructivist approach.

However, the path of constructing European law is also fundamentally marked by the conflict between European legal harmonization and the integrity of national legal traditions. Accordingly, the member states set limits on the expansion of European legal harmonization again and again, above all by their concerted action. For instance, the effect of ECJ judgements was alleviated by a protocol added to the Maastricht Treaty. In turn, the ECJ forced the member states to assume government liability for not implementating EU law. The German constitutional court tied the legitimacy of European law to the respect of fundamental rights, which it examines itself. Such conflicts show that the development of European law is not an automatism, but a matter of political struggles. However, it is not only the availability of power resources that matters, but also the framing of a conflict through the Community Treaty (Garrett 1992, 1995; Mattli and Slaughter 1995). The latter, above all, is an important power resource of the ECJ. It is a kind of symbolic capital (Bourdieu 1991a). The member states more or less agreed upon the Treaty of Rome without completely foreseeing its long-term sovereignty-restricting effect. In doing so, they left the interpretation of the Treaty to the ECJ. The ECJ can use the Treaty's spirit as a legitimatory source for its decisions tying the member states to their own intentions. In particular, it is the ECJ's acknowledged competence to interpret the Treaty and the commit-ment of the member states to the EC Treaty which give the ECJ a substantial degree of power in its conflict with the member states. Analogous to the thought model used by Thomas Gehring (2002) in an analysis of EU decision-making processes, the first member states negotiated an agreement under a veil of ignorance, according to Rawls (1972), which tied them to decisions they were unable to foresee in detail. The Treaty forced them to hand some part of their power over to the European bodies, above all the ECJ, which they cannot regain at will without endangering the European integration project and thus their own long-term interests.

The chances for conflicts between the European harmonization of law and the integrity of national legal traditions to lead, at least sometimes, to a back-lash in the sense of a hold-up or even retrenchment of legal integration rather than to a further spillover has been emphasized by Karen J. Alter (2000). In order to allow EU jurisdiction to change national law, four hurdles have to be crossed: (1) EU law has to offer a legal foundation for the challenging of national policies; (2) private plaintiffs have to be mobilized to use EU law for their strategic aims; (3) national judges have to present cases to the ECJ and have to apply its interpretation; (4) success in jurisdiction has to be trans-ferred into a change of national policies. Whether or not such hurdles are overcome depends on the national legal systems, the legal area in question and the chances of success of an ECJ preliminary ruling as compared to other strategies (Alter 2000: 509–11). Alter (2001) has also stressed the institu-tional interest of lower court national judges in making use of the preliminary reference procedure to strengthen their position against higher courts in their national judicial system, whereas the high and supreme courts of the member states have resisted the ECJ's claim to supremacy of European law as much as possible. The same is true for national governments. However, higher national courts and national governments have not been able to turn around the process of constitutionalization of European law, though they would have had the power to do so. There is therefore more at work, at least in the medium and long term, than the institutional interests of the relevant actors playing in the field of constructing Europe by jurisdiction.

For reasons of disciplinary specialization, the approaches to European integration prevailing in political science do not explicitly address the deeper transformation of solidarity, legal order and justice, coming about with the emergence of a European society superimposing itself on the segmentally, dif-ferentiated family of European nations (Münch 2001a, 2001b). The answer to this question needs a genuinely sociological approach to European inte-gration. Such an approach has to focus on the transformative power of European legal integration (cf. Swedberg 1994; Bach 2000; Müller 2007).

In looking for a genuinely sociological approach to explaining the emer-gence of a European society from a family of European nations in the process of European integration, it is helpful to draw on the basic ideas presented by Emile Durkheim (1964) in his classical study, *The Division of Labour in*

Society. According to Durkheim, the driving force of social integration beyond the borders of relatively closed communities is cross-border labour division resulting from increasing specialization. In terms of classical economic theory, cross-border labour division between two countries results in economic gains for both countries. According to Adam Smith (1776/1952) goods and services will be produced where costs are lowest in a system of free trade, which is beneficial for all nations included in free trade. David Ricardo (1817/1977) has demonstrated that a country would profit from specialization and cross-border trade even if it was able to produce an imported good at lower costs. This will be true as long as specializing in exporting one product while importing another product results in higher gains than producing both products at home. It is implied that capital and labour can be invested in the most profitable branch of production (Marrewijk 2002: 26–27, 42–43). In the world of classical and neo-classical economics there are, however, no transaction costs. This is exactly what is effective in the real world and what is of interest to the sociologist. For Durkheim, the transition from an existing level of labour division to a new, farther-reaching and transborder level of labour division implies a U-turn from the security of tradition towards considerable insecurity, involving anomie, distributive conflicts and erosion of consensus on the meaning of justice. Therefore, resistance to such change is quite normal and has to be overcome if the cross-border division of labour is to advance. It is this overcoming of resistance that has to be explained. In the real world of people facing the disadvantages of eroding traditions, advantages calculated by classical economic theory do not explain why people engage in increasing cross-border labour division. In Durkheim's eyes, it is first of all external constraint that leaves people no other option but to take the way of increasing specialization and corresponding cross-border labour division. This external constraint is increasing material density (i.e. shrinking distance between people), which has come as a consequence of population growth or improved means of transport and communication.

Increasing material density intensifies competition on scarce resources. There are a number of alternatives to cope with such intensified competition, such as war, emigration, increasing rates of suicide (or, for a limited time, improved productivity, as argued by Rueschemeyer 1982) and specialization with corresponding labour division. As various functional alternatives have proven to imply higher costs, specialization and international labour division have a greater chance of selection and progress. Durkheim was, however, well aware of the fact that the division of labour could only proceed along with a legal order representing the basic relationships of solidarity. The latter provides for the trust between people, without which no continuous economic exchange is possible without distraction into violent conflict. He also knew that this functional requirement would not produce the emergence of solidarity and legal order by itself. Functional necessity needs to be complemented by historical causation. Solidarity and legal order do not emerge by themselves from market transaction as spillover effects, but they need genuine construction by forces producing solidarity and legal order. In fact, displacement of national labour division and law by European labour division and law is harmful and by no means a direct advantage for everybody; resistance to such change is quite natural. This is what Durkheim (1964: Book 2, Chapter 1) means when he says that increasing labour division cannot be explained by growing happiness, which is contrary to the opinions Adam Smith and David Ricardo, who do not take transaction costs into account. Starting from a situation of segmental differentiation into nation states clinging to internal collective (mechanical) solidarity and national legal orders representing basically a justice of collectively shared equality of results (i.e. high level of status maintaining social security and low earnings dispersion), there must be pioneers who break up national solidarity and the national legal order. This is the work of transnational elites founding and administering transnational institutions and organizations. Managers, scientists, politicians, civil servants and lawyers play this role. Transnational solidarity created by such elites is a kind of 'organic solidarity' of specialized and mutually dependent parts of a new, more encompassing whole, in Durkheim's terms. Going beyond Durkheim's notion of an organic 'whole', we had better introduce the notion of a network of mutually dependent parts that might be more or less densely woven and open to including new specialized parts.

In as much as such institutions and organizations founded and administered by transnational elites become firmly established, they promote the further superimposition of transnational solidarity and law on national societies, thus provoking a conflict with forces representing the traditions of national solidarity and law. Step by step, this conflict shifts towards favouring the forces of transnationalization as much as the international division of labour proceeds under the protection of transnational institutions and organizations. It is therefore the tacit coalition between the self-catalyzing progression of cross-border labour division and transnational elites which puts the conflict between the forces of transnational order and the forces of national order increasingly on unequal terms, thus favouring the advancement of the transnationalization of solidarity. This is the logic behind the increasing transnationalization of the law. It is different from a spillover effect insofar as it needs particular sources of the transnational construction of solidarity and law beyond market transaction and entails a fundamental conflict between transnational and national forces in shaping the real process of the transnationalization of the law.

Following Durkheim, we want to know more about this process of transnationalization of solidarity and law. We want to learn how their nature is changing. According to Durkheim (1964), it is the change from mechanical to organic (or network) solidarity accompanied by a change of the legal order from repressive law focused on the collective's right over the individual to restitutive law focused on the protection of the rights of the individual against infringements originating from the collective or from other individuals.

Taking up Durkheim's visionary view of an emerging European society – right before two world wars originating in the heart of Europe – the European legal order is the basis of the 'cult of the individual', reaching beyond the national traditions of expanding the rights of the individual. This Durkheimian (1964) view is currently invoked by the notion of the 'EU rights revolution' (Kelemen 2003). European law is a major force in advancing individual autonomy by emancipating the individual from traditionally established national constraints. In this way of strengthening the individual, national collectives are losing in homogeneity. They become internally more differentiated and pluralistic. Internal pluralization, differentiation and individualization break down differences between previously homogeneous cultures so that the nations become more similar to each other by way of internal differentiation. This process helps to advance transnational ties between individuals emancipated from national constraints. What is emerging in this process is a European society establishing a new type of solidarity and a new type of legal order focused far more on the cult of the individual than the national legal orders did before. A major part of this process is the functional differentiation of European law from national constraints and legal traditions. Compared to national law framed by cultural traditions and political constellations, European law stands more on its own. It is more a product of legal experts and specializes in coordinating the rights of autonomous individuals. Because it develops in close connection with the market, it translates the model of market exchange between autonomous individuals into the law spreading from economic law to other areas of the law.

Neither functional spillover (Haas 1958) nor intergovernmental bargaining (Moravcsik 1993) help to understand and explain why cross-border trade and labour division and the construction of a legal order are advancing in the face of a situation that brings about a fundamental transformation of solidarity, legal order and justice for the average citizen thus far protected by national solidarity, legal order and justice. It is very unlikely that such a harmful process would be advanced by functional spillover from expanding trade to legislation and jurisdiction because national resistance can be expected. Because of that resistance, it is also unlikely for this process to spread from purely intergovernmental bargaining. From the point of view of a genuinely sociological theory, such a process of harmful institutional transformation depends on a whole set of favourable conditions. There must be a shift of legitimate power, the definition of the situation and the construction of a legitimate and meaningful order from the national to the transnational level:

1   Institutionalize formal European judicial power: Formal institutional procedures of legislation and jurisdiction have to provide a firm grounding on which a transnational elite can realize its vision in everyday decision making, favouring the transnational project.
2   Establish a substantial conception of control: A substantial leading idea and conception of control (Fligstein 2001) has to help the transnational

elite to define the situation in such a way that conflicts will be settled in favour of the transnational project in a way that is accepted as legitimate by both sides in the conflict.

3   Establish a dominant European legal community and turning politics into juridical technique: The transnational elite has to apply legitimate power based on procedural rules in such a way that national resistance is overcome in a way that is accepted as legitimate by both sides in the conflict.

4   Turn functional adjustment into constructing a legitimate order: The transnational legal order constructed by way of conflict settlement between the transnational elite and the forces of national traditions has to attain the status of a new order which makes sense and appears just as a whole and can therefore successfully claim legitimacy, thus transforming the traditionally given national legal orders and ideas of justice.

The following paragraphs will focus on ECJ jurisdiction in the perspective of the outlined theoretical model derived from Durkheim's study on the division of labour. The ECJ's work will be assessed step by step, according to the four outlined requirements of replacing national traditions by European law. The hypotheses specifying the requirements are not tested in this study; they are rather presumed to be confirmed by common sociological knowledge. The study is no test of hypotheses; it is rather a systematically guided explanation of an historical transformation of solidarity, legal order and justice. On the one hand, its task is the sociological framing of the subject matter to be explained, that being the transformation of solidarity, legal order and justice (*explanandum*). On the other hand, its task is to supply a sociological explanation of this transformation based on a theoretical model spelled out in four hypotheses (*explanans*) (see Figure 2.1).

What is substantiated in the study on ECJ jurisdiction is evidence pointing towards the superimposition of transnational network solidarity, restitutive law and justice as equality of opportunity on national mechanical solidarity and 'repressive' law and justice as collectively shared equality of results (*explanandum*). The evidence for that is the corresponding meaning of ECJ jurisdiction in individual cases. This meaning certainly has to be disclosed by an interpretation in the light of the assumed transformation. There is always the possibility of other interpretations and other cases contradicting the interpretation given in this study. What can be said in support of the interpretations advanced here is that they are compatible with established juridical commentary and interpretation so that the sociological framing does not seem to be in conflict with established juridical knowledge.

It is a well-established fact that the ECJ has played a crucial role in constructing a European legal order in technical terms, based on legal rationalism and formalism (Shapiro 1992). Therefore, European law has largely evolved in close connection with the economic needs of market integration and much less in connection with political needs of market regulation

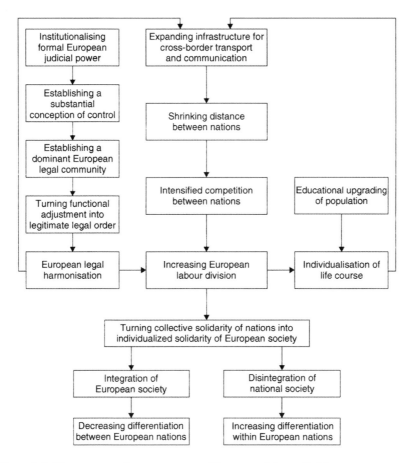

Figure 2.1 The causes and consequences of European labour division

(cf. Cappelletti, Seccombe and Weiler 1986; Höland 1993; Gessner 1994; Joerges 2003). The aim of this study is to point out, in sociological terms, how the ECJ's jurisdiction has contributed in the context of increasing European labour division to a fundamental change of solidarity. Starting from this change, the focus is on the corresponding paradigmatic change of the legal order and on the judicial construction of a European society that increasingly penetrates the family of European nations.

Institutionalizing formal European judicial power: preliminary reference, direct effect and supremacy of European law

This first step has to explain whether or not (and if so, why) ECJ jurisdiction can rely on legitimate power in order to complement and shape the dynamic force of European labour division, which is primarily advanced by shrinking distance and transnational elites promoting cross-border economic exchange. Without such legitimate power there would be no successful construction of a genuinely European legal order. The major assets empowering the ECJ are the institutional rules of preliminary reference, supremacy and direct effect of European law and the principles of judicial rationalism. These are the formal preconditions for constitutionalizing the European legal order as a prerequisite of transforming national legal traditions by European jurisdiction.

The ECJ is an essential driving force behind the developmental dynamics advanced by the functional differentiation of European law from national collective constraints and legal traditions. In this context, it retains a particularly strong position in the European Union's structure of institutions, especially as national interests are still strongly making their way in the Council, since Parliament possesses very limited decisional power only and the Commission ultimately depends on both Council and Parliament's agreement with its proposals. Consequently, the ECJ represents the interest in the European integration's progress in its utmost purity, with only a minimum of opportunities for blockading existing for national interests. Compared to national systems, jurisdiction is therefore more pronounced than legislation on the European level. Accordingly, the limits to the functional differentiation of law from moral and/or political constraints seem to be less tight than in the different member states. We may therefore assume that the ECJ's judicial practice particularly promotes this process of the functional differentiation of European law from collective constraints and traditions, thus giving a substantial boost to developmental dynamics and the change in legal order as compared to national developmental paths and the power of persistence of national traditions. To be able to play this role of change, the ECJ has to occupy a prominent position in the EU's structure of institutions, but it also requires its acknowledgement by the member states, its invocation by national courts and private plaintiffs and the acceptance of its decisions as legitimate. It is true that this position of the ECJ has been drafted in the Community Treaty, yet it had to be brought to life by the judges in their judicial practice. This has happened to a great extent indeed, as can be seen from a whole series of facts (Brown and Kennedy 1995; Dehousse 1998; Arnull 1999; Stone Sweet 2000, 2004; De Búrca and Weiler 2001; Vesterdorf 2003).

The heart of European judicial power: the preliminary reference procedure

Since 1965, procedures concerning violations of the Treaty as well as preliminary rulings according to Article 234 (ex 177) EC have increased year by year, with the preliminary rulings having gained clear dominance since the 1970s (Dehousse 1998: 31). This offers first proof of the ECJ's continually expanding activity in constructing a European legal order based on apparently legitimate and effective power. The ECJ's decisions in the preliminary reference procedure do not relieve the national courts of their judicial responsibility, yet they form an essential basis for jurisdiction, which the national courts keep as a rule (Dauses 1995; Sciarra 2001). The fact that the inferior national courts have to enter into a direct dialogue with the ECJ and do not have to go via higher national courts is of essential significance. The latter are even expressly deprived of their power since the ECJ is solely responsible for interpreting European law. This procedure is to guarantee the uniform interpretation and implementation of European law. It is the resulting increase in power of the lower national courts alone, as compared to the higher courts, which serves as a stimulus for them to use the tool of preliminary rulings. It is in their institutional interest to do so (Burley and Mattli 1993: 62–64; Alter 2001). National courts may, however, decide a case on their own, without submitting it to the ECJ, if precedents allowing for a clear and precise judgement exist in the court's case law or if the relevant EC law is obvious enough to ensure a clear-cut decision. The latter is explained by the ECJ as *acte clair* strategy in CILFIT (C-283/81). Nevertheless, it is the firm position of the ECJ that national courts act as its delegates in applying European law, even if they decide on their own (cf. Rasmussen 1984; Mancini and Keeling 1991). In fact, the lower national courts have more and more frequently seized the chance of preliminary references and have thus raised the number of such procedures from just a few in the 1960s to an average of 50 per year during the 1970s, to an average of 100 during the 1980s and up to more than 250 in the 1990s and then back to just below 200 at the end of the 1990s (Dehousse 1998: 31; Stone Sweet and Caporaso 1998: 104; Alter 2000: 499–500; see Figure 1.1 in this book). It is shown that, of course, larger member states are more frequently engaged in preliminary rulings than the smaller ones. Nevertheless, measured by the population, Luxembourg heads the list, followed by Belgium, the Netherlands, Denmark, Germany, Italy, Ireland, France, Greece, the UK, Portugal and Spain (Dehousse 1998: 32). Through the presentation of cases by national courts, the preliminary reference procedure has opened the gate to the ECJ for individual litigants, a way that would otherwise be rather restricted. Therefore, individual litigants and their problems have become a major driving force behind European integration. In this sense, European integration is not only advanced by legislation from above, but also by acts of litigation from below. A mutual building up of increasing cross-border trade and legal integration of the EU by jurisdiction as well as legislation in the sense of Ernst Haas's (1958) neofunctionalist integration theory has occurred. There is spillover from economic to political and legal integration. This development has been documented by Stone Sweet and Caporaso (1998) as well as by Fligstein and Stone Sweet (2002) in empirical quantitative terms.

Constitutionalizing EU law: supremacy and direct effect

Spillover from economic transactions to the construction of a European legal order does, however, not occur automatically. The construction of a European legal order needs its own juridical sources, which are legitimate power of EU legislation and EU jurisdiction. As regards jurisdiction, the legitimate power of the ECJ is at stake. For the ECJ's ability to change national legal traditions by European jurisdiction, the growing constitutionalization of the common legal order and establishment of a European rule of law has been of greatest importance (Dehousse 1998: 36–69; Maduro 1998: 7–34; Weiler 1999: 10–63; Wind 2001; Arnull 2002). The Treaty and the Community's established law form a legal order ranking above the law of the different member states. The ECJ plays the role of a constitutional court deciding upon the compatibility of national law with the higher-ranking European law. The two principles guaranteeing this status of the European legal order are the principles of direct effect and supremacy of European law.

All binding EC law is directly effective in the member states in as much as it is regarded as clear, precise and unconditional enough to be litigable in legal practice. According to the ECJ's case law, treaty provisions, regulations and decisions, as well as international agreements, are directly effective if they fulfil the requirement of litigability. Directives are generally not directly effective. However, they are indirectly effective because member state courts are expected to interpret domestic law so that it conforms to Community directives. Furthermore, directives may have incidental effects in legal proceedings between private litigants. If directives are not implemented in due time, the state is liable for damages resulting from that noncompliance as ruled by the ECJ in *Francovich and Bonifaci* (C-6/90 and 9/90). The meaning of 'direct effect' varies between the broader notion of EC law to be invoked before a member state court and the narrow notion of EC law to confer rights on individuals to be enforced by member state courts. The ECJ laid the foundations for its doctrine of direct effect as early as in 1963 in the now-famous case *Van Gend en Loos* (C-26/62), which dealt with the question of whether or not citizens of a member state may refer directly to the ban on an increase in tariffs as stipulated by Article 12 EC and can institute legal proceedings at a national court. Responding to a complaint by a Dutch company and supported by the ECJ's Advocate General, three member states raised the objection that the Treaty binds the member states but does not create any directly valid law to which individuals or authorities might refer. Nevertheless, the ECJ opted for just the latter interpretation, ruling that Community law not only creates mutual obligations for the contractual partners (as does ordinary international law), but creates a new legal order to the benefit of which the states have restricted their sovereignty within a limited area of legislation so that the subjects of this legal order comprise of the member states themselves and their citizens. In doing so, the Court did not simply follow the wording of Article

12 EC, but in the ensuing sequence followed the spirit, general scheme and wording of the text. Both the spirit and the general scheme precede the wording. By adopting this way of interpretation, the ECJ has created greater latitude of interpretation, which has been utilized in further jurisdiction, essentially in favour of advancing the Community's legal integration, for itself. Accordingly, the ECJ's jurisdiction has given a highly effective boost to European integration. The case in which the court went well beyond the state of implementation of treaty provisions in EC legislation is *Reyners* (C-2/74). In this case, the Court applied its method of teleological interpretation of the treaty to fill gaps by way of envisaging future implementation. While such implementation measures could be predicted in that case (freedom of establishment under Art. 43, 44 and 47 [ex 52, 54 and 57]), such a prediction was much less possible in *Defrenne II* (C-43/75), which regarded equal pay of men and women. Nevertheless, the Court's ruling in this case implied direct effect of Art. 141 (ex 119), with enormous intervention in the domestic law of member states (cf. Craig 1992; Dauses 1995: 5–17, 43–52; Craig and de Búrca 2003: 178–229).

The supremacy of European law over national law is also owed to an ambitious interpretation of the Community's Treaty, according more to its spirit and objective – the creation of an integrated single market – than its wording (Dauses 1995: 17–20). According to Article 10 (ex 5) EC, the member states are requested to take all necessary steps to meet the obligations resulting from the Treaty. In terms of the wording, however, this does not mean that in the case of conflict Community law will automatically receive primacy over national law. It might be left to the member states to decide how they are going to live up to their obligation to accomplish the Community Treaty so that there is no automatic primacy of Community law over national law. It is precisely this argumentation that was carried out by the Italian government when a shareholder of a nationalized electricity company filed a law suit with reference to Community law, to which Italian law did not conform. In the corresponding preliminary ruling (C-6/64 *Costa v. ENEL*) the ECJ concluded, however, that, in contrast to ordinary international law, the Community Treaty has created a legal system on its own. It has become an integral part of national legal systems so that it can be applied by the national courts without using the detour of national legislation or higher national legal instances. Once again, the limitation of the member states' sovereignty rights is emphasized in the framework of Community law. In a case handled later on (C-106/77 *Simmenthal*), the Court ruled explicitly that Community law would enjoy supremacy over both old and new national law in any case. This clearly highlighted the Community law's constitutional character. In a case of conflict between European and national law, national courts are obliged to apply European law and ignore the national law. In the case *IN.CO.GE.'90* (C-10-22/97), the Court explained that national courts are not expected to nullify national law, which would be beyond their competence. Nevertheless, they must not apply national law that is in conflict with European law. With this phrasing of the subject matter, the Court avoids constitutional conflicts with national constitutional courts.

However, the member states have not accepted the Court's supremacy doctrine easily. They prefer the interpretation that the supremacy of Community law only results from the explicit national agreement due to articles in a national constitution, such as the French *Conseil d'Etat* as well as the *Cour de Cassation*, referring to Article 55 of the French constitution, and that even examination of European law by the national court of justice is required, such as the Italian court of constitution referring to Article 11 of the Italian constitution. In its Maastricht judgement, the German constitutional court links the supremacy of Community law to the agreement of the national parliament, which has the people's sovereignty as its sole source of legitimation; it even reserves the right to assess the compatibility of European law with fundamental rights since there is no equivalent for this on the European level. Nevertheless, it is prepared to accept European law as long as (*Solange*) the ECJ, above all, guarantees sufficient protection of the fundamental rights (*Solange I* judgement, BVerfG 37/1975, 29.5.74; *Solange II* judgement, BVerfG 73/1987, 22.10.1986; Maastricht judgement, BVerfG 89/1994, 12.10.1993). In the UK, the supremacy of Community law is derived from the British Parliament's European Communities Act of 1972. In fact, these interpretations are constructions trying to leave a loophole for deviations from the ECJ's legal interpretation and make the factually practised supremacy of Community law compatible with national patterns of legitimating law, more or less for their own reassurance. It is, however, a matter of fact that the ECJ's legal interpretation has made its way in practice. In individual cases we can definitely assume that European law enjoys supremacy over national law. This supremacy of European law stretches straight into national legal procedures. According to the principle of effectiveness (*effet utile*) applied by the ECJ, these should be formed in such a way that European law will immediately enter into effect without taking the detour of higher national legal bodies. A delay caused by national detours is to be avoided (C-106/77 *Simmenthal*; C-213/89 *Factortame*). Nevertheless, two languages of that reality still exist side by side. On the one hand, there is the European Court's monistic language of supremacy. On the other hand, there is the dualistic language of national constitutional courts seeing the legitimacy of EC law still depend on national constitutional provisions (cf. Kumm 1999).

Basically, the Community Treaty can be interpreted as a constitution granting rights to the citizens of the Union by establishing duties for the member states and the acting individuals; the citizens may enforce their claim by legal action. In fact, this has become a widely used practice in both national and European jurisdictions (Harlow and Rawlings 1992; Dehousse 1998: 46–53). This is what can be called the European 'rights revolution' within the boundaries of the European Union (Kelemen 2003). Beyond the EU's boundaries this rights revolution is complemented by the work of the Council of Europe and the European Court of Human Rights. Focusing on the European

Union, we see national courts in a dialogue with the ECJ, practising a legal examination of national law's conformity with the rights of individuals as they are granted by Community law. In this sense, jurisdiction, according to European law, acts as the essential driving force behind the individual's emancipation from the restrictions of national legal traditions (i.e. as the pacemaker of individualization), offering wider latitudes of action to the individual. Of course, this means that such latitudes of action can be further exploited the more the individuals become capable of leading an autonomous life. Typically, single individuals (and certainly also companies interested in trade liberalization) are working as pioneers, helping European law initiate preliminary rulings and paving the way for implementing the new ethics of individualism. This applies to the majority of cases. Especially well-known cases are: *Defrenne v. Sabena* (43/75), where a female Belgian flight attendant requested equality; *Cassis de Dijon* (120/78), where an importer enforced the entry of French liquor into the German market against national minimum requirements of alcohol content; and *Bosman v. Royal Club Liègeois* (C-415/93), where a footballer attained the removal of financial restrictions involved in changing from one club to another.

At the beginning of the 1990s, the ECJ went one step further in its jurisdiction by introducing state liability for cases where failure to respect the deadline stipulated for the transfer of EU directives into national law made it impossible for individuals to exercise their rights in line with the directives. The breakthrough was achieved with the cases *Francovich and Bonifaci v. Italian Republic* (C-6/90 and 9/90), where the Italian state was held liable for two employees' unsatisfied wage claims in the case of their employer's bankruptcy. At the time in question, a guarantee for this should have existed, according to EU Directive 80/987, but this was not the case due to the lack of implementation of the EU directive by Italian law. The Court explained that the Community law's effectiveness would be impaired if the member states could not be held responsible for the compensation of damage resulting from a lack of implementation of EU directives by national law contrary to contract. The Court underlined its interpretation of the law in two other cases, namely *Brasserie du Pêcheur v. Federal Republic of Germany* and *Factortame III* (C-46-93 and 48/93); at the same time, it specified the terms under which a right to compensation by the state in question has to be granted. The violated law has to be laid out to granting individual rights and the case has to concern a sufficiently serious violation of the contract; the latter has to be in causal relationship with the damage suffered by the plaintiff. The amount of compensation for the damage has to be adjusted to comparable regulations in the corresponding national law. Against the criticism to be expected from several member states, the ECJ justified its reasoning with the job of guaranteeing the validity and implementation of the European legal order against possible violations, and even against the interests of member states (Dehousse 1998: 53–56). There are three principles applied by the ECJ to ensure an effective implementation of individual rights against traditional restrictions by national law: (1) the Community Treaty creates rights that can be legally enforced by private persons, (2) the preliminary reference procedure according to Article 234 (ex 177) EC allows for the transfer of the ECJ's legal interpretation into national jurisdiction and (3) the state's liability for violations of Community law promotes the effective realization of the individual rights created by Community law (Dehousse 1998: 46).

The logic of implementing European law also contains the ECJ's generally positive attitude towards strengthening Community competence and tightening control of the rights to autonomous legislation, which are claimed by the member states. The former applies, for instance, to international agreements where the Community represents the member states in the field of common trade policy (22/70, *ERTA*); the latter applies to educational policy, where Bavaria, for instance, was prohibited from refusing children of guest workers educational grants (C-9/74, *Casagrande*).

Protecting fundamental rights: European versus national prerogative

The item of protecting human rights has been particularly explosive (Jaeckel 2003). As the Community has no list of fundamental rights as long as the new Constitution with its opening paragraph on fundamental rights is not ratified by the member states, the constitutional courts of the member states may reserve the competence of assessing European law with regard to its compatibility with the fundamental rights granted by national constitutions. This position was adopted by the German constitutional court in the *Solange I* judgement (BVerfG 37/1995). Accordingly, the court claims the right to such an assessment as long as (*Solange*) there is no European guarantee of fundamental rights. The *Solange II* judgement admits that no such assessment is required as long as (*Solange*) the protection of fundamental rights is in good hands, above all with the ECJ (BVerfG 73/1987). This judgement of the German constitutional court was preceded by an increasing readiness on the part of the ECJ to assess Community law with the yardstick of human rights (Dehousse 1998: 62–66; Weiler 1999: 102–29). After an initially hesitant attitude based on the lack of a European list of fundamental rights and on the fact that a reference to national constitutions would involve abandoning the supremacy of Community law, the ECJ finally adopted the position that the member states share common traditions of guaranteeing fundamental rights, which may serve as a guideline for European jurisdiction (C-11/70 *Internationale Handelsgesellschaft*). Moreover, the Court explained that it was unable to validate measures contradicting fundamental rights granted by the member states' constitutions (C-4/73 *Nold*). In a further step, international treaties concerning the protection of human rights and ratified by the EU member states were made the yardstick of assessment procedures (C-36/75 *Rutili*; C-44/79 *Hauer*). This decision referred to the European Convention on Human Rights.

The claim to protecting human rights by the ECJ has been of great importance for safeguarding the supremacy of Community law in the face of the position of national constitutional courts to consider the protection of individual rights their most prominent task and to carry out an assessment of European law in the light of fundamental rights. If they did so in fact, the postulate of Community law supremacy would be a matter of the past. This is demonstrated in a particularly precarious way by the German constitutional court's *Solange I* judgement. The *Solange II* judgement attenuates the conflict by suspending it provisionally, but not by removing it (Windolf 2000). In fact, the German constitutional court's *Maastricht* judgement recalls the safeguarding of the democratic legitimation of European law by the national parliaments (BVerfG 89/1994). The more it moved away from this path, the more it would violate the fundamental right of democratic participation according to the judgement of the German constitutional court. In this case, the German constitutional court would once again claim the supremacy of the national constitution's protection of fundamental rights and would thus annul the ECJ's legal interpretation in this significant item. The ECJ can avoid such conflicts only by forestalling the national constitutional courts with its own active protection of fundamental rights. It is above all this latent conflict between the ECJ and the national constitutional courts which compels the ECJ to adopt an active stance in constitutionalizing Community law. The Court has to do so if it wants to strengthen its position as against the national constitutional courts in its own institutional interest and also in the interest of the integrationist ideas behind the Treaty of Rome; this seems to be a plausible assumption at least.

The social basis of constitutionalizing EU law

An orientation to the Treaty of Rome's spirit and goal instead of its mere wording gave a substantial boost to the Community's legal integration. It was in the institutional interest of the Court to base its judgements on this guideline. However, institutional interest is a necessary but in no way sufficient condition for the effective constitutionalization of Community law. What has shaped this process in particular is the very logic of legal rationalism, which cannot be easily contested by member state interests in maintaining sovereignty. It is the ECJ's uncontested task to give reliable validity to European law against an always possible derogation on the part of the member states, and thus to meet the legal principle of determining exactly what is lawful and what is unlawful. Seen from this viewpoint, the ECJ's legal interpretation is nothing but a consequent application of the most general principle of jurisdiction: protecting the Community's legal unity and avoiding legal uncertainty due to differing and contradictory law. Accordingly, the constitutionalization of Community law is housed in the logic of differentiation and institutionalization of cross-border transnational law. If the ECJ had acted less in favour of the Community and had implemented the direct effect and supremacy of Community law less consistently, the consequence would have been the validity of highly differing law within one and the same legal unit. Its own jurisdiction would have decided this way today and that way tomorrow. It would have become highly inconsistent and incalculable. As a result, a maximum degree of legal uncertainty would have reigned. The ECJ had to act the way it did solely for reasons of consistency. One judgement laid the foundation for further judgements, which then had to stay in the same line for reasons of consistency and, as a rule, judgements proceeded along the same path. Very far-reaching judgements, such as *Dassonville*, were not cancelled but were specified further in their application, as in the *Cassis de Dijon* and the *Keck* cases. Amendments do not mean a turnaround, but rather a more precise specification of the terms of validity of preceding general explanations. We may therefore assume that the way towards today's level of differentiation of European law from national constraints and legal traditions and its firm institutionalization as a transnational law possessing direct effect and supremacy has been paved with the establishment of the ECJ. It could have been stopped solely by a massive turn-away of the member states from the initiated path of single market integration. In this way, the member states set a train in motion; they could have stopped it only at a high cost. Once started, they had to leave it rolling, although they had to pay tribute to the growing legal integration by sacrificing their freedom of legislation (Weiler 1999: 10–63).

The common commitment to the standards of the legal profession – contractual strictness, drawing a line of exact distinction between the lawful and the unlawful, justiciability and legal certainty – and to the modern Western constitutional traditions, with their guarantee of fundamental rights, were enough to gear the ECJ's jurisdiction into tracks involving the progressing constitutionalization of Community law. The transfer of the common features of commitment to professional standards and fundamental rights into jurisdiction has been supported by a certain *esprit de corps* resulting from long years of cooperation and the common French language. The dependence of the judge's appointment for a second term after six years on the corresponding national government obviously has not impeded the implementation of the legal logic, especially as certainly any jurist should have internalized the ethical principle that he or she will be more appreciated the better he or she is at doing his or her job. The secrecy of the court's internal debates and the announcement of the judgements as the result of a unanimous or majoritarian decision among colleagues protect the different judges against direct pressure. Accordingly, the governments' influence on the different judges is practically nonexistent. This is even more so as judges retiring from the ECJ cannot complain about a lack of attractive jobs after the end of their term. For instance, the German ECJ judge, Manfred Zuleeg, had no problem returning to his job as a professor at Frankfurt University after his six-year term in Luxembourg.

The jurist's professional ethics, which is to ensure legal certainty and the protection of fundamental rights and to provide solid jurisdiction based on the existing legal texts avoiding any uncertainty, has essentially marked the ECJ's active role in the Community's legal integration (Arnull 1993; Bengoetxea 1993; Anweiler 1997; Maduro 1998: 12–25; Sacco 2003). With their orientation to the general scheme, the spirit and the objective of the Community Treaty, the judges in Luxembourg have followed the academic tradition of legal interpretation on the European continent, especially as a great many of them come from an academic teaching background. Additionally, the Anglo-Saxon tradition of inductive procedure plays an important role insofar as pioneering decisions of the Court serve as the starting point for a whole series of specifying decisions built on them. Building up chains of precedents has reduced uncertainty of decision making for judges, lawyers and litigants. The most prominent case law in this respect is the chain from *Dassonville* to *Cassis de Dijon* to *Keck* (Stone Sweet 2004: 9–11, 118–20). In the sense of Max Weber's (1922/1972: 456–59, 503–12) classical study, the legal profession is the carrier of legal rationalism and the legal construction of the modern world. This is what the judges in Luxembourg are doing on a new level of constructing a European society by jurisdiction. Their ability to establish the direct effect and supremacy of Community law based on the preliminary reference procedure and the strict adherence to the tools of judicial rationalism enhanced the legitimate power of the ECJ in such a way as to provide a solid basis for playing an active role in superimposing a genuinely European order on national traditions of law.

After all, the Court's guideline is the interpretation of Community law as regards the Treaty's general scheme, spirit and goal. This interpretation method, which is marked by the academic spirit on the European continent, has ensured that the Court is able to elaborate Community law and to provide boosts to legislation wherever the Treaty turns out to be open and vague and whenever legislation stagnates. This can be said for European law to a substantial degree. According to a commonly shared assessment, the Community Treaty is extremely vague when compared to national legal systems. Yet this is not really astonishing in view of the necessity of a unanimous agreement of governments following their own ideas and interests and their wish to not abandon too much of their sovereign rights. The Community Treaty provides a framework requiring specification through directives in order to achieve an effective realization. This set a whole series of tasks of the European Commission. These are tasks which failed to be accomplished due to the constraint of reaching unanimous agreements until the qualified majority vote was introduced in the European Council by the Single European Act of 1986. The institutional crisis of 1965–66 (France's policy of the empty chair) paralyzed legislation for quite a while (Egan 2001: 60–82). In this situation it was left to the ECJ to provide the most essential stimuli for the Community's legal integration. Its active role was required by the Treaty's vagueness and by legislation's paralysis since the judges had to fulfill their legal task of constructing a transnational space for protecting fundamental rights and making an exact distinction between right and wrong. The principles of direct effect and supremacy of Community law served as the foundation from which the necessity of specifying the contractual terms according to the spirit and the goals of the Treaty unavoidably followed.

The preliminary reference procedure and the supremacy and direct effect of European law have made the ECJ a continuously working driving force of superimposing a genuinely European legal order on the different national traditions of law. With the Treaty of Rome, the founding governments of the European Economic Community have set in motion a process that is no longer fully under their control. This institutional choice has introduced a central element of supranationality with significant and lasting long-term effects. The penetration of the member states by a common legal order with enormous transforming effects on their national legal traditions would have never gone as far as it has if the founders had not established this crucial element of supranationality. The member states had to accept a whole series of decisions in favour of the supranational order, which had been harmful to the integrity of their national legal traditions. This was demonstrated by all Court decisions, implying that member states had to abandon regulations that had been considered meaningful and necessary within their own tradition of law for a long time. We learn here that again and again European integration has proceeded against the inertia of established national legal traditions involving a transformation process with high transaction costs. From the point of view of the forces behind the national traditions, transaction costs would have been mostly too high to voluntarily engage in such processes of change. Establishing the ECJ's responsibility for that change has been the crucial institutional device that has made the advancing of the economic integration process independent of such utility calculations. Economic integration has been able to advance, though it has always involved enormous transaction costs, calling for resistance. What otherwise would have been a matter of unresolvable conflicts of interests between governments has become a technical matter of sound judicial reasoning based on the very premises of the Treaty and its basic aim of economic integration. Bargaining has been replaced with arguing in the hands of the ECJ as the crucial agency of guaranteeing the legal foundations of economic integration (cf. Gehring 2002).

The Treaty has established a European judicial field of discourse with the ECJ at the centre. The game is played in the language of adjudication. Judges, lawyers, legal commentators and litigants are the players. They have to frame their objectives in the language of this field. What determines their chances of winning is symbolic capital earned in this judicial field (Bourdieu 1986, 1991a). Symbolic capital helps to define the situation and to frame solutions to problems. The ECJ has accumulated symbolic capital with every new ruling. The Court has established lines of precedents to build frameworks within which cases can be handled in a consistent way. The preliminary reference procedure has become the crucial bridge to transmit the ECJ rulings down to the level of member states so the member states can fundamentally change their legal traditions. It is impossible to understand the establishment of the European judicial field of discourse and its repercussions on national legal traditions in terms of the delegation of power from the member states (principals) to the ECJ (agent), as intergovernmentalism prefers to do (Garrett 1995; Moravcsik 1998), because such an approach ignores the emergence of its own field with its own language and rationale (Stone Sweet 2004: 7–9). The claim to European law's supremacy is certainly still in conflict with the interest of national governments to remain masters of the treaty and of national jurisdiction to maintain the internal consistency of national law against implanting contradictory European elements in national law. National courts can simply ignore European law by not making use of preliminary reference procedures. However, there is the day-by-day practice of such procedures that contributes to the growing factual supremacy of European law without greater public attention.

The preliminary reference procedure has established the ECJ as a crucial force for advancing European economic integration. Direct effect and supremacy of European law have become powerful tools in the hands of the ECJ. They have shifted juridical power from the national level to the European level in all matters of market integration, as well as other fields affected by that process. With the creation of the European single market the distance between potential competitors has shrunk. The resulting intensified competition has been put on the track of Europe-wide specialization and corresponding European labour division because European law, as continuously advanced by the ECJ in preliminary rulings, has provided the necessary legal framework. Removing barriers has intensified competition. Creating a legal framework for the single market has reduced uncertainty and has enabled economic actors to engage in exchange across national borders. The Court's judicial activism has not only complemented legislation, but has also given legal harmonization through legislation a crucial push. In the theoretical perspective applied in this study, ECJ jurisdiction has played two complementary roles: on the one hand, it has intensified competition on a European scale; on the other hand, it has provided directly (and indirectly, by pushing legislation) the legal foundation upon which such intensified competition has been turned to increasing specialization and European labour division. This harmful process has advanced only because the Treaty of Rome, and the way it has been interpreted by the ECJ as formal institutional asset, has shifted power to the side of market integration. These forces have been bundled in the collaboration of the ECJ, national courts and private litigants with an interest in making profit from breaking down (national) barriers to market access.

Establishing a substantial conception of control: free movement and nondiscrimination

In this step, it has to be explained whether or not (and if so, why) the ECJ has been able to establish a leading idea and conception of control (Fligstein

2001) for jurisdiction in the transnationalized field of judicial discourse. An item for such a conception of control is the rigorous application of the mutually linked ideas of free movement of goods, services, capital and persons and nondiscrimination in any regard. Removing trade barriers means nondiscrimination of foreign suppliers of goods, services, capital and labour. With this link to trade liberalization, nondiscrimination as the more general idea has received a boost as the basic principle of justice, which could be more easily extended to other fields on this basis. This conception of control has replaced the traditional idea of collectively shared equality of privileged groups within the nation entailing discrimination of non-nationals, females and minorities of any kind. In this process, tackling exclusion and promoting social cohesion have assumed new meanings, replacing traditional ideas of national welfare. By establishing such a leading idea and conception of control, European jurisdiction is shaped in a substantial way to conform to substantial ideas of 'good' jurisdiction.

After the legislative legal harmonization in Europe had come to a halt during the 1970s and 1980s, until the introduction of the qualified majority vote by the Single European Act of 1986, the Community's legal integration was overwhelmingly in the hands of the ECJ (Capelletti, Seccombe and Weiler 1986). Though the ECJ's actual power in the integration process has been questioned (Garrett 1992, 1995), there is still considerable evidence of such power (Mattli and Slaughter 1995). It was therefore thanks to the then very expansive jurisdiction of the ECJ that integration made any progress at all. It was also obvious that such progress, according to the logics of legal rationalism, went towards a removal of national restrictions as regards protecting subjective rights constituted according to European tradition. The removal of trade barriers to market access in cross-border economic transactions has been the pioneer of this liberalization of the legal order. In doing so, the European philosophy of market integration as a tool of protecting subjective rights had to make its way against the nation states' philosophy of collective market closure and regulation for protecting the individual against undesired effects of the market. The general direction of this jurisdiction was removing discrimination in the access to markets, social security, schools, grants and public service. The ECJ succeeded in so doing in a number of pioneering judgements. With the ECJ assuming the role of a driving force behind European integration for an essential period of time, European law has become, at the same time, a tool for constructing the paradigm of the liberal order of a market society, strengthening the individual's subjective rights and reaching right into the member states. The Court has established comprehensive nondiscrimination as the new conception of control in the field of judicial discourse, replacing the national conception of collectively shared equality within the nation privileging nationals, males and majorities. Complementing the formal establishment of direct effect and supremacy of European law, the principles of free movement and nondiscrimination play the role of shaping the European legal order in a substantial way. They do not follow directly from procedure; they have, in fact, to be established by themselves.

In a series of judgements, the Court replaced the lacking legislative specification of the Community Treaty in directives by jurisdiction or triggered such specifications and produced innovations adopted by legislation later on (Dehousse 1998: 70–96; Egan 2001: 83–108). In the *Reyners* case (2/74) the cross-border freedom of establishment when exercising a freelance job was interpreted according to Article 43 (ex. 52) EC as being directly valid for individuals upon expiration of the provided transition period, although there was no harmonization of the terms of admission then. Until that judgement it had been assumed that observing this right would only be possible upon enforcing corresponding harmonization directives. According to the Court's opinion, the lacking harmonization was not allowed to hinder the realization of the Community Treaty's objective. In specific terms, it concerned the ban on discrimination due to nationality included in Article 43 (ex. 52) EC. As far as the control of company mergers is concerned, the ECJ decided that both the spirit and objective of the Community Treaty allowed for a control of mergers by the European Commission with reference to Articles 81 (ex. 85) and 82 (ex. 86) EC (6/72 *Europemballage and Continental Can v. Commission* 142/84 and 156/84, *British American Tobacco and Reynolds v. Commission*). Following this decision, both the member states and the tobacco industry were prepared to cooperate with the Commission in working out a corresponding European regulation on merger control (1989) after they had fiercely resisted a previous European merger control spearheaded by the Commission.

Free movement and nondiscrimination: goods

The pioneering judgement for enforcing the free movement of goods according to Art. 28 (ex 30) EC was *Dassonville* (C-8/74). The court specified its interpretation of Art. 28 along with the qualifications according to Art. 30 in *Cassis de Dijon* (C-120/78) and *Keck and Mithouard* (C-267/91 and 268/91) (Alter and Meunier-Aitsahalia 1994). The three cases stand for three phases of the Court's case law on the free movement of goods, with *Dassonville* representing the first phase of breaking down trade barriers in the 1970s; *Cassis de Dijon* represents the second phase of specifying the circumstances under which national regulations could be upheld, even if they have a negative effect on cross-border trade, in the 1980s; and *Keck and Mithouard* represents the third phase of stepping further towards allowing member states regulations with negative trade effects under specified conditions in the 1990s (see Stone Sweet 2004: 109–45). Whereas Article 28 interdicts any regulation measure resembling a restriction of the volume (quota), Article 30 (ex 36) EC specifies the terms under which national governments are entitled to apply such measures (e.g. public morals, safety and health protection). In its *Dassonville* judgement, the Court explained in a very general way that national technical requirements are not permissible if they act like quantitative import restrictions. In the *Cassis de Dijon* judgement, this interpretation of the law was confirmed, and it was also specified that such import restrictions would only conform with the Treaty if they fulfilled mandatory requirements, that is if they were proven to be necessary and required by public interest (e.g. tax control, fairness, health and consumer protection) (cf. Craig and de Búrca 2003, 659–77). Compared to *Dassonville*, the *Cassis de Dijon* judgement explicitly acknowledges market regulations adopted by member states under Article 30.

In the face of the very slowly growing harmonization of product regulations on the European level, the Court introduced the principle of validity of regulations in a product's country of origin for all member states. This implied a policy of mutual recognition of product standards by the member states. This policy was adopted by the Commission in order to promote the completion of the single market by the end of 1992. By introducing this principle, the ECJ has established a strong counterweight to the member states' inclination to abuse state regulations according to Art. 30. What is allowed by Art. 30 has to be approved by the ECJ in the last instance and has to undergo a fierce review process.

The line of the ECJ's judicial policy therefore does not simply approve of trade liberalization without any consideration. The requirement to be respected by national governments is, on the one hand, avoiding discrimination between imported and nonimported goods and, on the other hand, avoiding trade-restricting measures. In as much as market regulations affect imported and nonimported goods in the same way, and if they do not restrict trade in the single market in an unjustified way, there is no reason for the Court to interfere in such regulations. The Court has made it quite clear that import restrictions are allowed under Article 30 if they do not entail any discrimination of imported goods in favour of domestic goods and if they do not set unjustified restrictions to trade. A number of judgements represent this line of jurisdiction. In *Kaasfabriek Eyssen* (C-53/80) the Court approved a Dutch ban on imports of soft cheese containing nisin because it implied risks for consumers' health. In *Commission v. Denmark* (C-302/86) the Court accepts the Danish system, which obliges firms to take back the packaging of beer and soft drinks. It is considered nondiscriminatory and justified by reasons of environmental protection that imports have to conform to the requirements stipulated by this system. In *Cinéthèque et al./FNCF* (C-60/84 and 61/84) the Court argued in favour of a French regulation which allows the distribution of movies on video no earlier than one year after their release in cinemas. The relevant reason is protection of cultural goods. In *Torfaen BC/B&Q* (C-145/88) the Court's judgement saw prohibition of Sunday trading in the United Kingdom as being compatible with Article 28 (ex 30) EC as long as it did not discriminate between imported and domestic goods. It was justified because it helps to preserve social and cultural traditions of a region or country (see also C-155/80 *Oebel*) (see Craig and de Búrca 2003: 580–677).

If, however, no necessity of an import restriction can be proven in the public interest, products admitted in their home country can be launched on the market of any other member state without restriction. This means that any member state is obliged to recognize the admission rules of any other member state as being equal to its own admission rules. This interpretation of the law has essentially contributed to the acceleration of single market integration since the time-consuming schedule of harmonizing technical product standards became practically dispensable. In fact, the Commission joined this interpretation of the law and adopted the principle of the mutual acknowledgement of technical product regulations to accelerate single market integration. Following initial criticism on the part of the member states and the Council, the Commission gained the upper hand with this principle. In the White Book on the Completion of the Single Market of 1985 this was bindingly stipulated and was accepted by the Council and the member states with the magical date of December 31, 1992 in mind (Egan 2001: 109–32).

Going beyond *Cassis de Dijon*, the Court advanced a considerable step towards approving trade regulation by member states in *Keck*. This development can be interpreted as a crucial move away from far-reaching trade liberalization and priority of the Community in matters of market regulation and towards greater leeway for market regulation in general and regulation on the member state level in particular. Shortly after *Keck*, this line of argumentation was consolidated in *Huenermund* (C-292/92) and *Leclerc-Siplec* (C-412/93). According to *Keck*, member state regulations are lawful in terms of Art. 30, even if they might have negative effects on the volume of cross-border trade, if they do not refer to products directly but to selling arrangements only. The requirement for the legality of such regulations according to Art. 30 is equal treatment of foreign and domestic goods. There must not be any discrimination of imported goods. Nevertheless, such measures have to meet the requirement of proportionality in relation to their objectives. With regard to products directly, *Keck* does not change the *Dassonville/Cassis de Dijon* framework. The major reason behind *Keck* was the increasing invocation of Art. 28 by litigants in cases with no immediate link to intra-Community trade, such as the British Sunday trading cases (C-145/88, *Torfaen*) and the French video of films cases (60 and 61/84, *Cinéthèque*). These cases can be regarded as preparatory for *Keck*. Commentators say, however, that it is difficult to decide on what is only a selling arrangement and what is not part of the product itself. This holds particularly true for static selling arrangements, which may be part of the product itself, as compared to dynamic selling arrangements, such as special strategies of sales promotion (cf. Weatherill 1996).

Free movement and nondiscrimination: services

Beyond the free movement of goods, the ECJ has ensured that cross-border market access for services no longer has to fail because of national particularities in terms of admission, according to Art. 49 EC. Germany, for instance, had to open its market to foreign insurance companies, even if they do not run an establishment in the country. Nevertheless, admission procedures can be considered legitimate in the interest of consumer protection. However, they have to respect the terms under which a company is operating in its own home country. This was the Court's position in *Commission v. Federal Republic of Germany* (C-205/84). In the wake of this judgement, the European regulation of the insurance market progressed further after a long period of paralysis. Moreover, a strong stimulation of harmonization on the political level through a boost of new directives was one essential consequence of the ECJ's legal interpretation based on the mutual acknowledgement of standards and the Commission's subsequent turnaround to this line. This new boost of harmonization can be explained by the fact that the qualified majority vote, which was introduced by the Single European Act in 1986, removed the paralysis created by the constraint to unanimity. The member states' governments prefer to accept harmonization from that side rather than being exposed to the ECJ's jurisdiction, which has increasingly been sensed as a threat to their national sovereignty. Health service has become a particularly impressive field of expanding European integration, which is contrary to all expectations on the basis of this formerly national policy domain. There is the Working Time Directive (WTD) (93/104) used by the ECJ to challenge member state regulations in health service regarding the working time of trainees and junior professionals. *Sindicato de Médicos de Asistencia Pública* (C-303/98) and *Jaeger* (C-151/02) were particularly crucial in this context. Compliance with the Court's rulings imposes enormous costs on the member states in terms of employing thousands of new doctors in order to run hospitals in accordance with the WTD. Further, the court has helped patients to receive medical services across borders on the basis of their health insurance (C-158/96, *Kohll*; C-120/95, *Decker*) (Davies 2002; Greer 2006).

Free movement and nondiscrimination: from a worker's right to a citizen's right

Following the faster growing free movement of goods, the free movement of persons has also increased steadily, though it has proceeded on a lower level. Currently, about five per cent of EU citizens live in a member state other than their state of origin. The ECJ has ensured the free movement of persons along the lines of furthering market integration and removing barriers to the free exchange of production factors and to free competition. Whatever could hinder workers to work in a member state other than their home country has been abolished by the Court as far as it is compatible with maintaining legitimate rights preserved for nationals only, such as public employment related to security. The crucial criterion is the status of a worker. That means that one has to move as a worker and to make a contribution to market integration to come under the free movement principle, have equal rights compared to nationals or have access to social rights in the country of actual residence. In this field of jurisdiction, the Court's rulings have moved from a stricter interpretation of the worker status towards a less strict interpretation, eventually including part-time workers, unemployed people, students having been employed or seeking employment, persons in training programs and family members. The Court has also gone from a narrower definition towards a broader definition of benefits to be granted (O'Leary 1996; Weiss and Wooldridge 2002). Relevant cases for extending the group of persons covered by the principle of free movement include *Walrave and Koch* (C-36/74), *Ministère Publique v. Even* (C-207/78), *Levin v. Staatssecretaris van Justitie* (C-53/81), *Lair v. Universität Hannover* (C-39/86), *Lawrie-Blum* (C-66/85), *Stanton v. INASTI* (C-143/87), *Konstandinidis* (C-168/91) and *Baumbast* (C-413/99). Relevant cases for extending the kind of civil and social rights covered by the principle are *Salvatore Uglioa* (C-15/69) and *Sala* (C-85/96). Up until 1990, economic activity was the precondition for free movement (Arts 39, 43 and 49 EC). With three directives (90/364, 90/365 and 93/96), the Community has extended free movement to include students, the economically inactive and retired persons. The ECJ paved the way for this extension of free movement in *Lair v. Universität Hannover* and *Lawrie-Blum*. The Maastricht Treaty has made free movement a right of EU citizenship, going considerably beyond the requirement of economic activity. Ever since Maastricht, the crucial requirement has been economic self-sufficiency so that the resident will not be a burden to the hosting member state's welfare system. The ECJ began to treat free movement as a citizenship right beyond economic activity no earlier than in 2000 in *Ursula Elsen* (C-135/99). In this respect, the ECJ lagged somewhat behind legislation.

Removal of trade barriers means abolishing inequality of access to markets between nationals and non-nationals. It breaks down the differentiation between in-group morality and out-group morality, replacing it by an internally and externally valid equality of opportunity, both across and within national borders. This is a first step to constructing a legal order for a European society beyond the family of European nations. It is, however, a step that remains limited to establishing a common market, but it does not necessarily imply the extension of constructing an internal market order going beyond trade – particularly labour and social law – and to a coherent private legal order. However, nondiscrimination of non-nationals can be regarded as the core from which ECJ jurisdiction – along with EU legislation – most likely goes on to construct the legal order of the emerging European society. Beyond the removal of market barriers, nondiscrimination of non-nationals has become the core of constructing a European society of empowered individuals. Article 12 (ex 6) prohibits any discrimination on the grounds of nationality. This general principle has been carried out in further Articles and regulations on employment, business and professions, services, professional sports, trade union activities, housing, social benefits, education, vocational training, tuition fees and maintenance grants. The ECJ has progressively ruled out discrimination of non-nationals in these matters. Just referring to matters of education in *Forcheri* v. *Belgium* (C-152/82), the Court made it clear that the Italian wife of an Italian Commission official had to be treated like a Belgian student with regard to tuition fees; in *Lair* v. *Universität Hannover* (C-39/86), the Court ruled that a French national had to be treated like a German national with regard to access to maintenance grants for students; in *Brown* v. *Secretary of State for Scotland* (C-197/86) the Court's judgement was the same. Nondiscrimination of non-nationals has become the cornerstone of the emerging European society, which acknowledges equal rights of nationals and non-nationals across national borders. In so doing, EU law and ECJ jurisdiction have in fact constructed a European citizenship, which has become consolidated by the introduction of Union citizenship in Articles 17 to 22 (ex 8, 8a-8e). Many cases were handled under the free movement rules. Beyond that, the ECJ ruled increasingly in the interest of nondiscrimination of non-nationals in cases where the free movement rules were not directly applicable (Reich 2003: 180–81; Davies 2003). The introduction of Union citizenship has strengthened the rights of Union citizens in member states outside their home country (Wiener 1998). The ECJ has made use of this tool to extend the groups of persons and subject matters to fall under the principle of nondiscrimination (Fries and Shaw 1998; Reich 2003, Hailbronner 2004; Koenig 2007). Relevant cases are 9/74 *Casagrande*, 186/87 *Cowan*, 120/95 *Decker*, 158/96 *Kohll*, 85/96 *Martinez Sala*, 273/96 *Bickel and Franz*, 184/99 *Grzelczyk*, 224/99 *D'Hoop*, 431/99 *Baumbast*, 200/02 *Chen*, and 209/03 *Bidar*.

Equal treatment of men and women

Along this line of nondiscrimination, equal treatment of men and women is a second feature of a European society consisting of empowered individuals (Hoskyns 1996; Dashwood and O'Leary 1997; Ellis 2000; Stone Sweet 2004: 146–97). Gender equality has been promoted by EU legislation and put into practice in the member states by ECJ jurisdiction. This can particularly be demonstrated with the application of Article 141 (ex 119) EC. It requires equal pay for equal work for men and women. There is also the Equal Pay Directive 75/117, the Equal Treatment Directive 76/207 and the Equal Treatment in Social Security Directive 79/7. Equal treatment has become a major field in which ECJ jurisdiction has promoted the move of national legal practice away from historically established discrimination, above all as regards employment, working conditions, promotion or vocational training of men and women. In a whole series of judgements, the ECJ has established nondiscrimination as basic legal principle. It provides for equal access to opportunities of self-fulfilment for men and women. Equality of opportunity of autonomous individuals is the guideline of this legal reasoning. The legal practice in this field started with cases of direct discrimination, but it has been extended to ban any kind of indirect discrimination from social practice. The

major breakthrough of making the obligation of the member states to guarantee equal treatment of men and women a directly effective individual right
came along the cases *Defrenne I* (C-80/70), *Defrenne II* (C-43/75) and
Defrenne III (C-149/77). It was established in *Defrenne II*, that is *Defrenne
v. Sabena* (C-43/75). In this case, the ECJ ruled that Ms. Defrenne was treated
unequally when she had to quit her job as a stewardess with the Belgian air-
line Sabena to take another job either within or outside the company at the
age of 40, while male stewards only had to do so at the age of 55. The crucial
point was making equal pay a directly effective individual right and the
expansive interpretation of equal pay in the spirit of removing any kind of discrimination. Further judgements of the Court have continued along this line
of argumentation. In *Defrenne III* (C-149/77) equal treatment was made a
general fundamental right. Three directives have complemented this jurisdic-
tional path by legislation: the Equal Pay Directive of 1975, the Equal
Treatment Directive of 1976 and the Equal Treatment in Social Security
Directive in 1979 (Caporaso 2003: 381–84). The objective is constantly the
removal of discrimination (Wobbe 2003).

   Continuing along this line, direct and indirect discrimination came under
attack. Indirect discrimination results, for instance, when regulations taken
by a company affect women to a considerably higher degree than men in statistical terms, although no unequal treatment had been intended. This
applies, for instance, to the limitation of benefits to full-time jobs as against
part-time jobs since women form the majority of part-time workforce. The
breakthrough regarding this kind of indirect discrimination came with
Jenkins v. Kingsgate (Clothing Productions) (C-96/80). *Jenkins* was a breakthrough in equal treatment like *Dassonville* in trade law, but it called for specification like *Cassis de Dijon*. This specification was attained in the case
Bilka-Kaufhaus v. Weber von Hartz (C-170/84). It was presented by the
German labour court according to Article 141, saying that any type of indirect gender-specific discrimination is inadmissible (Blomeyer 1995: 55–62;
Reich 1999: 212–32; Stone Sweet 2004: 160–62). That case dealt with the
justification of excluding part-time employees – mostly women – from a non-
contributory pension scheme granted to full-time employees. This benefit
was rated as an economic incentive for working full time so that the company
would be able to cover evening hours and Saturday hours, which were regularly avoided by part-time employees. Here the ECJ specified under what conditions unequal treatment of part-time workers is justified compared to
full-time workers. Economic reasons are required. The means applied have to
cover a genuine need of the company and they have to be appropriate and
necessary to meet the purpose. The *Bilka* framework was further extended in
Rinner-Kühn (C-171/88) (Stone Sweet 2004: 162–64). The differentiation of
rights to claims, which could previously be justified for factual reasons
according to German law, is no longer covered by European law. This has
resulted in a substantial need for change in national law. Until all changes
have been made, there will inevitably be contradictions that did not

previously exist (Blomeyer 1995: 62–64). A similar effect was exercised by ECJ judgements on the right to compensation in the case of a discriminating refusal of employment and on the continuing of employment in the case of company takeovers (Blomeyer 1995: 65–71). The Community's legal integration unavoidably advances at the expense of a certain legal disintegration of the member states (Dehousse 1998: 173–76).

The power of a leading idea and conception of control: promoting paradigmatic change of the law

Free movement and nondiscrimination as a substantial conception of control in the European judicial field of discourse have shifted power in favour of competitive companies and individuals seeking the advantages of a European market without national barriers. Both principles legitimize a legal order for empowered economic actors, both companies and individuals. It is, therefore, not surprising that powerful and competitive actors are the pioneers advancing a process that not only involves benefits, but also costs, particularly for such economic actors who are less powerful and competitive. Free movement and nondiscrimination are the substantial legitimate principles that enhance competition on a European scale, on the one hand, and form the legal framework within which European labour division is advancing, on the other hand.

With free movement and nondiscrimination as conception of control, the ECJ has contributed to the beginnings of a shift of paradigm away from the welfare of national collectives and status groups and towards the inclusion of empowered single individuals in the equal access to opportunities of any kind, independent of nationality, gender and ethnicity, in an emerging European society, thereby transcending the historically established family of European nations. This is well established in trade law as the core of the common market – it is under way in constructing the internal market beyond trade law, and in labour law in particular – but it is only in its beginnings in private law (Micklitz 2005). What is crucial, however, is the fact that the guideline and conception of control are going to establish a semantics and even paradigm of a transnational legal order, which increasingly dominates legal and political discourse across and within nations to change not only European legal reasoning across member states but also legal reasoning within member states well beyond the strict implementation of European law in individual member states.

For some time, change might remain rhetorical with no real change of legal and social practice in member states. Rhetoric introduces, however, new ideas that call historically established social practice into question. With their diffusion, such practice is losing legitimacy and giving way to changes that were not imaginable before. The more a binding semantics (i.e. being more consistent and demanding than mere rhetoric) is established, the more pressure of change will be exerted on social practice. With every step of jurisdiction, as well as legislation, new elements that contradict established tradition are implanted in legal practice. This contradiction can be solved by separating the general core of the historically established national paradigm (i.e. basic principles) from the new special programmes (i.e. acts of jurisdiction and of legislation). The more new special programmes abound, the greater the chance of a change in the paradigm's core in the long run. This would be the case with the replacement of the principle of collective welfare of national collectives and status groups by the principle of transnational and national equality of opportunity.

Summarizing the court's judgements in core cases establishing the substantial guideline of its jurisdiction and the conception of control of European legal discourse, a common meaning can be identified: the removal of any kind of unjustified barrier to free movement and discrimination. It tends towards replacing the guideline and conception of control established in national legal traditions that focus on the protection of national collectives and shared equality within national collectives and inequality between them.

European unity versus national varieties of law: establishing a dominant European legal community and turning politics into juridical technique

In this next step it has to be explained whether or not (and if so, why) the ECJ has been successful in enforcing a genuinely European legal order with a new sense of justice against the persistence of national variety, as represented by national constitutional courts and national governments. The major forces in support of Europeanizing the legal order are the legitimate power of the ECJ as addressed above, the legitimacy of the *acquis communautaire* making a reversal of Europeanization very costly for national governments, the consistency requirements of judicial reasoning keeping divergence of ECJ jurisdiction from the established path within narrow limits, the support of the Europeanized legal order by transnational elites and the individualization of life careers. What has particularly enabled the forces of European legal integration to overcome the resistance of national varieties of law is the establishment of a dominant European legal community and the replacement of political struggle by juridical technique.

Legal rationalism as tool of binding member states to European law

The ECJ's crucial role in constructing a European legal order along technical terms of jurisprudence with little political interference has been largely supported by the firm establishment of a genuinely European legal field in Bourdieu's (1986, 1991b) sense. A European elite of academics, judges, officials, clerks and lawyers working for the big law firms is clearly in the dominant position of this field, while representatives of national law and jurisprudence are in the dominated or even marginalized position. This is demonstrated by Schepel and Wesseling's (1997) survey of three long-established European law journals (*Common Market Law Review, Europarecht* and *Cahiers de Droit Européen*).

The ECJ's significance for the European integration process reviewed thus far is additionally mirrored by the fact that it has been repeatedly employed by actors in the European political arena to protect their rights in the decision-making process. The European Parliament, for instance, used a number of procedures to extend the volume of its codetermination rights with the support of the ECJ's legal interpretation (C-138/79 *Roquette vs. Council*; C-13/83 *Parliament vs. Council*; C-294/83 *Les Verts*; C-302/87 *Parliament vs. Council (comitology)*; C-70/88 *Parliament vs. Council (Chernobyl)*). By using the principles of legal rationalism (i.e. conceptual sharpness, legal security and protection of fundamental rights), the tools of direct effect and supremacy of Community law, as well as the guideline of a far-reaching interpretation of the Community Treaty in line with its spirit and objective but less in line with its wording and free movement, as well as nondiscrimination as conception of control, the ECJ has pushed legal integration far beyond the Treaty's vague prerequisites. In doing so, it accelerated integration above all during the period of political paralysis from the mid-1960s to the mid-1980s. It is unanimously agreed that the ECJ has played a very active role in the promotion of integration and the corresponding restriction of the member states' rights to sovereignty. The institutionalization of the transnational European legal space is, to a very high degree, due to the jurisdiction of the ECJ. Without the latter's establishment and its active and extensive judicial construction of the single market, this transnational European legal space would not have been differentiated so clearly from the national legal systems and would not have been institutionalized as being unmistakably binding. In the different member states, European law is binding; it is uniformly interpreted by the ECJ for the member states through preliminary rulings and is integrated into the practice of national jurisdiction by the national courts. Consequently, the question arises as to what factors have contributed to the ECJ's powerful role and why its extensive legal interpretation has been accepted as legitimate without any noteworthy actual resistance despite its occasional critical appreciation as doing too far-reaching jurisdiction in the sense of a judge's law, above all from the part of the member states in response to the judgements on state liability (Weiler 1999: 188–218; Dehousse 1998: 117–47). A major prerequisite for the acceptance of the ECJ's extensive legal interpretation of the Treaty by the Community's other bodies, the member states' governments and the national courts, above all the constitutional courts, which act as critical observers, has been its derivation from legal rationalism's basic principles (i.e. from the consequent application of professional standards), above all in the sense of the continental European academic interpretation method according to legal unity, spirit and objective of the Treaty. The development of lines of precedents to build up consistent frameworks for dealing with various kinds of cases has also been important.

The Court's activity has consequently been of a technical nature and has therefore largely been kept away from political controversies. The Treaty's vagueness is added to this. It has more or less called for an extensively specific legal interpretation to set the Treaty's spirit and objective in motion at all. Another role was played by the political paralysis from the mid-1960s to the mid-1980s, when little progress in integration through European legislation was attained. In this situation, the ECJ was called on to compensate for lacking harmonization by legislation by way of the Treaty's interpretation so as to remove the biggest obstacles to the integration project. In this way, the Commission was relieved and, at the same time, ground was prepared for subsequent harmonization. The Parliament's right to a say has been strengthened. Under the dictate of unanimity, the Council made little progress in harmonization for a long time. In this situation, the ECJ guaranteed that the single market project was not abandoned completely.

Increasingly, the member states had to forego their rights to sovereignty. This is why representatives of their governments most frequently criticized the judgements harshly when the law was interpreted in a rather extensive way. Nevertheless, they subjected to the extensive interpretation of the law and did not obstruct its implementation. Their readiness to abide was most certainly due to the fact that a counter-position to the ECJ's legal interpretation could not be justified with regard to the spirit and objective of the Community Treaty and had no chance of obtaining support in legal discourse. Since, however, the member states have made a commitment to the common Treaty, they are bound to accept the ECJ's integration-minded interpretation of the law as legitimate, not least of all for reasons of consistency. A withdrawal from the Treaty, or failure of the integration project at all, would, moreover, have involved high costs for the different member states. After the disaster caused by the First and Second World Wars and in view of the chance to have affluence promoted in all member states, integration has gained such high priority that there is no reason to seriously endanger the integration project just because of some losses in sovereignty, which have to be expected anyway. For the governments of the member states there has, therefore, been no other choice but to accept the ECJ's extensive interpretation of the law, even if this involves losses in sovereignty.

The situation has been very similar for the national constitutional courts. Their institutional interest in maintaining their position as the guardians of fundamental rights and as the supreme body of legal interpretation in the national court system has not been able to avoid the ECJ's extensive interpretation of the law making its way and thus restricting their sovereignty. The foundation for this constellation has been the preliminary reference procedure according to Article 234 (ex 177) EC, which makes the ECJ the directly responsible interpretation body for European law for the national courts, without any detour of national bodies and authorities. Article 234 (ex 177) is, therefore, a tool for Europeanizing law, which mirrors the common will of the governments, but which is to the detriment of the national legal systems' independence. In conflict with the national constitutional courts, the ECJ therefore holds the suitable tool whose utilization has forcibly brought the constitutional courts into the position of an observer whose hands are bound, however, when it comes to active interference. The ECJ has been able to create facts with its extensive interpretation of the law right through to claiming protection of fundamental rights, which has factually raised it on to the position of the supreme legal authority above the national constitutional courts. The role remaining for the national constitutional courts has solely become that of symbolically calling to mind their right to sovereignty to their own jurisdiction if a favourable occasion comes up. It is in this context that we should consider the corresponding judgements of the German constitutional court, namely *Solange I, Solange II* and *Maastricht*. None of these judgements has actually changed anything in the ECJ's legal interpretation and position as the factually effective supreme authority and in the progressing Europeanization of the law. At best, they represent reservations to which the member states could refer, should the improbable case of a demand for returning to national sovereignty occur in legal discourse. If this case happened, in fact, it could only be handled on a political level. The legal reasoning could at best supply legitimate reasons for a political step like this. There is every reason to believe, however, that such a step is not to be expected (Windolf 2000).

The daily progressing of integration in judicial practice tends to prevent a regression of the transnational European legal space's integration. In that practice, preliminary rulings are being used to an ever increasing extent. This daily practice of jurisdiction does not require a central boost, but it is rather fed by a wealth of minor individual cases issued by individuals or authorities. In the framework of the preliminary reference procedure, private plaintiffs, national judges and the ECJ cooperate on the basis of their related interests in the liberation from national restrictions, in the reduction of legal uncertainty and in the creation of legal unity in the European Union (Burley and Mattli 1993: 50–65). They are triggering a process that makes European law penetrate more widely and deeply into national legal systems in its uniform interpretation by the ECJ and its specified application by the national courts. The individual or corporate actors initiating preliminary rulings act as pioneers of Europe's legal integration. As a rule they make use of European law in order to free themselves from restrictions of the national legal systems. For these pioneers of European legal integration, European law is a source of emancipation. In the framework of a European legal culture geared towards the emancipation of the individual from traditionally rooted yet rationally no longer justifiable rule and derived from the Enlightenment, the new paradigm of European law also has legitimatory reasons on its side. The individual and corporate pioneers benefiting from the Europeanization of law are therefore the first and foremost advocates of accepting the legitimacy of European law and the ECJ's extensive interpretation of the law. Since it is the elite of actors actively involved in jurisdiction that count in the legitimation of law, but not the mass of people not participating, the Europeanization of law could make its way even without any greater resistance from the national populations.

As we have seen so far, the process of European integration constantly involves the latent conflict between the European forces of change and the national forces of persistence. This latent conflict may manifest itself at any time and slow down the process of the functional differentiation of European law from national collective constraints and legal traditions or it may slow it down for a certain time or even reverse it to some extent. Karen J. Alter (2000) has pointed out this possibility in a particularly clear way. It would therefore be wrong to understand the functional differentiation of European law as it occurs, in fact, as a linear, frictionless, forcibly and automatically ongoing process. Yet it would be as wrong to see nothing but power struggles between European and national authorities or merely power struggles between national governments in the sense of strict intergovernmentalism. Neorealism and intergovernmentalism cannot recognize any direction of development; they have to strictly deny it. They cannot say anything about the deeper meaning and the underlying paradigm of the emerging order as a social construction. Our analysis as it has been carried out so far shows, however, that it is reasonable to consider the formation of European integration through the developmental dynamics of the differentiation of European law by the ECJ as the essential driving force behind this process and its victory over the countervailing forces of national inertia and developmental paths. This does not prevent us from asking why the ECJ's power of advancing legal change made its way against the persistent strength of national legal traditions and national governments. The ECJ's position in the legal structure of the EU institutions and the way in which it has been filled by the European judges have given the ECJ necessary legitimacy, which has allowed it to play the role of a power differentiating European law from national collective constraints and traditions. This legitimate definitional power has been the crucial weapon in the struggle against the national forces of persistence and inertia in the field of discourse on European unity and national varieties of law.

In a series of judgements, the ECJ has undertaken a relatively far-reaching interpretation of European law, resulting in the judicial extension of law and the complementing of individual rights by remedies in the case of their violation, which has become a matter of conflict with national governments. Evidence of this can be shown by three cases concerning the acknowledgement of rights that had not been granted according to national legal practice. In the *Emmott* case, an Irish plaintiff was accorded back payment of social benefits for the good of equal treatment of men and women, although the deadline for filing a suit had expired according to national law. In conformity with the principles of direct effect and effectiveness, it was established that directive 79/7 had not been properly transferred into Irish law so that it had not been possible for her to respect the deadline for filing action in line with Irish law (208/90, *Theresa Emmott v. Minister of Social Welfare and Attorney General*). In the *Francovich and Bonifaci* case, the Italian state was compelled to assume state liability for damages caused by the nonimplementation of an EU directive. Two employees had gone to court because their wage claims raised against a bankrupt employer were not met, although directive 80/987 demands an institutionalized guarantee for this (6/90 and C-9/90, *Andrea Francovich v. Italian Republic, Danilo Bonifaci et al. v. Italian Republic*). Contrary to German competition law, in the *Yves Rocher* case it was decided that cross-national advertising including price comparisons was admissible in sales leaflets. It was decided that a ban would mean an import restriction that is not justifiable as being necessary according to Art. 30 EC so that no validity can be claimed (126/91, *Schutzverband gegen Unwesen in der Wirtschaft e.V. v. Yves Rocher GmbH*). Because of the relatively wide latitude of interpretation, these judgements have been criticized as being too far-reaching in their intervention in the member states' sovereignty. The fact, however, that no general movement aiming to restrict the ECJ's competence has resulted from these cases speaks for the ECJ's legitimate power and acknowledged status in the member states' practice of jurisdiction.

European forces of change versus national forces of persistence

The process of European integration constantly involves the latent conflict between the European forces of change and the national forces of persistence. This latent conflict may manifest itself at any time and slow down the process of constructing a European legal order against national collective constraints and legal traditions or it may slow it down for a certain time or even reverse it to some extent.

Whether or not the national governments are still the masters of the Treaty or whether or not the ECJ has been successful in establishing a European constitution and rule of law that cannot be turned around by the governments of the member states is a much-debated question in political and legal research (Garrett 1995; Mattli and Slaughter 1995; Rasmussen 1998; Slaughter, Stone Sweet and Weiler 1998; Garrett, Kelemen and Schultz 1998; Wincott 2000; Beach 2001; Theodossiou 2002). In this sense, the functional differentiation of European law is nothing but a permanent power struggle for the formation of the legal order in the multilevel system of the European Union. For this power struggle, however, the ECJ possesses a sharp and effective weapon, enabling it to interpret its role very extensively and to advance the functional differentiation of European law very far against the persisting national powers of inertia. We may admit, in any case, that the functional differentiation of European law is rich in conflicts, precarious and always threatened by setbacks for the course and direction of which, however, the ECJ's position in the structure of EU institutions, its application of the logic of legal rationalism and its legitimate definitional power (i.e. symbolic capital) as well as its support by a dominant European legal community are of crucial importance and are essentially responsible for the formation of the paradigm of a liberal order in the European multilevel system. This is the case even when the forces of persistence and inertia of the member states resist it and may possibly achieve one or another victory in the power struggle. Added to this situation is the fact that the logic of legal rationalism is powered by the boosts of individualization resulting from growing transnational entanglement. Therefore, the member states have limited power only, which is not sufficient for them to fully counteract the functional differentiation of European law and the constitution of the new paradigm of a liberal order in the European multilevel system.

This perspective helps us to correctly assess the ECJ's greater respect for the member states' regulatory competence, which seems to have started in the 1990s. Nevertheless, this is less of a real backlash and more a specification of the ECJ's case law. It is essential, above all, that the philosophy of pure market liberalization meets recognizable legitimatory limits so that a sharper distinction is drawn between real and fictional discrimination when entering the market than before. Nevertheless, there is no complete turn away from the policy of ensuring free movement and removing discrimination when entering the market. We may, however admit straight away that a point seems to have been reached in the 1990s, where the pure liberalization of the order of the European multilevel system has hit its legitimatory limits and where the forces recalling the necessity of national market regulation on the one hand, and the possibility of a legislative European market regulation on the other hand (i.e. the re-embedding of the disembedded economy) (Polanyi 1944) have gained in legitimacy and thus in strength of accomplishment. In fact, European legal harmonization has substantially gained in momentum after the introduction of the qualified majority vote by the Single European Act of 1986. The liberal order of the European multilevel system was accompanied by several elements of the collective protection against the risks of markets, science and technology. Let us now tackle the question as to whether or not, how far, in what sense and why a turnaround as regards the granting of more scope for national regulation can be recognized in the ECJ's jurisdiction since the 1990s.

Ever since the turnaround in public opinion during and after the negotiations on the Maastricht Treaty, which was finalized in February 1992, towards a critical attitude with regard to a too far-reaching transfer of competence on to the European level, the ECJ has also faced tougher headwinds. While it had been able to advance the process of legal integration without any major public attention for around two decades, including the corresponding limitations in the member states' sovereignty rights, and even against occasional criticism from their governments, the latter were now more willing than ever to set limits to the ECJ's judicial activism (Dehousse 1998: 148–76; Maduro 1998: 61–102; Weiler 1999: 63–101; Alter 1998, 2000). With reference to a series of more recent judgements, the ECJ is now claimed to have left the path of expansive interpretation of the law and to have followed a more careful line that leaves the member states a wider latitude for national legislation. In the Maastricht Treaty, the member states have also changed the ECJ's portfolio of tasks (Curtin 1993). By reformulating Article 230 (ex 173) EC according to the ECJ judgements in the cases *Les Verts* (C-294/83) and *Chernobyl* (C-70/88), the possibilities of a nullity suit were regulated in such a way that this path is now also open to the European Parliament. Moreover, Article 228 (2) (ex 171 (2)) EC has enabled the ECJ to impose monetary sanctions on member states that do not abide a decision of the ECJ in an infringement proceeding. At the same time, the areas of common foreign and security policy and common justice and home policy have been withdrawn from the ECJ's jurisdiction.

In the Amsterdam Treaty, however, the common justice and home policies have again been assigned to the ECJ's jurisdiction, though with some limitations in preliminary reference procedures applying also to visas, asylum and immigration. Additional protocols on the Maastricht Treaty have restricted the effect of ECJ judgements on the member states. For instance, in the *Barber* case (C-262/88), the ECJ decided that the principle of equal remuneration of both sexes according to Article 141 (ex 119) EC also applied to company pensions. The suing British employee, Barber, had been dismissed for internal reasons at the age of 52 without any claim to company pension payment since this was only available to men aged 55 and older, while women were entitled to such payment from the age of 50. The ECJ adjudged a pension claim in Barber's favour, yet excluded the applicability of Article 141 (ex 119) EC to potential pension claims dating prior to the announcement of the judgement on May 17, 1990, apart from claims filed before that date. The governments of the member states, which were influenced by the insurance lobby, responded to this judgement with an additional protocol added to the Maastricht Treaty saying that payments from company pension schemes on the basis of employment prior to May 17, 1990, do not represent remuneration according to Article 141 (ex 119) EC.

In the case *SPUC v. Grogan* (C-159/90 [1991] ECR I-4685), the ECJ decided that advertising foreign abortion clinics in Ireland comes under the principle of free cross-border services according to Article 50 (ex 60) EC. However, Ireland's ban in line with the Irish constitution was considered compatible with Community Law since it affected mainly student organs and not clinics wishing to launch their services onto the market. This still appeared too threatening to the Irish government, which obtained an additional protocol added to the Maastricht Treaty confirming that this Treaty did not contain anything affecting the ban on abortion in the Irish constitution. The argument was that student organs did not provide a commercial service so that they were not covered by the EC Treaty, which includes commercial services only. However, it has to be taken into account that the ECJ was released of accounting for the freedom of information because the same case was handled by the European Court of Human Rights in exactly this respect at the same time (Weatherill and Micklitz 1997: 282–83). In the judgement *Commission v. Greece* (C-305/87), the ECJ declared a ban on the acquisition of second homes by foreigners to be incompatible with the freedom of residence guaranteed by the Community Treaty. The Danish government, in contrast, succeeded in being granted precisely this kind of ban by an additional protocol added to the Maastricht Treaty. The common effort of all member states to put a brake on the transfer of competence to the European level and the resulting loss in sovereignty was finally specified with the adoption of the principle of subsidiarity in Article 5 (ex 3b) EC. Accordingly, the Community shall only become active outside its exclusive sphere of competence when an objective cannot be attained on member state level and the Community is definitely better suited for it.

Paralleling the efforts of the member states to set limits on the expansion of the Community bodies in the Maastricht Treaty (Curtin 1993), there has been jurisdiction on the part of the ECJ since the beginning of the 1990s. This jurisdiction at least seems to more strongly take into consideration the member states' particular regulation requirements (Mancini and Keeling 1995; Shuibhne 2002). Obviously, the terms and conditions under which the member states can make their own regulations are interpreted in a less restrictive way. In the judgement on *Commission v. Belgium* (C-2/90), the region of Wallonia was allowed to stop accepting dumps for a limited period of time, although this hindered the free circulation of goods. In *Keck and Mithouard* (C-267/91 and 268/91), a French ban on the sale of goods under cost price was declared admissible. The Court rejected the complaint that this would discriminate against imports. It emphasized in its judgement that not every market regulation might be interpreted as a limitation of cross-border goods flow but that, in contrast, the member states are free to implement such regulations if they prove necessary according to Article 30 (ex 36) EC and if they do not include any discrimination of foreign goods against domestic goods. As compared to *Dassonville* and *Cassis de Dijon*, the latitude for national regulations seems to be extended again here, though judgements have always respected national regulation if they are nondiscriminatory and justified as necessary according to Article 30 (ex 36) EC. It has to be taken into account that by passing the *Keck* judgement, the ECJ struggles against a flood of complaints aimed at removing any market regulation by referring to European law, even if the reference to an import-restricting effect is completely far-fetched. The Court clearly and unmistakably says that a restriction of imports is only given if there is a discrimination of foreign goods as compared to domestic goods. This kind of restriction can be traced in the *Cassis de Dijon* case, but not in the *Keck* case. Consequently, this is not a complete U-turn, but rather a specification along the lines of preceding jurisdiction aimed at stopping the abuse of the argument of import restriction according to Article 28 (ex 30) EC (see Stone Sweet 2004: 139–44). If we take into account the judgements on state liability, which were passed at around the same time (C-6/90 and 9/90 *Francovich and Bonifaci v. Republic of Italy*; C-46/93 and 48/93 *Brasserie du Pêcheur v. Federal Republic of Germany* and *Factortame III*) and caused considerable costs for the member states, the thesis of a U-turn appears even less plausible. As a rule, it is explained by the fact that the

ECJ has been under increased pressure from member states since Maastricht and is therefore less courageous now when it comes to interfering with their sovereignty rights. This argumentation, which is fed by the approach of inter-governmentalism, appears far too superficial, however, since it insufficiently takes the logic inherent in legal work into account. This work is determined by the standards of legal interpretation more than anything else. Of course, from a secondary point of view, no court will be able to completely free itself from currents of thought and political pressures. Nevertheless, the courts may certainly precede both currents of thought and politics with pioneering judgements, putting them on a certain track. This goes, for instance, for the jurisdiction of the American Supreme Court on civil rights and the ECJ's jurisdiction promoting integration, which has worked without much public attention for a long time.

When ECJ judges expressly emphasize that legal harmonization is a matter of legislature and not of the courts, it is merely a matter-of-fact consolidation of the difference between legislation and jurisdiction (Joliet 1995: 451). It might gain special attention against the backdrop of an expansive legal inter-pretation over at least two decades and the interpretation of more recent judgements as a U-turn. However, the new line of ECJ jurisdiction can be understood and explained simply from the boost given to legislative legal har-monization by the Single European Act. Up until the mid-1980s, the ECJ's jurisdiction compensated for the paralysis of legislation; ever since the boost to harmonization in the wake of the Single European Act and after jurisdic-tion also paved the way for integration, the Court has been able to dedicate itself to specification and fine tuning. Added to this was its involvement in lit-igations concerning the balancing of competences between Community bod-ies and the member states, whereas the mere removal of obstacles to goods flow was pushed to the background. One example is the explanation given by the ECJ to the Council's question as to whether or not Art. 308 (ex. 235) jus-tified the Community joining the European Convention on Human Rights. The Court said 'no', arguing that Art. 308 (ex. 235) does give the Community the competence to act without any specific order in the interest of accom-plishing the objectives of the Treaty, yet it does not allow a step that might look like a complement to the Treaty (e.g. the Convention on Human Rights). Such a step would have to be backed by the specific arrangement of such an addition on the part of the member states (statement 2/94). In the light of the Maastricht debate, the Court's statement might once again be interpreted as a sign of reverence to the member states, especially as the ECJ follows in the footsteps of the German constitutional court in its Maastricht judgement of 1993 (BVerfG 89/1994). Nevertheless, it might also be seen as a neat professional interpretation of the Treaty. We can therefore say that political developments can influence legal interpretation only to the extent that it does not involve distortions which might not withstand criticism according to the yardsticks of legal rationalism in legal discourse. In this sense, we may maintain that after Maastricht the ECJ has remained the essential force in the interpretation of European law according to the logic of legal rationalism.

In its most recent case law, the ECJ went as far as giving precedence to the economic interests of enterprises over the national law regulating strikes. In the *Viking* case (C-438/05), the Court prohibited trade unions in Finland to go on strike against a shipping company about to change its flag from Finland to Estonia. With this measure, the union wanted to prevent the replacement of more expensive Finnish workforce with less expensive Estonians. According to the ECJ's ruling, such a measure violates the freedom of choosing one's place of business guaranteed by European law. In a similar way, in the *Lavall* case (C-341/05) the Court ruled that a strike initiated by a Swedish trade union against a wage agreement according to Latvian law offered by a Latvian company doing business in Sweden was incompatible with the free cross-border exchange of services. In the *Rüffert* case (C-346/06), the government of Lower Saxony in Germany had to accept that Polish construction workers were employed below the German wage agreement at a public construction measure. In the *Luxembourg* case (C-319/06), the implementation of the European directive for sending employees to work in another member state was categorized as incompatible with the free cross-border exchange of service. The sending directive that was originally intended to prohibit wage dumping was subjected to a very restrictive interpretation by the ECJ in this way.

These recent examples of ECJ case law highlight in a most striking manner that the legal integration of Europe, in close connection with economic cross-border exchange, gives precedence to the rights of private citizens and private companies to make use of their economic freedoms over the nationally bound political and social rights of state citizens. The ECJ as the responsible judicial institution of interpreting European law is a control pillar of Europe's liberal order. Under the latter's precedence, the republican traditions bound to the nation states lose in significance and effectiveness.

Whether or not a balance between liberalism and republicanism, bourgeois and citoyen might ever be restored is a much-debated question. Therefore, attempts at regaining political sovereignty in regulating the economy are directed at strengthening the intergovernmental character of the European Union. Such a strategy implies allowing the member states to resist too extensive an elaboration of European law by the ECJ by way of threatening non-implementation of such rulings unless they are confirmed by a majority of votes in the Euorpean Council. The decision would be taken on the intergovernmental level of the European Union in this case (Höpner 2008; Scharpf 2009). In this way, it would be guaranteed that all European law came into being exclusively through the filter of national republican procedures and that economic liberalism was put in its place by political republicanism. This strategy would not change the fact that in the transnational space the economy gains precedence over the polity, just as the law gains precedence over politics and liberalism over republicanism. This tendendcy is obviously demonstrated by the ECJ's much stronger position in the institutional framework of the EU as compared to the judicial branch of the governments in the nation state.

Nevertheless, these recent rulings do not mean that the ECJ would no longer ackowledge any national regulation under Article 30. If such regulation can be justified as necessary for protecting the health of consumers, for example, there are chances of approval by the Court, as was recently demonstrated with regard to the rather strict German law allowing only approved pharmacists to sell drugs. In purely economic terms, the Court has confirmed the legitimacy of a professional monopoly. This came as a surprise for many commentators. The public anti-market mood after the global financial crisis may have contributed to this favourable turn towards national regulations.

Anyway, European legal thought is increasingly penetrating the member states' jurisdiction through preliminary reference procedures, especially as such processes have been used more and more frequently. In these cases, national courts submit individual legal questions to the ECJ for preliminary rulings from the viewpoint of European law and refer to them in their own binding decisions. In this way, national courts are in fact increasingly administering justice according to European law and are gradually developing a uniform European legal practice through their cooperation with the ECJ, which is amalgamated with the national legal traditions. This practice, which is applied above all by the lower national bodies, attributes a degree of acknowledgement to European law in the different member states which could not be attained by European jurisdiction penetrating the member states directly. The lower national courts consider their right to initiate preliminary rulings as a means of gaining power against the higher national courts. Therefore, they make extensive use of this tool (Weiler 1999: 197). Their anchoring in the national legal system and their direct involvement in litigations in everyday practice help translate European law into national daily life. An increasing Europeanization of the legal practice results from national jurisdiction. Since this is a creeping process, great resistance does not arise as a rule.

It is the legal practice in preliminary rulings that also leads to the legalization of the relationship between European jurisdiction and national governments. This development is demonstrated by national governments having increasingly made use of submitting observations to the ECJ in preliminary reference procedures since the 1990s, compared to the 1970s and 1980s. In doing so, they turn from the role of sovereign states to members of the Union as supranational unit. Certainly, they submit observations in order to exert influence in their interest on the development of Community case law. However, they have to comply with the established rules of jurisdiction and have to apply judicial language and sound legal reasoning in order to be respected in the court procedure. The master of this procedure is the ECJ. In order to be effective in this process, member state governments need to dispose of the necessary legal culture and armament. In this respect there is a great difference in making use of submitting observations between member states, with France, the United Kingdom, Germany and Italy in the lead, so that claims for equal equipment and access and greater transparency are being made (Granger 2004).

Beyond intergovernmental bargaining: the logics of legal integration

We can say that the greater respect for national market regulation – as represented by decisions on cases like *Keck* – does not justify an argument for a fundamental change in the Court's guideline and conception of control devoted to the principles of free movement and nondiscrimination. Thus, there is ample evidence speaking against intergovernmentalist claims arguing that the member states are still the sovereign masters of the Treaty and the managing directors of the integration process, as put forward paradigmatically by Moravcsik (1991, 1993, 1998, 1999), Garrett (1992, 1995), Garrett, Kelemen and Schulz (1998) and Tsebelis and Garrett (2001). The evidence supports the neofunctionalist argument, saying that supranational agencies, and especially a trustee like the ECJ, have been able to construct an autonomous European legal framework. This framework has increasingly run beyond the reach of the national governments. It is the very basis for transforming national legal traditions, even against member state resistance in the line of neofunctionalist reasoning, as put forward by Sandholtz and Stone Sweet (1998), Stone Sweet, Sandholtz and Fligstein (2001), Fligstein and Stone Sweet (2002), Stone Sweet (2004) and Caporaso and Jupille (2005).

Summarizing the argument in the above paragraph, we can say that the central role of the ECJ in the judicial construction of the European single market, borne by a dominant European legal community, has been to turn politics into juridical technique. This dominance of the juridical field over the political field has undermined intergovernmentalism. In this way, European forces of change, namely the ECJ itself and pioneering private litigants, have been empowered. Correspondingly, national forces of resistance have been weakened because such resistance would have appeared as politics at the wrong place, namely the place where juridical technique and legal reasoning matter more than interests and political power.

Making sense of legal change: turning functional adjustment into constructing a legitimate order

In this step it has to be explained whether or not (and if so, why) the process of Europeanizing the legal order outlined so far involves a fundamental transformation of solidarity, legal order and justice. The generally shared meaning behind individual cases of jurisdiction has to be revealed. It has to be demonstrated whether or not (and if so, why) legal change advanced by ECJ jurisdiction makes sense in the broader framework of constructing a European society which transcends the traditional European family of nations. Superimposing European network solidarity, restitutive law and justice as equality of opportunity on national mechanical solidarity, repressive law and collectively shared equality of results makes sense of a very harmful transformation process, provides legitimacy and helps to keep resistance within manageable limits.

Let us tackle the question as to whether or not a paradigmatic change can be recognized from the functional differentiation of European law from national constraints and traditions. The fact that the development occurs as a struggle of power between European forces of change and national forces of persistence and inertia in no way excludes such a change. This kind of change is shaped by the problems to be coped with by the legal order and by the existing structural conditions. Development may, in this context, be regarded as a search for solutions that can be stabilized. This search may over and again involve inadequate results that cannot be stabilized. If, however, a solution matching the existing structural conditions has been found, it may be easier to institutionalize that solution firmly than any other solution as long as the structural conditions do not change. In this sense, we may interpret the international division of labour as an adequate solution to be stabilized in the long run to cope with the struggle for scarce resources; it replaces other solutions prevailing for a long period in history and having been based on wars for territorial expansion. It organizes higher complexity and allows for the peaceful coordination of action beyond nation states.

Here the subsequent problem of legally ordering the transnational space is arising. This problem has to be solved under structural conditions that are very different from the nation states' conditions of clear-cut external demarcation of their boundaries and strong internal homogenization of their population. The transnational legal order has to gain validity to a greater extent than national legal orders, irrespective of collective solidarity. Far more than national legal orders, it has to be a legal order for the interaction of autonomous individuals. To a greater extent, it requires the functional specialization on this interaction and the corresponding structural differentiation in the European multilevel system according to the principle of subsidiarity. It has to exercise a sufficient amount of inclusive strength for a far more heterogeneous population. Moreover, it needs a greater abstraction of its idea of justice as the basis of legitimation, for justice, in the sense of sharing equal conditions of living, there is less room than in the nation states. In contrast, there is more room for achievement, equal opportunities and fairness being the yardsticks of justice. Among strangers, the right is given preference over the good.

The European cult of the individual: equal opportunity and individual achievement

Looking at the deeper meaning underlying the European legal order, we will recognize that, as compared to national law, it takes a step in the direction of a vocabulary, semantics and paradigm, emphasizing individual achievement, equality of opportunity, individual empowerment and fairness instead of status security, equality of results and collectively shared welfare. In this sense, the European legal order is also promoting a transformation of solidarity and justice. Of course, there is no guarantee whatsoever of factual development always following this direction. This process is a search for adequate solutions that can be stabilized for a longer term. If and to what extent this process will succeed is a matter of the concrete development of law, which may deviate from it, but will then suffer from substantial adjustment problems and tensions as it does not match the structural conditions of transnational social interaction. These adjustment problems and tensions are expressed by setbacks in transnational integration and a relapse of an intergovernmental conflict settlement instead of transnational cooperation. Looking at the European legal order that has developed so far from this point of view, we will widely recognize the formation of an order specialized in regulating interaction between autonomous individuals in the above outlined direction.

This promotion of a European society of empowered individuals by European integration unavoidably implies a latent conflict between the better skilled and equipped individuals making profit from the extended European space of action on the one hand, and the less skilled and equipped people on the other hand. This is proven by the former's far greater support of European integration and the latter's sticking to national solidarity (European Commission 2003: B30) (see Table 2.1).

The construction of a European society is the work of elites forming transnational networks and weakening the primacy of national solidarity. This dialectic of constructing a European society and deconstructing nations has especially been promoted by the ECJ. Apparently this transformation process invokes a deep and long-lasting conflict between the avant-garde of transnational integration and the less equipped and less mobile people who cling to traditional securities guaranteed by the nation state. The dialogue between the ECJ and national courts contributes to promoting the rise of a European identity claiming its own significance as against an exclusively national identity.

A field where the promotion of the normative model of a European society composed of knowledgeable individuals (Giddens 1984) by European law is paradigmatically visible as the law focusing on consumer protection, which includes, for example, the law regarding misleading, comparative and uninvited direct advertising. This is demonstrated by ECJ jurisdiction regarding Arts. 28, 30 and 49 EC on advertising cases, as well as by European secondary law in directives 84/450 and 97/55 on misleading and comparative advertising as interpreted by the ECJ. In European law, the average informed, attentive and understanding person has become the guideline for legislation and jurisdiction. Protecting persons who do not meet this average standard would imply greater barriers to trade and competition, which would counteract the Community's aim of promoting the single market. The German law

Table 2.1 To be national/European in the future (% by demographics)

EB 60.1	TOTAL	SEX		AGE			
	EU 15	Male	Female	15–24	25–39	40–54	55+
n=	16171	7804	8367	2392	4445	3999	5336
National only	40	35	44	33	33	39	49
National and European	47	49	45	48	51	49	42
European and national	7	9	5	10	9	7	4
European only	3	5	2	4	4	4	3
Don't know	3	3	3	5	4	2	3
TOTAL	100	101	99	100	101	101	101

MAIN ECONOMIC ACTIVITY

	Self-employed	Managers	Other white collars	Manual workers	House persons	Un-employed	Retired
n=	1419	1488	1857	3380	1831	965	3793
National only	32	24	31	44	49	44	49
National and European	52	57	56	44	42	40	41
European and national	8	12	7	6	4	8	5
European only	5	4	3	4	2	3	3
Don't know	3	3	4	3	2	5	2
TOTAL	100	100	101	101	99	100	100

	TERMINAL EDUCATION AGE				EU MEMBERSHIP		
	15<	16–19	20+	Still studying	A good thing	Neither good nor bad	A bad thing
n=	4325	6866	3499	1481	7802	4973	2379
National only	53	42	25	26	22	49	70
National and European	39	45	57	54	61	42	22
European and national	4	6	10	13	11	4	2
European only	2	3	5	4	5	2	2
Don't know	2	3	3	4	2	3	3
TOTAL	100	99	100	101	101	100	99

Source: European Commission 2003.

on unfair competition (UWG) and legal practice regards an advertisement as misleading and therefore illegal, when a hasty, inattentive, uncritical and unreasonable consumer does not understand a spot. Thus, it aims to protect the minority of weak consumers, which can be estimated at ten per cent. The ECJ, however, has made use of quite a different image of the consumer. Interpreting the rather open European law, the Court has applied the image of an average consumer, who is average in being informed, attentive and reasonable. The Court is aimed at the typically empowered and knowledgeable consumer as a self-responsible market citizen. Relevant cases include *Mars* (C-470/93), *Gut Springenheide* (C-210/), *Verbraucherschutzverein e.V. v. Sektkellerei Kessler* (C-303/97), *Lloyd v. Klijsen* (C-342/97), *Estée Lauder v. Lancaster* (C-220/98), *Linhart v. Biffl* (C-99/01), *Pippig v. Hartlauer* (C-44/01) and *Douwe Egberts v. Westrom Pharma* (C-239/02). In consumer law, it becomes very clear how much European law – with the ECJ as crucial interpreter – is reflecting and changing the structure of solidarity. While the German tradition of consumer law has aimed at protecting the weakest through collective solidarity represented by the state, European law in the hands of the ECJ counts on the empowered, knowledgeable individual and disregards the minority, which does not live up to the standards of a knowledgeable agent.

Vice versa, we can say that the single market project needs at least normally empowered individuals to be eventually realized. This is the message of European law in jurisdiction and in legislation. It is in blatant contrast to the German tradition of protecting the weakest of the consumers, as well as weaker suppliers, who are particularly middle-class entrepreneurs, against the market power of the big corporations. The law on unfair competition (UWG) has long been considered a pillar of the German domestication of capitalism. However, under the rule of European law, as well as the changing image of the consumer, empowered by broad educational upgrading, German jurisdiction and legislation, too, have changed in the direction of the guideline of the average informed, attentive and reasonable person. In Britain and France, there has never been such far-reaching protection of weak consumers and suppliers. In Britain, this would have contradicted the tradition of voluntarism and little governmental regulation of the market. While the 1970s and 1980s saw some movement in the direction of the stronger German philosophy of consumer protection in the member states and on the European level, the liberal market philosophy is clearly prevailing today. This is how a society of empowered individuals is being inaugurated as a normative model in European law, jurisdiction and legislation (Schwarze 1999).

Doubtless, European law strengthens the individual against his or her community of origin and, in the case of migration into another EU member country, also against the community of indigenous citizens of his or her country of residence. The ECJ has progressively ensured that individuals cannot be deprived of their rights established by Community law or by national legislation or administration in neither their country of origin nor their country of residence, as established in *Casagrande v. Landeshauptstadt München* (C-9/74) and recently confirmed in *Sala* and *Grzelczyk* (C-85/96 *María Martinez Sala v. Freistaat Bayern*; C-184/99 *Rudy Grzelczyk v. Centre public d'aide sociale d'Ottignies-Louvain-la-Neuve*; see Jacqueson 2002). European law forms society from the viewpoint of the market citizen who uses his or her liberties on the market to realize his or her own ideas of value, ideals of life and interests. The market citizen exploiting his or her liberties on the market is also the cell from which originates a legal citizen developing a feeling of what is right or what is wrong in legal terms in the extended European space and liberating himself or herself from national blindness, above all the kind of blindness including some form of discrimination when it comes to market access.

It appears logical that on the way to generalization, the sense that all kinds of discrimination are unlawful is growing (Bell and Waddington 2003). Race, nationality, religion, gender, age and other features are banned from the list of legitimate criteria in regulating access to market, employment, education, public discourse and the like. As compared to national legal traditions, European law goes one step further in this direction of strengthening the individual and his or her personality by liberating him or her from collective constraints. In this sense, the European legal order advances institutionalized individualism (Parsons and White 1964) and the 'cult of the individual' (Durkheim 1964) to a new level that is beyond the limits existing in the nation state. The ECJ is a focal point of this cult. Free movement, nondiscrimination and self-realization of the individual is the focus of the new paradigm promoted by the European legal order. In this way, it corresponds to the individualization of living conditions resulting from the ever more finely tuned international division of labour and the correspondingly growing network solidarity. Both sides (i.e. law and social structure) complement and support each other. This is made obvious, for instance, in the dwindling force of morally founded regulations of alcohol consumption in the Scandinavian countries and of abortion in Ireland in the wake of joining the EU (Kurzer 2001).

We may assume that Europe's judicial construction helps the basic principles of legal rationalism achieve a new breakthrough against particularism and privileges based on the concerted influence of organized interests: calculability through abstraction and analytic thought, freedom from contradiction and formal correctness, freedom, equality before the law and self-responsibility. This is very much in line with Max Weber's (1922/1972: 503–13) classical analysis, pointing to the rationalizing, formalizing and generalizing work of the legal profession in constructing modern 'rational' law as compared to the particularizing effects of legislation aimed at the attainment of particular goals or substantial justice. It has to be taken into account, however, that the ECJ's jurisdiction is oriented towards the consistency of Community law and does not pay attention to creating inconsistencies in national law. Therefore, the Europeanization of law forms substantial contradictions within the national law of the member states – at least for a certain transition period – which will enforce revisions that are aimed at re-establishing consistency. This is complained about, above all, in Germany due to the extremely high importance attached to consistency as an element of the rule of law (Blomeyer 1995). In the interest of matching European and national law, national courts in Germany make extensive use of preliminary rulings, while British courts are more reluctant to do so (Dehousse 1998: 32, 173–76; Harlow 1995).

The predominance of legal rationalism is the reverse side of the European Union's democratic deficit if we start from the principles of representative democracy (Maduro 1998: 103–75). Given the weight of Europe's judicial construction (Stone Sweet 2004), it seems obvious to pay particular attention to the extension of this side of the European Union and to create better pre-requisites for making the subsequent standard setting in committees and the administrative processes on both the European and the member state level more transparent and for facilitating access to information on such processes and on legal procedures – above all through joint law suits – so that interested citizens, particularly citizens' initiatives, can create more critical public control (Gerhards 1993, 2000; Eder, Hellmann and Trenz 1998; Eder and Kantner 2000). The more the legal order moves in this direction, the more it will turn away from the predominant model of sectoral consent among selected experts and go towards an adverse procedure, according to a competitive model of decision making.

According to Micklitz (2005), there is a disproportion between the ECJ's objective of providing for horizontal integration in the sense of looking for the equal application of Community law in each member state and the national courts' interest in vertical integration in the sense of making European law and national law consistent. The ECJ leaves this task to the national courts. The result is an existing gap between advancing horizontal integration promoted by the ECJ, which proceeds occasionally somewhere in the clouds, and vertical integration, which remains weak. Therefore, member state legal practice is torn between the two extremes of ignoring European law and endangering the consistency of national law by applying European law. All this means that the ECJ is constructing a legal order for a European society. There is, however, still a considerable amount of work in progress. However, the contours of an emerging European society are clearly visible in this work in progress.

Choices for democracy and choices for an economic constitution in the European multilevel system

What has emerged with the central role of the ECJ in advancing the European integration process is a kind of 'judicial democracy' in the sense of Tocqueville's (1945, vol. 1: 98) classical analysis of the peculiar traits of democracy in America. This is a kind of democracy that does not remedy the widely lamented 'democratic deficit' of the European Union because such complaints take representative democracy as a yardstick. In this type of democracy, power centres on the parliament of representatives regularly elected by the people, in this case by the ideal construction of Europeans as one people. Anyway, this is only an ideal construction that does not even meet the reality of pluralism within nation states. Therefore, under conditions of increased pluralism in the European multilevel system, it is much more realistic to conceive of democracy as a complex set of institutions which help to keep political, administrative and legal decision making transparent, accessible and open to revision; likewise, they should ensure that people in powerful positions are responsible for their actions. A system of checks and balances is more capable of managing the complexity of such a pluralistic system than a fully fledged representative democracy. Such checks and balances are also important for models of deliberative supranationalism, which otherwise would lean towards the rule of wise experts who are out of touch with the real world (cf. Joerges and Neyer 1997).

Miguel Poiares Maduro (1998) has interpreted the evolution of the Court's rulings from *Dassonville* to *Cassis de Dijon* to *Keck* as opening up avenues for developing an economic constitution for the European single market along the lines of European traditions, which differ in their stronger political regulation of the economy from the tradition of a liberal economy, as is paradigmatically represented by the United States. While *Dassonville* has opened the door for establishing a market economy with no political regulation beyond the political devices of guaranteeing equal opportunity and free competition, *Cassis de Dijon* has demonstrated that the liberties of the market might end where fundamental requirements of public order and the protection of the consumer would be undermined. If the Community or the member states arrived at such a conclusion and it was approved by the Court with regard to its mandatory character, nondiscriminatory nature and proportionality in regards to its objective, such a measure of regulation would be acceptable. After *Keck*, there is even greater space for political regulation. There are three models of an economic constitution: a liberal model, a centralized model of regulation on the community level and a decentralized model of regulation on the national level. The decentralized model is particularly attractive in the face of limited chances of concentrating regulative power on the Community level. This is a logical, sound argument. However, in empirical terms, we have to take into account the structural changes of solidarity brought about by the legal integration of the European single market, along with other factors of Europeanization and globalization. These structural changes of solidarity set limits on the effective and legitimate choice for the economic constitution of the European single market, both on the Community level and on the national level. These structural changes of solidarity are in favour of an economic constitution that focuses more on equality of opportunity and individual achievement than on far-reaching equality of living standards, collective achievement and comprehensive protection of the individual by the state. European law empowers the individual, thus it promotes the change of social order towards greater emphasis on the inclusion of the individual into society through activation instead of protection. It empowers particularly competitive companies to build European economic powers while the organization of industrialists and trade unions is increasingly weakened by this process. Fritz Scharpf (1996) sees the precedence of negative integration over positive integration in this feature of the emerging European society. Wolfgang Streeck (1999: 67) has coined the concept of 'neovoluntarism' for this new economic order. It replaces the old order of neocorporatism. Such an activated society turns what has been under state control into a market. It inevitably creates the problems of dividing society into more or less active individuals and marginalizing those individuals who cannot be activated. Greater inequality within national societies is the consequence of this structural change. It is the disintegrative side of increasing European integration predominantly advanced by mobile elites. Legal integration is part and parcel of this process. There is no European integration without national disintegration. This is what a sociological analysis has to contribute: pointing out the limited chances of realizing empirically different models of an economic constitution for the European single market.

From the European family of nations to a European society

The functional differentiation of law as an institutional order for avoiding and settling conflicts among autonomous individuals or between these individuals and state authorities beyond the boundaries of particular communities has occurred through the formation of the European nation states. Functional differentiation of the law means focusing on the ordering of a society composed of autonomous individuals who do not share a densely woven collective tradition. This function is fulfilled by protecting individual rights, determining their latitude and distinguishing between lawful and unlawful behaviour. This is accomplished by rational techniques and procedures of decision making, precluding any influence of collective constraints and substantial conceptions of justice as far as possible (Weber 1922/1972: 456–58, 503–13; Luhmann 1983: 55–135). The big legal codifications on the European continent (i.e. the General Prussian Land Law, the French Code Civil, and the German Civil Code) were, above all, projects designed to consolidate the nation state by submitting the entire territory to uniform law. In England, jurisdiction according to the common law, along with the legislation of the sovereign parliament, has created a strong tradition of national law overcoming particularism. The respect of law and jurisdiction has essentially been fed by the formation of nations by way of the external demarcation of their boundaries and the internal homogenization of their population. Quite clearly, though with differing success, heterogeneous regions, classes, strata and denominations in multi-denominational states have been transformed into nations which boast a certain feeling of solidarity and a unique collective identity. The construction of nations with a relatively strong feeling of solidarity and a collective identity helped to overcome the segmentary differentiation into families, clans, local communities, regions and, in part, denominations and the stratificatory differentiation into estates. The liberation from particularistic bonds and the formation of the individual's autonomy as a binding ideal of life have gone hand in hand with the emergence of a new type of all-embracing community: the nation. Being the carrier of the constitution guaranteeing human and civil rights, the nation is the stronghold of the individual's autonomy. It is the union of citizens sharing the same individual rights and committing themselves to mutually respecting their individual rights as a result of their loyalty to the nation. Different to all older forms of society, the nation of citizens is a union of autonomous individuals aimed at the mutual protection of their autonomy. As a result, the legal bonds of autonomous citizens depend largely on experienced solidarity, commonly shared traditions of a legal spirit and the respect of others as fellows sharing common law. In the framework of the coalescence of this nation of citizens, an ever more comprehensive granting of civil, political and social rights has emerged in the European welfare states. This has, in turn, strengthened the feeling of solidarity of the nation of citizens (Marshall 1964). The legal order has been able to interfere more in the formation of equal conditions of living for all. Jurisdiction, which has comprehensively developed in the settling of conflicts, has been abided by and respected; it has been considered legitimate since the nation of citizens has provided the necessary resources of commitment. The community of individuals has therefore benefited from a new kind of association. Seen from a European or global perspective, this has still been a form of segmentary differentiation coupling internal cohesion with external division and internal legal order within nations with an external lack of order between nations.

In the light of this nation building, the question arises as to what the functional differentiation of law from national traditions means in the process of European integration. After all, it concerns law and jurisdiction beyond the segmentary boundaries of nations of citizens without there being a similar association on a European level. The European Community does not possess that quality of solidarity and shared legal traditions (i.e. mechanical solidarity) that might fuel the sharing of human and civil rights in the framework of a common legal order and jurisdiction and that provides all those resources of commitment, which are essential for legitimately respecting legal order and jurisdiction. What matters here, therefore, is the creation of a legal order and jurisdiction for a space that is still considerably differentiated in segmentary terms and is not supported by dense cross-national ties. Consequently, the concrete question is whether or not uniform law may exist without a cross-national legal community and without a legal culture being the foundation of stabilization and legitimation. The progress made by legal harmonization within the European Union proves that this is not an undertaking doomed to complete failure after all. The development is facilitated by the national legal traditions' formation as branches of a legal family with common roots in a legal order building on human and civil rights. The differences refer to nuances and specific practices in the service of one and the same matter, but they do not refer to unbridgeable contrasts. It is therefore certainly possible to discover the core of a uniform legal culture within the different national legal traditions. Moreover, the legal communities are not cut off from each other. Instead, an increasing entanglement has resulted from the exchange of information about the different models of how to solve legal problems. It is, above all, contractual terms beyond national borders which acquaint the pioneers of economic exchange (i.e. the lawyers concerned) with the legal practices of the home countries of contract partners. Nevertheless, it is the advancing legal harmonization resulting from the cooperation of jurists from all member countries in the Commission's committees (i.e. comitology) which is crucial (Joerges and Neyer 1997; Joerges and Vos 1999; Neyer 2000). They create a European legal vocabulary, semantics and paradigm by way of formalizing and abstracting national traditions. European law being incorporated in the national legal systems thus creates an increasing harmonization of national traditions of law. The jurists cooperating in the committees in Brussels form an elite, spearheading a European legal community that grows with each step of legal harmonization and European jurisdiction. Consequently, we may well talk about a European legal community *in statu nascendi* (Zuleeg 1995).

We even dare to say that the European Community can be considered essentially as a judicial construction markedly following the logic of legal rationalism (Stone Sweet 2004). In this sense, the project of European integration can certainly be compared with the big legal codifications, having created the European nation states as legal entities, without which no order and cohesion would have been possible within an extremely heterogeneous structure. The crucial feature has been the functional differentiation of law as an independent system of the order of social intercourse between individuals who are otherwise not tied to each other and its liberation from being embraced by particular communities and local or religious traditions. This development has been accompanied by the emancipation of the individual from collective constraints and the emergence of a new societal community of autonomous individuals. Contrary to habits, traditions and conventions, law is a rational construction, is independent of traditions and merely refers to the function of guaranteeing the ordered coexistence of free individuals. According to its internal logic, law does not reflect the constraints of action imposed upon the individual by collectively shared traditions. Its task is rather the creation and maintenance of an order between free individuals beyond such traditions. The more law actually moves away from such traditions, the more it will functionally specialize on creating an order within which the individual may exploit his or her latitude of action insofar as it does not restrict the latitude of others. Since law, according to its internal logic, forms and secures an order between free individuals who do not share any tradition of proven values and norms, it ultimately leans towards favouring a liberal order.

Deviations from this legal trend, for instance towards more comprehensive collective regulation, redistribution and life provision, are fed from different sources. Above all is the source of collective association and the collective formation of will, which always goes hand in hand with external demarcation of boundaries and an internal, leveling homogenization of the population and restriction of individual liberties. The European welfare states have followed this path for a considerable time. Evidence of this includes indicators such as government spending, public welfare spending, redistribution and regulatory depth as regards the control of economic action and the 'degree of decommodification' of human labour (Esping-Andersen 1990: 35–54). In terms of regulation theory, the accumulation regime of industrial mass production and the mode of regulation of Keynesianism supported each other in the regime of Fordism, which was closely tied to the powerful nation state. However, this also included preconditions such as strong external demarcation of boundaries and internal homogenization of the population, which set relatively narrow limits on the functional differentiation of law and its emancipation from collective solidarity and collective traditions.

From the point of view of regulation theory, the accumulation crisis of stagflation in the 1970s put an end to the 'golden era' of Fordism and gave way to Postfordism. Postfordism was a new accumulation regime based on product diversity and supply-side economics of neoliberalism as the new mode of regulation (Boyer 1990). In this perspective, the European single market program is a promoter of this fundamental shift in societal formation, and the ECJ plays an important role in the promotion of this regime change (Bieling and Deppe 1996; Ziltener 1999). This story told by critical integration theory embodies some truth. It is, however, only half of the truth because the existing economic bias of this theoretical approach fails to adequately recognize that the change of the economic regime is only part of a more fundamental change of societal organization on the way from Europe as a family of nations to the emergence of a European society. To understand and explain this change we have to address, in particular, the change in the structure of solidarity and in the cultural idea of justice taking place in the process of European integration.

The establishing of the European single market bursts the bonds of national, collectively tied legal orders and enforces a new boost of the functional differentiation of law and its emancipation from the particularism of national legal traditions. The more it is left to on its own to do so and the more the unfolding of its internal logic is not restricted simultaneously by a countermovement of external demarcation of boundaries and internal homogenization of the population comparable to that of the nation-states, the more it will create a liberal order, freeing the individuals from national restrictions and transforming the national legal bonds towards a more liberal order in view of the supremacy it enjoys and the direct effect it exercises in the different member states. Obviously, the interrelation between law and collective regulation, redistribution and provision of life meets closer limits on the European level than on the level of the nation states since processes of external demarcation of boundaries and internal homogenization of the population will not come into effect to the same extent. The detaching of the individual from collective national traditions is the very vehicle allowing European law to foster the cross-border cooperation of many single individuals. This cooperation of many single individuals is the essential driving force behind European integration. It is shown, above all, in the growing cross-border division of labour. According to Emile Durkheim's (1964) model, the latter is the cement of an organic solidarity, which increasingly eclipses the mechanical solidarity of nation states differentiated in segmentary terms, though it does not remove it completely. Beyond Durkheim's approach, we may describe the new type of cross-border solidarity as solidarity of networks. While organic solidarity fits the individual strongly into status groups and into a whole demarcated against the outside, network solidarity goes one step further on the way towards establishing a liberal order. In view of the less marked strength of the individual's collective integration and in view of the pluralization of group memberships and the individualization of conditions of life, it is gaining significance on the European level.

In our explanatory model, the functional differentiation of European law from national collective ties plays an essential role. Indeed, clear specifications have been set, namely the prominent role assumed by the ECJ in the European Community's legal integration. We may even say that the ECJ has a far greater influence on the EU's legal order in the concert of European institutions (i.e. Commission, Council and Parliament) than the national courts, including the constitutional courts in the nation states. This gives clear supremacy to the logic of legal rationalism as compared to the political formation of will, which collectively restricts the latitude of individual action. With this in mind, we may say that the functional differentiation of law from collective constraints goes further on the European level than on the national level. Since law regulates the coexistence of free individuals beyond collective traditions, the farther-reaching functional differentiation of European law from collective constraints and traditions involves a trend towards the emergence of the vocabulary, semantics and paradigm of a liberal European order, which gradually eclipses the collectivistic national orders. The ECJ is the driving force behind this process, alongside its inherent logic of legal rationalism, which joins an ethic of individualism. This ethic is moreover fueled by the process of cross-border division of labour, cooperation, interaction and communication extending latitudes of action. The logic of legal rationalism and the logic of individualization work hand in hand, thus producing a new liberal European model of society. In this context, the ECJ's strong position as the driving force behind the differentiation of European law from national collective constraints plays a crucial role.

In a nutshell, in the hands of the ECJ naturalistic functional adjustment of the legal order to shrinking distance and the advancement of European labour division have become a meaningful and legitimate order. This is a legal order made for competitive economic actors. It is more appropriate for the market citizen of liberalism than for the political citizen of republicanism or for the social citizen of welfare states in the social democratic or conservative sense. The ECJ has been a driving force of shrinking distance across national borders as well as the central instance that has turned this naturalistic process into a meaningful procedure aimed at the construction of a new legitimate order. The construction of that order is an ongoing and much-debated process. ECJ jurisdiction has, however, made a fundamental contribution to setting it on a track in a clearly discernible direction.

Concluding remarks

The ECJ has assumed a dominant position in framing the European legal order because of its ability to exploit the powers allotted by the Treaty of Rome and because of the greater weakness of the other European political bodies (i.e. Commission, Council and Parliament) compared to the typical national fields of politics. It has been called for by increasing transnational trade to make use of its power. It has been enabled to do so by acquiring a reputation as guardian of the EC Treaty and embodiment of sound legal reasoning dealing with technical (but not political) matters. In this way, ECJ jurisdiction has attained legitimacy in establishing a European legal order that penetrates the national law of the member states. On the formal institutional basis of preliminary reference procedure, supremacy and direct effect of European law and judicial rationalism, the ECJ has established a substantial 'conception of control' (Fligstein 2001), invoking free movement and nondiscrimination as opposed to national, collectively shared protection of advantages and equality of results. In so doing, the ECJ has contributed a great deal to establishing the European paradigm of a legal order focused on protecting individual rights and equal opportunity and prohibiting discrimination against national resistance. By penetrating national law, the ECJ's decision making promotes paradigmatic changes in national legal orders. Due to their overlap with the European legal order, national legal traditions converge with every step of EU legislation and jurisdiction. National peculiarities remain in areas not affected directly by European law, but they are affected indirectly by the diffusion of the vocabulary and semantics of the European legal order. In this way, a European society which imposes itself on the historically evolved family of European nations is emerging.

Our analysis of the position and role of the ECJ and its jurisdiction has shown that we will arrive at a more comprehensive and deeper understanding of European integration if we explain this process with the help of a theoretical approach derived from Emile Durkheim's (1964) study on the division of labour in society. The process entails a permanent conflict between European forces of change and national forces of persistence, European developmental dynamics and national developmental paths; the distribution of power is crucial to the result of this. However, it is not simply power that is relevant, but also the kind of power resources available to the relevant actors. It has turned out that due to its unique position in the European Union's structure of institutions, the ECJ assumes a crucial role in this power struggle. It has been able to fulfill this role very effectively with the help of the definitional power (i.e. symbolic capital) available to it. The settling of the power struggle, however, does not tell us anything about the deeper meaning of the order created in this process. In a move to understand the meaning of this order, we have to grasp the process as functional differentiation of European law from national collective constraints and national legal traditions, a social construction of legal experts according to the logic of legal rationalism and free movement and nondiscrimination as substantial conception of control. We also have to explain that process as an adjustment of the law to the structural conditions of transnational social intercourse and the accompanying individualization of the conditions of life. Any explanation of European integration based on part of this whole process only will be insufficient. Our goal cannot be a mere causal explanation of European integration in a positivistic sense. We also have to try and obtain an adequate understanding of the emerging new paradigm of social order within the European multilevel system in a hermeneutic sense. What we see in this broader view is an emerging European society of autonomous individuals superimposing itself upon the previous Europe of nations. Individualization as promoted by the European rights revolution is the vehicle for overcoming Europe's segmentary differentiation into nations and producing a new transnational European society that is composed of empowered individuals and a plurality of self-organizing associations of autonomous individuals. This does not mean that the family of nations will be completely replaced by the European society of empowered individuals; however, the latter is increasingly superimposing itself upon the former. The corresponding tensions will fuel conflicts on Europeanization versus the preservation of national collective solidarity for a long time to come.

3 The French dilemma
Postnational republicanism against economic liberalism

The public role of the French intellectual was formed during the Dreyfus Affair at the end of the nineteenth century. Emile Zola's article '*J'accuse*' remains the paradigmatic exemplar of the public role of the intellectual in France. The intellectual is a custodian of truth and justice. He or she belongs to the enlightened elite at the heart of the community. He or she is the warden of the nation's political conscience. His or her task is to combat false beliefs and resist the seduction of public opinion. Reflection on the correct course of the world and critique of dominant grievances are incumbent upon him (Levy 1987: 19). He or she should publicly espouse the results of his or her reflections, conclusions and values. In his or her role, he or she significantly influences the fate of his country in crucial phases of history (Ory and Sirinelli 1986/1992). Nonetheless, the cross-party advocacy of truth and justice has, since the Dreyfus Affair, remained a disputed intellectual mission that continues to provoke critical reactions (Benda 1927).

The process of European integration, which eventually culminated in the failed proposal for a European constitutional contract, has, at latest since the referendum concerning the Maastricht Treaty, become a significant object of intellectual debate in France. French intellectuals are the bearers of European thought in the heart of the hexagon, the signposts of its development and the architects of its possible design. In the following, the significant contours of the French intellectual discourse on the institutional design of Europe will be examined beyond disciplinary boundaries.

On 29 May 2005 the French said 'no' to the European constitutional contract. For the contract's draftsmen, their supporters and their opponents, the results of the referendum were a fundamental turning point in the European project. Some see this as a chance to construct a different Europe and the others see it as the end of further European institutional construction. In any case, the referendum left behind a helplessness concerning the future of Europe and it revealed that there is a basic tension between French traditions of political thought and the construction of a legitimate system of European governance. The following sections will uncover the basic tension between the French idea of state and society and the inclusion of France in the emerging European system of multilevel governance (Guéhenno 1995). The core of the French theorizing of state and society is constituted by the semantics of republicanism. This semantics is unique in its understanding of freedom as resulting from state law that is formed on the basis of democratic decision making of civic citizens who are united by the bonds of the one, indivisible nation. The first part of the following considerations will deal with the institutional construction of Europe; the second part will deal with the evolution of a European identity.

The institutional construction of Europe

The French intellectual discourse concerning the institutional construction of Europe is marked through and through by the tension between the republican tradition and the political elite's commitment to the European integration project. Therefore, the debate is characterized by profound conflict. This is demonstrated by three contradictions: (1) economic liberalism versus economic anti-liberalism, (2) federalism versus anti-federalism and (3) liberal democracy versus political republicanism. These contradictions will, by way of exemplary comments, be elaborated upon in the following sections.

Economic liberalism versus economic anti-liberalism

The 1957 Rome agreement concerning the foundation of the European Economic Community clearly gave the economic integration of Europe priority over political integration. Under the terms of the method favoured by Jean Monnet, step-by-step legal and political integration was supposed to be spurred on by economic integration. This method corresponds to the functionalist concept of spillover from economic to legal and political integration. The decision to place priority on economic integration also implies a strengthening of economic liberalism that not only characterizes the European project, but also increasingly affects member states by way of increased integration. In France, this development provoked criticism of Euro-liberalism which is, however, countered by liberal positions that have followers within, particularly, big business management and followers who play a role in the intellectual discourse.

In the French intellectual discourse, the political left wing sees liberalism as playing the role of a global villain particularly marked by the culture of the US. However, this does not mean that there is complete consensus on the topic. Representatives of the liberal doctrine are also to be found in the intellectual discourse. An example of a contribution to this position is Alain Minc's book, *La mondialisation heureuse* (1997). According to Minc, the free market economy is the only economic system with long-term viability, and this is even more so the case in the context of globalization. Making use of the market as the dominant mechanism for the allocation of resources and preferences is only natural as the market is not a cultural phenomenon, but a natural reality. According to Minc, Europe, like the rest of the world, is working towards the realization of the liberal model of society. Even the Rome Treaty is inscribed with the logic of the liberal model. Deregulation, deregimentation, the European harmonization of law and the end of state monopolies are results of the European integration process. These measures do away with obstacles of economic competition and therefore ensure the functioning of markets.

Globalization, according to Minc, subjects governments to a new economic game. In this context, the Keynesian policy of demand management only generates growth of the national deficit. At the same time, budgets lean more towards saving than spending in times of crisis. Growing national debt with increasing interest payments then becomes an almost insurmountable barrier to economic growth. In accordance with the conditions of liberalized foreign trade, a country loses competitive capacity when it has to bear a large national deficit with a heavy burden of interest payments. The European Economic and Monetary Union, with the common currency and the limitation of national deficits to three per cent of the gross domestic product, has imposed further restrictions that prevent the return to a Keynesian spending policy upon member states. Having established the independent European Central Bank in line with the model of the German Federal Bank prevents a European monetary policy geared towards accelerating demand. Both measures bind the hands of policy at the national and European levels. According to Minc, the advantage of restrictions on economic and monetary policy is the promotion of market forces. On the one hand, Europe becomes more independent from the fluctuations of the US dollar and increases its competitive capacity vis-à-vis the American currency. On the other hand, the growth-restricting effects of large national deficits and correspondingly high interest payments are kept under control. According to Minc, these are the advantages that Europe can gain from the liberalization program that is inherent in the European integration project.

The liberal European integration program is, contrary to the propagated advantages exemplarily illustrated by Alain Minc, an object of intense criticism from, above all, the political left wing of the French intellectual discourse. Jacques Sapir's *La fin de l'euroliberalisme* (2006) is a representative example of this criticism. It deals with the debate concerning the European constitutional contract and, in particular, the question of the extent to which the selection of a certain economic policy may be laid down in a constitution. This question has led to an animated debate. In essence, the debate is concentrated on two questions: the question of the ideological character of the decision on liberalism and the refutation of the hypotheses fundamental to this program and the question of whether or not it is at all acceptable to include a particular political path (i.e. liberalism) in the body of the constitution, especially because a constitution is a text by which the long-term organization of societal life orients itself. Sapir (2006: 73) speaks of a 'new betrayal' of the experts and a part of the French intelligentsia because they are promoting the revival of an economic doctrine marked by errors and highly controversial assumptions. From his point of view, the average citizen may not be able to measure the validity of expert positions in the discourse, but he or she has the right to know that experts respect the rules of critical review or abstain from opinion (Sapir 2006: 18). Sapir accuses the doctrine of economic liberalism of being disproved by numerous analyses. This would particularly apply to the assumption of the balancing powers of competition, above all because the prerequisites of a perfect market with market participants' complete information and without any informational asymmetries can never be achieved. Pricing is not merely dependent on supply and demand. Asymmetries of information are inherent in the market and are dictated by relationships between market participants and not by external factors. Accordingly, it does not help at all to pursue the realization of conditions for perfect markets because it is known that spontaneous market development tends to produce conditions of market failure. What we call market failure is in reality a failure of the competition mechanism itself. Market failure does not first spring up from particular exogenous factors, but from the structure of competition itself. Therefore, without institutions that limit the field of competition, market failure is unavoidably structurally programmed by unlimited competition. By this argument, the significance of nonmarket decision-making processes by way of organization and hierarchy is confirmed (Sapir 2006: 34–35). Despite these misapprehensions, orthodox liberal thought has achieved dominance. Advocates of the liberal policy objectives of the constitutional contract would, in the name of truth, represent a position that is, at its base, marked by fundamental errors. Making competition the sole principle of economic organization would be utterly wrong. The constitutional contract would be a manifesto of liberal theology (Sapir 2006: 44). The designers of the constitutional contract, using anchoring in the constitution, would have, in one crucial action, submitted politics to rules – rules of economic policy – that, in reality, could only be the result of political decision-making processes themselves. In so doing, they would have used their temporary power to set limits on the decision-making latitude of future generations, especially as concerns vital questions regarding the lives of citizens. The procedure of achieving unanimity among the member states would make later amendments or changes to the text all but impossible. This judicial guise makes clear the intention to eternalize economic positions that are, in reality, based on a decision for a particular ideology. One should therefore be reminded of Article 28 of the French declaration of human and citizens' rights of 1793, which gives the public the right to, at any time, review, reform and change its constitution and forbids any generation to irreversibly subject future generations to its laws. For this reason, the constitutional contract would be founded on breaches of the principles that define a democratic constitution (Sapir 2006: 63–64).

Federalism versus anti-federalism

The concept of sovereignty occupies a place of significant importance in the Europe of national states. In order to grasp the problems of 'sovereignty' in the context of European integration, it is first necessary to understand the term in its historical context.

Jean Bodin (1530–96) introduced the concept of sovereignty as a pillar of state theory. According to him, the republic has the right to rule over multiple households and their common ground with sovereign power (in the terms of legitimate rule). The authority of the state is the source of law. Its sovereignty is absolute, and its power is indivisible. The state has the power to make laws, and, according to its own will, give orders and defend without having to respond to demands and without the right to opposition to its instructions. The state decides on peace, war, taxes and alliances. Loyalty, devotion and obedience from both the nobility and the common people are legitimately claimed by the state alone. If we follow Bodin, the sovereignty of a state can be recognized in the fact that its legislature is not subordinate to any higher power. Nothing limits the legislative power of the state. These are the tenets of Bodin's (1994) sovereignty doctrine that must be considered in order to be able to understand the French intellectual debate concerning the division of power in the European multilevel system. The evocative questions are whether or not the national state will remain the sovereign legislator, to what extent legislative force should be shifted to the European level, whether or not and how legislative force should be divided between the European and national levels and what overall loss of sovereign political legislation results from the implementation of economic liberalism (Sapir 2006: 114–15).

In a country in which the concept of state sovereignty was developed, the loss of sovereignty resulting from increasing international interdependence is particularly painful. The globalization of the economy is seen as a dangerous limitation on state sovereignty. The state loses sovereignty over economic policy by having to subordinate itself to the laws of global competition. In the tradition of Bodin's concept of sovereignty, the continued sovereignty of the state is maintained despite the altered conditions of state action. Accordingly, the exercise of state sovereignty is only possible by means of differentiation of independently operating institutions with specific competencies. However, this form of governance by no means does away with the state's sovereignty over the establishment of these institutions and the delegation of their competencies. The institutional differentiation of competencies does not change the form of the state or the fact that there is ultimately one sole, undividable state sovereignty (Goyard-Fabre 1991). According to this concept of the state, it is wrong to derive a basic limitation or division of sovereignty from the practical restriction of state sovereignty following from international treaties and the *Pacta sunt servanda* principle. Thus, international law is a form of coordination between sovereign states, but it does not imply the subordination of states to a higher power (Dupuy 1963, quoted in Sapir 2006:

116). Following this line of argumentation, the postmodern thesis – as represented by Jean Marie Guéhenno (1995) in an exemplary way – which states that sovereignty in the European and global multilevel system will be increasingly fragmented, is rebutted by the argument that it is marked by a lacking distinction between democracy and rule of law and legitimacy and legality (Sapir 2006: 116). Legislation without legitimation by a democratic decision-making process would require an omniscient and well-meaning legislator. As this, however, does not exist, legality without legitimacy, or, in other words, the validity of law without a democratic legislative process, would end in tyranny (Sapir 2006: 117). This would mean rule by judges, not rule by the people (Sapir 2006: 120).

For advocates of national state sovereignty, the main issue is that, to date, adequate democratic decision-making processes have only been institutionalized on the national level, but not on the European or global levels. Adherence to national state sovereignty is not to be confused with essentialist nationalism (Sapir 2006: 121). Nations and national decision making should by no means be seen as homogeneous and overriding. Rather, national state democracy is the only form of democracy in which it has been possible to institutionalize conflict resolution and decision-making processes that can be identified as democratic. On the one hand, the project of European federalism is seen as a logical continuation of national state democracy on the European level. On the other hand, the project is described as being dependent on the development of a European nation and a European people that have a realistic content and represent more than mere metaphor. However, Europe is, according to the perception of advocates of national state sovereignty, still a long way from this level of development. From this perspective, Euro-federalists adhere to a utopian idea that is far removed from reality (Sapir 2006: 124).

The doctrine of democratic sovereignty is set in opposition to a purely legal reading of international treaties. According to this reading, international treaties create obligatory law which concerned states can no longer allot at their will. Following the tenets of the hierarchy of legal sources (H. Kelsen), this means that international law has priority over national law (Quermonne 1994: 266–67). If nation states have entered into such treaties, they must ascribe unlimited validity to the resulting law, thus restricting their own latitude for action and their sovereignty. This legal reading of international treaties allots national states only a limited authority within a de facto federal system. The European Union has in fact already made considerable progress in this direction. European law based on treaty agreements has priority over national law and direct validity for Union citizens. Advocates of nation state sovereignty object to this development, stating that European law is a matter of law created by lawyers without democratic legitimation, and that the member states, as lords of the treaties, can be the only source of the legitimacy of European law. Accordingly, European law binds sovereign nation states to contractually stipulated law, which they can terminate at any time by way of contract amendment or withdrawal from the contractual alliance (Soin 2005: 17).

Arguments for the lingering sovereignty of the nation state in the European multilevel system can be based on the position of the French Constitutional Council (*Conseil Constitutionnel*). Article 54 of the V. Republic of 4 October 1958 specifies that, in cases where the Constitutional Council determines that consensus on a clause of an international agreement is lacking, this clause can only be ratified by French Parliament if the constitution has previously been amended accordingly (Quermonne 1994: 268). The precedence of the French constitution over international and European law is thereby established. French Parliament can only authorize the government's international agreements if they do not conflict with the constitution. The French Constitutional Council has confirmed this precedence of the national constitution in several cases. The constitution allows for the restriction of national sovereignty only in cases of peacekeeping by way of international treaties in accordance with the principle of reciprocity. It is up to the people to exercise this sovereignty by delegation to their representatives or by way of referendum (Quermonne 1994: 269). The constitution does not allow the transfer of national sovereignty to an international organization. Regarding European law, this means that neither approval of the popularly and directly elected European Parliament, nor a decision by the European Council implies the shifting of sovereignty from the national to the European level. However, this does not at all mean that the French government's hands are fully tied when making international agreements or establishing international organizations and arranging their competencies. In a ruling on the Maastricht Treaty, the constitutional council unmistakably decided that the constitution explicitly authorizes the French government to do just these things. However, according to the understanding of the constitutional council, this is a matter of agreements between nation states that do nothing to alter the fact that these agreements are the states' sovereign decisions and can therefore be revised at any time (Quermonne 1994: 270). Along the same lines, the state council (*Conseil d'Etat*) and the court of cassation (*cours de cassation*) recognize the precedence of European law over French law in the sense that the validity of European law is ultimately founded on the national sovereignty of the member states. Critics, however, see this practice to be an increasing depletion of the notion of sovereignty, which will become an empty concept if de facto legislation lacking the legitimation of the French people is enacted (Quermonne 1994: 270).

In summary, two positions concerning the question of sovereignty are represented in the French intellectual discourse. One position is that of the postmodernists who profess a dissolution of sovereignty, originally subject to the nation state and ultimately subject to the people, in the European multilevel system. They see this development to be the unalterable end of democracy as Europeanization and economic globalization are unstoppable forces which undermine nation state sovereignty. The other position is represented by the advocates of nation state sovereignty who maintain that, despite the internationalization of politics, nation states, as sovereign contractual partners, retain the final power of decision. They are therefore called upon to exercise this power when international agreements intervene in the sovereignty of national populations to an excessive extent, as in the case of the liberally programmed European constitutional contract. Postmodernists and advocates of sovereignty share the belief that, to date, democratically legitimate sovereignty can only be exercised within the framework of the nation state. However, whereas postmodernists take this sovereignty to be part of an inexorable process of erosion, advocates of sovereignty still believe democratically legitimate nation state sovereignty, even in the context of the European and global multilevel system, to be the source of all law.

The question of sovereignty is, in the context of the debate concerning the appropriate institutional form of the European Union, also a question of the feasibility of a European federation. In this point, the federalists and antifederalists in the French intellectual debate seem to be locked in an almost irresolvable conflict. It is difficult to design any model of a European federation in France as federalism in the tradition of Bodin's sovereignty doctrine and its translation into the indivisible sovereignty of the people during the French revolution never fell on fertile grounds there. Federalism is fundamentally foreign to French thought.

Liberal democracy versus political republicanism

The republican tradition rooted in France has been at odds with liberalism since the beginning. Whereas liberalism sees the freedom of citizens as protected by the setting of tight constraints on the state's interference in the people's affairs, republicanism regards the state as the embodiment of the polity in which citizens collectively decide on the laws to which they wish to subject themselves. According to the republican view, the polity is a place of freedom in which citizens make laws for themselves. From the liberal point of view, even a state, in the republican sense, is a threat to its citizens because its laws limit those citizens' freedoms. The more competencies the state has, the more it limits the freedoms of the citizens. There is therefore a need for constitutional limits on state competencies and the guarantee of citizens' inalienable freedom rights (Sadoun 2002).

In the same way that republicanism represents a contrast to liberalism, it also represents a contrast to democracy, where the implied democracy is the Anglo-Saxon liberal model of the kind put into practice in the USA. With this in mind, Regis Debray (1992) differentiates between the French idea of the republic and the Anglo-Saxon idea of democracy. According to his understanding, freedom and reason (*raison*) come together in the republic. The reasonable argumentation of the assembled citizens of the republic allows for the identification of the common interest, common welfare and public good and their separation from particularistic interests. Citizens do not subordinate themselves to any external power, not even God; they subordinate themselves only to their own freely reasoned law. The republic is therefore laical. Its laws are made by free citizens who are only following their collective reasoning (*raisonnement*). Thus, the republic harmonizes freedom and reason. Participation in the matters of the polity trains citizens in the public virtue of caring for the public good (Sadoun 2002). As civic citizens (*citoyens*), they create themselves the common good that defines the framework within which private citizens (bourgeois) can pursue their interests without harming the interests of others or doing harm to the common good (Rousseau 1762/1964). A functioning republic requires schools that are responsible for raising young people as citizens who are committed to the public good. Debray (1992) states that the republic of virtuous citizens is the legitimate foundation for the validity and due process of the law and the guarantee of fundamental equality of citizens and social justice.

In contrast, according to Debray (1992), the Anglo-Saxon, and especially the American, idea of democracy rests on the precedence of the private citizen over the civic citizen, and the private citizen's mistrust in the activity of the state, which always implies interference in his freedom of action. The liberal model of democracy has particularly been formed by the Anglo-Saxon and Protestant countries. In these countries, the citizen is primarily a member of a prepolitical cultural and/or religious community, and he only secondarily aligns himself with the larger political community. The recognition of citizens' self-organization in prepolitical communities, to which religious communities particularly pertain, is an integral part of modern liberal democracy. Hence, pluralism of prepolitical identities has precedence over the development of a broader political identity. The liberal democratic model is meant to protect this pluralism of prepolitical communities. This model is not, in contrast to republicanism, meant to overcome this pluralism by way of the development of a civic identity. From the republican point of view, liberal democracy is therefore always threatened by fragmentation that can lead to a struggle of all against all, wherein the stronger prepolitical communities prevail over the weaker ones. Politics exhausts itself with the mere creation of compromise and finds no possibility for the definition of a common good that is equally valid for all. As Debray argues, the school of liberal democracy accordingly aligns itself with the society. The school is a reflection of societal pluralism and therefore cannot nurture political identities beyond pluralism. Society dominates the state. This also means that the economy rules politics because the state cannot develop enough binding power to keep the forces of the market under control. In Debray's eyes, France has already significantly moved away from its own long-established republican tradition, moving towards the model of a liberal democracy. Referring to the resistance movement against the French revolution in the Vendée, he believes that the Vendists would oust the Jacobins. The more the one indivisible and laical republic would be weakened, the more the contours of a kind of postmodern feudalism would appear.

There are also two contradictory forms within republicanism that must be distinguished: national republicanism and postnational republicanism (Ferry 2002). Whereas national republicanism is more closely connected with Jean-Jacques Rousseau's thinking, postnational republicanism is closer to that of Immanuel Kant (Sadoun 2002). National republicanism is rooted in the feeling of interconnectedness between a national collective and a common political history of internal homogenization within the boundaries of the state, along with external dissociation from other states. In contrast, postnational republicanism requires less common ground and relies on the binding strength of citizens' participation in matters of the polity and public deliberation on the common good. It is also less outwardly dissociated. It follows Kant's model of a cosmopolitan federation of European states. Whereas national republicanism has fundamental reservations about a European federation that exceeds the level of a confederation of sovereign nation states, it is considerably easier for postnational republicanism to conceive of Europe as a federation with a strong federal level of the political union.

However, national republicanism rather than post-national republicanism is more strongly rooted in the history of French thought. However, national republicanism has increasingly become a fiction that does not correspond with political reality. This applies to French domestic conditions and especially to the country's integration into the European Union. According to the ideal notion of republicanism, the participation of the citizens in public deliberation and the handling of public matters creates the common republican spirit, which bolsters the cohesion of the citizenry. The republic requires no prepolitical community (e.g. a religious one), but rather it spawns a civic community from within itself. This is the fundamental difference between republicanism and communitarianism. From the republican point of view, the nation as a solidary community does not exist independently, but rather it is the product of republican praxis and the republican spirit. A strong republic transcends pre-existing cultural differences and assimilates its new members by means of its praxis and spirit. The republic is also the bearer of civil rights because citizens can only be sure of their rights to the extent that they are upheld by republican praxis and the republican spirit. Nevertheless, a republic cannot be drawn up theoretically. It needs time to develop processes of internal homogenization and external dissociation. Only in this way can a solidary nation, which then forms the solid foundation for republican praxis and the republican spirit, emerge from political practice. This, however, results in problems with carrying over the idea of republicanism to the postnational age. Several processes have contributed to the fact that the national idea of republicanism is decreasingly backed up by reality, and there are no real chances for bringing reality back towards the idea. In reality, politics is a far cry from the model of republican praxis. Politics has become a matter of the technocratic and administrative elite. The political elite can now only engage in public debates in the shadow of medial orchestration. The average citizen is not a participant in political practice, but a spectator who cannot develop a feeling of belonging or political responsibility. Without vital repub-lican praxis that incorporates citizens, the society degenerates into insur-mountable group particularism. Accordingly, France has not been successful in making its North African immigrants a coequal part of the nation. The results of the republic's weakness are, on the one hand, a lack of integration of immigrants and, on the other hand, rampant right-wing extremism. The shifting of a majority of legislation to the European level has significantly contributed to the depletion of the idea of republicanism in real political life. The European harmonization of law forced by the European single market proceeds far away from the citizens. It is, first and foremost, a technical process. Political involvement does not take place in the form of public rea-soning, but in the form of extensive lobbying according to the law of the strongest. The medial orchestration of politics in order to influence public opinion has increasingly taken the place of public reasoning. However, pub-lic opinion formed in this way no longer represents a common good arising from public reasoning in the republican spirit, but a momentary sentiment that can change at any time.

These are the political realities that, according to Jean-Marc Ferry (2002: 140–47), have made national republicanism an idea without real content. National societies' heterogeneity does not allow itself to be forced into the national model of the republic and the national republic is not sovereign enough to actually serve as the dominant political venue. For this reason, Ferry logically looks for chances of realizing postnational republicanism at the European level. Ferry thereby uses the concept of postnational republi-canism rooted in the tradition of Kant to build a bridge to Habermas. Accordingly, the link between republicanism and nationalism is indebted to the specific historical situation of the Westphalian system of states, in which nations, as solidary foundations, were created from the formation of states by way of internal homogenization processes within the nation and external dis-sociation from other nations. In the age of advanced European integration, the union of republicanism and nationalism has inevitably been unravelled. Therefore, in order not to perish with nationalism, the development of a post-national European republicanism is required. Otherwise, liberalism prevails on a broad scale. This means the precedence of private citizens over civic cit-izens, society over the state, the economy over the polity, the egotism of pri-vate interests over the common good and the particularism of prepolitical religious and cultural and ethnic communities over the political community. If Europe does not wish to fall victim to these consequences of unchecked lib-eralism, a constitution that constructs Europe as a political space in which Europe-wide public reasoning creates the basis for a European polity and a European sense of belonging, is, according to Ferry, necessary. Such a European polity can only arise from a long, historical process. This, however, requires impetus from a suitable constitution in order to have any chance for development. Only within the framework of such a European community will it again be possible, according to Ferry, for European citizens, in the perspective of the common good, to define the scope of private citizens' rights in such a way that they do not cancel each other out or fall victim to a system of 'might makes right' (Ferry 2000).

European identity based on a common cultural heritage?

The semantic construction of Europe from above, using models of the polity, is paralleled from below by the semantic construction of a European community beyond the union of nations, a European identity beyond national identities and a European culture beyond national cultures. In this matter, sizeable obstacles stemming from the French tradition of thought also come to the fore. In contrast to the German idea of the culture-nation, the French state-nation, according to the exemplary understanding of Ernest Renan (1947), needs no roots in a common culture, language and/or religion. Anyone can become a Frenchman as long as he or she shows his or her loyalty to the French nation and fulfils the civic duties connected therewith, including paying taxes, attending school and, as a male citizen, serving in the army. Nevertheless, the French state-nation, which differs from the German culture-nation, is the result of a long, historical process of internal homogenization within the nation and external dissociation from other nations in which a national sense of belonging formed as the foundation of the national republic. Accordingly, a strong demand for the citizen's identification with the nation characterizes the idea of the French state-nation. His or her undivided loyalty should apply to the nation above all other memberships. Because of this understanding of a citizen's strong identification with the nation, which has grown from a long, historical process, it is difficult for French thought to imagine that this process could repeat itself on the European level in the foreseeable future. The development of nation states is unique in European history. It has led to the generally improbable fusion of the state and the nation. This could, as in France, occur from above, whereby the state created the nation and subjected it to a central bureaucratic system, or, as in Britain, from below, whereby a state was formed from the civil organization of the society.

Accordingly, there is a fundamental tension between European integration and the idea of the nation as stronghold of republican freedom. In the following sections this will be made clear by means of examples dealing with two pertinent issues: (1) the idea of the nation and the European space with variable borders and (2) European identity versus European identities.

The idea of the nation and the European space with variable borders

According to Dominique Schnapper's (1994) republican understanding, the nation is a community of civic citizens. It is nothing more than a political entity whose sovereignty is recognized by other political entities. The nation integrates population groups into a community of civic citizens from whose existence the state's foreign and domestic actions receive legitimacy. The civic

citizens give up their particular group identities and are prepared to participate in the democratic game based on equality for all. The nation is therefore
a form of political organization that is bound to the democratic process. The
state is the instrument of the nation. It has the instruments and means of control and coercive power at its disposal. Its functions are the domestic integration of population groups by way of citizenship (*citoyennetté*) and the
protection of the nation from foreign threats (Schnapper 1994: 59).

Accordingly, the nation is not an objective factor of community formation
following from the same race, culture or religion, but a political construct
that desists from such differences between people. According to this idea, the
nation is therefore a universalist project, but in reality it is always the result of
historical coalescence of population groups into a nation as a particular entity
with a specific identity that distinguishes it from other nations and it has difficulties in really incorporating every group of people as equal citizens
(Schnapper 1994: 165–69). An accordingly tense relationship exists between
the universalist idea and the historical particularism of the nation. The nation
is not merely an idea, but a social reality that is concretely positioned in time
and space. Both sides cannot be separated from each other (Schnapper 1994:
80–81). It is not possible to have one without the other. One cannot realisti-
cally implement the idea of citizenship without its objective and subjective
historical preconditions for existence. Consequently, projects concerning
postnational and supranational citizenship are difficult to put into practice.
This is also true for the European project. This type of citizenship can be
designed on the drawing board of intellectual discourse. However, it cannot
be put into practice in the foreseeable future as the European unity of institutions, culture, history and feelings is insufficiently developed for reaching
this goal.

As Robert Soin (2005: 188) asserts, the European Union has made a number of advances towards the realization of a European citizenship. However,
he doubts that these advances have noticeably bound the citizens to the
European Union as their own political community. The Maastricht Treaty
established Union citizenship and expanded rights to political participation.
Economic liberalism was to be complemented with first steps towards a political union. Union citizenship should be added to state citizenship, but it
should not replace it. National state citizenship retains its priority, and Union
citizenship, although superordinate, is less of a priority. National citizenship
is the basis for Union citizenship. Robert Soin therefore expects that Union
citizenship will do little to change primary identification with the nation and
will achieve only minimal identification with the Union. Even expanded
political rights (e.g. the right to vote in local elections in an EU host country,
petition and ombudsman) are poorly suited to binding citizens to the EU
because, in Soin's opinion, they are too difficult to manage and are rarely
used.

The author points out that, since 1979, Europeans are called on every five
years to elect their representatives to the European Parliament in a direct

election. In spite of the expanded codecision procedure introduced by the Maastricht Treaty, European Parliament does not come close to possessing rights that are a given to national parliaments. Therefore, European Parliament can hardly attract the attention of the citizens. By way of the Maastricht Treaty, citizens' participation rights in the process of European integration were expanded. Accordingly, undeniable steps towards the democratization of the Union have been taken. Regardless, this advancement has hardly brought the citizens closer to the Union, as Robert Soin, representing the critical intellectual discourse, has pointed out. The ratification procedure of the European constitutional contract offers a clear example of this. Citizens are asked for their consent to a prearranged agreement that they were unable to influence and that they cannot change. Other examples are the submission of a petition to European Parliament and the invocation of the ombudsman in administrative processes. Both practices are, in their implementation, quite complicated and are seldom used. Thus, Robert Soin draws the conclusion that the steps that have been made towards democratization do not contribute to the creation of a political space of European union citizens. The desired ability to allow the citizens' sense of belonging to the Union to grow must therefore be cast into doubt.

Dominique Schnapper (1994) argues that social space without borders is not comprehensible for the human being; a person's sense of belonging cannot emerge in such a situation. Even if one wishes to recognize a common European cultural heritage, the lack of consensus concerning the borders of Europe is proof of the indeterminacy of this common heritage. Two positions concerning the matter of the European Union's borders oppose each other. Whereas Great Britain leads on the side of member states that have advocated the expansion of the Union into middle-east and south-east Europe and have accelerated and continue to accelerate the admission of new members, France has wished for more of a political deepening of the Union without new member states. Preferred partnership with neighbours in the east and south should take the place of expansion. In this regard, Mitterand thought differently from Kohl and Chirac thought differently from Blair. Hubert Védrine (2005: 24–25) states that the goal of the French after Maastricht was, using the euro and a deeper Union, to create a strong Europe that can form a countervailing power to the global hegemony of the USA. From this perspective, a union without fixed geographic, historical, cultural and religious borders is a sort of United Nations at the regional level. It is a union without unrestricted, historically-rooted commitment to democracy, a nebulous entity that is held together neither by a sense of citizenship nor by a sense of belonging.

European identity versus European identities

In his work *Penser l'Europe* (*Thinking Europe*), Edgar Morin (1987) searches European cultural history for the common identity of Europeans and asks, based on this background, what the designation of Europe's history could be. As Morin asserts, Europe has never had clearly defined borders. In the south and the west, Europe is bordered by the Mediterranean Sea and the Atlantic Ocean, respectively. The border in the east, however, is not a natural one. Therefore, it is difficult for Europe to be defined by its geographic borders. In fact, Europe first emerged from political and cultural development in a historical way. It formed from its organization. Its history is marked by division and conflict, but also by treaties and the cultivation of unity. On the one hand, Europe's divisions are of a religious nature: the secession of Constantinople and Luther's Reformation. On the other hand, they have resulted from wars and the subsequent development of nation states. Europe's unity is based on the development of trade (i.e. Hanseatic cities and exhibition cities), the diffusion of technologies and the principles of diplomacy for the purpose of assuring a European balance. According to Morin, Europe is divided by everything from which it is formed, and everything that it divides contributes to its development. The nationalism of the nineteenth century is also a commonality in the development of Europe. Nationalism led to wars, including the First and Second World Wars of the twentieth century, and sealed its division until 1945.

Morin states that Europe, throughout its entire history, has passed through a series of metamorphoses. From the Europe made up of states, a Europe of nation states arose; from the Europe of trade, a Europe of industry arose; and a ruler of the world changed into a province under US protection (and wardship). Its identity does not arise in spite of its metamorphoses, but because of them (Morin 1987: 70–71). The existence of a European cultural space cannot belie the reality of cultural polycentrism. Even so, European culture has common roots: Jewish, Christian, Greek and Roman heritage. According to Morin, Europe has spawned a unique culture marked by spirituality, humanism, rationality and democracy (Morin 1987: 81). From these common roots, national cultures have developed; in each case they have developed as an osmosis of one with the other in which each is characterized by its respective dominant traits and prominent aspects (Morin 1987: 86–87). Modern Europe, born in the Enlightenment, developed its culture from the Jewish, Christian, Greek and Roman roots. Modern European culture arose from that which, in the medieval thought, formed one entitiy: faith, reason and nature (Morin 1987: 90–91). Since the renaissance, these three elements have had a simultaneously complementary and contentious relationship, from which a permanently heated dialogue has arisen. Within this permanently heated dialogue, Europe forms itself culturally by way of new theories and ideas that search for its own roots. This permanent dialogue is concerned with freedom and justice and reason and faith. Science is spurred on by discrepancies between rationalism and empiricism and imagination and verification. The original European cultural development strives towards universalism, which has its upsides and downsides. According to its nature, European universalism gives rise to the question of what can be regarded as specifically European.

Concluding remarks

The French intellectual debate's fundamental difficulty with achieving a consensually supported, coherent semantic construction of Europe lies in the internal tensions of political thought that are, on a national level, increasingly difficult to resolve. The dominant political categories shaped by republicanism make it increasingly difficult, on the national level, to master the challenges of a society that has become much more open and heterogeneous. They are particularly ill suited to the institutional design of a still more open and heterogeneous European Union. Liberal and federal positions occupy a dominated position in the French intellectual discourse. The principles found therein can neither be used for the rearrangement of the nation state, nor for the design of the European Union, such that an agreement concerning a new social model suited to the structural conditions of an open society would be possible in the foreseeable future. The debate will also continue to be marked by the contradictions between centralism and group particularism, republicanism and liberal democracy, a powerful state and a federalist division of powers and antiliberalism and liberalism. These contradictions that determine the design of society within the nation state also characterize the debate concerning the design of Europe. France's historical development, initially by means of absolutism and then by means of the republican nation state, levelled the particularisms and facilitated the containment of economic liberalism. However, this process cannot be repeated on the European level. The greater openness, heterogeneity and weight of liberal markets all work against it. The functional constraint to adapt to this new reality works to the advantage of the, in France, long-dominated pole of contradictions of political thought on the European level. But the historical path of development only allows for a very slow and persistently unstable adaptation to the new structural conditions. Especially now, this new reality still has no sufficient foundations for legitimation because the intellectual discourse is, as always, dominated by visions for which there are fewer and fewer opportunities for transformation into real institutions. Advocates of progressive integration (i.e. advocates of the European constitutional contract) consider themselves to be willingly or unwillingly forced to justify their visionary position with categories of thought from which reality is increasingly diverging. Advocacy of the constitutional contract thus appears to the citizens to be all the more implausible. These are the fundamental reasons for the failure of the referendum on 25 May 2005.

The French intellectual discourse is deeply divided on the issue of Europe. Since the founding years of the Union, the forces of orientation towards Europe have been strong. They desire a strong Europe in order to be able to live in a stable order, and so that they can exercise global political influence and keep the forces of globalization under control. Therefore, symbolic power can be found on the side of a strong Union. But the more the European project is exhausted by the promotion of economic liberalism, the more the resistance of opposing forces that adhere to the model of the national republic come to the fore. At the same time however, forces of economic liberalism in industry's management elite, who support the European integration project together with its expansion dynamic and without strong political design, are also articulated.

4 The German dilemma

Constitutional federalism
against unconstitutional
supranationalism

The political debate on Europe within the German intellectual landscape has, in recent years, been particularly marked by the discussion about a European constitution. The effect of legal thought in the German tradition of codification law is clearly expressed therein. This discussion's different positions can be placed at opposite poles: sceptics versus optimists. Constitutional scholars make up the majority of those among the constitutional sceptics, whereas prominent philosophers and political scientists are represented among the supporters of a European constitution. The sceptics operate in the tradition of Hegelian thought, by which, due to its democratic interpretation, every legal system requires legitimation. For the sceptics, this will only be possible in the foreseeable future in places where the sovereignty of the people can be truly, and not merely formally, exercised (Hegel 1821/1995). For them, this is the national level in the European multilevel system. The optimists operate in the tradition of Kantian thought, whereby law itself constitutes a legal community beyond particular traditional bonds, from which a postnational community of European citizens can in fact also emerge (Kant 1793/1964; 1797/1968).

Compared to the French and British theorizing of state, government and society, the German intellectual debate is marked by its preoccupation with the legal construction of Europe. This is why we can describe this type of theorizing state, government and society as semantics of legalism. This intellectual tradition conceives of society as constructed by constitution and law. Rights of freedom and equality at the heart of modern society have to be understood and accommodated through legal construction in legislation and jurisdiction. This means that the emerging European society and the inclusion of national government in the European system of multilevel governance have to be constructed in sound legal terms to be viable at all. The following considerations will uncover the problems of the legal construction of Europe that come to the fore when we think of Europe in the German tradition of theorizing state, government and society. We will start with the institutional construction of Europe and move on to the evolution of a European identity.

The institutional construction of Europe

Long before the European Union resolved to conscribe a convent for the composition of a contract concerning a constitution for Europe which would supersede the EC contract in favour of a standardized EU structure, Dieter Grimm and Jürgen Habermas waged a debate about the necessity of a European constitution that set a course for the subsequent intellectual debate in Germany. For this reason, Grimm and Habermas's contributions will be presented somewhat more elaborately, as they already contain significant arguments from other authors which will only be addressed briefly in the further course of this chapter. The debate is marked by a central conflict: the contrast between a closed model of democratic legitimation of law bound to the national state and an open model leaning towards supranational expansion (cf. Diedrichs and Wessels 2005; Liebert 2005).

Grimm's legal thinking becomes clear when he, in his essay 'Does Europe Need a Constitution?' (Grimm 1995), comprehends the two conflicting arguments concerning a European constitution being exclusively judicial. Accordingly, from the judicial perspective there can be only two understandings. On the one hand, there is the view that a constitution is unnecessary, as the available EC/EU treaties, as higher law already limit national states' freedom of action and thus function like a constitution. On the other hand, there is the view that a constitution is only necessary in the event that one asserts that the treaties are insufficient and therefore must be replaced by a constitution. If the treaties function like a constitution, it is necessary to determine what Europe is lacking and whether or not this shortcoming can, or even should, be remedied. If the treaties do not represent a constitution, the difference between a constitution and these treaties would have to be demonstrated.

By way of international agreements, the EU was actually granted sovereign power, whereby it may perform regulatory or directive intervention in the legal systems of national states. Accordingly, its domestic effect, particularly in policy areas which fall under its jurisdiction, can, for all intents and purposes, be compared to that of a sovereign state. In contrast, the limited supranational sovereignty of the EU can be recognized especially in the intergovernmental character of European foreign policy and security policy. The major problem of a European constitution identified by Grimm is the separation of the constitution from the state. This separation is accompanied by the lack of an EU bond to higher law. From Grimm's point of view, the EU exists, in the absence of an antecedent social substratum, merely as a legal community (Grimm 1995: 285). This is linked to the primary Community law which, although not stipulated in a constitution, is laid down in the treaties. Law ultimately constitutes the community, sets its greater goals, establishes its institutions, carries out the allocation of competencies and regulates procedure. For Grimm, the existing treaties are already a functional equivalent to a European constitution, even though he recognizes that fundamental constitutional principles like equality and freedom are, in the absence of basic rights, not adequately represented.

According to Grimm, it is particularly the concept of a constitution that poses problems. A European constitution could not be traced back to the people, but would rather, at best, possess the character of an international legal treaty (Grimm 2005). The decision criteria concerning this constitution are not derived from an abstract common good, but are rather rooted in national states. This lack of democratic legitimacy expresses a sort of democratic dilemma in which, although democracy does exist on a national level, regulatory competencies simultaneously vanish, whereas, at the EU level, the competencies continue to increase, but without being democratically legitimized. Grimm dispels hopes that the EU can be democratized by the expansion of the competencies of European Parliament with the remark that, besides parliamentarianism, democracy also requires other elements, such as mass media and a European public (Grimm 1995, 2004). Particularly with regard to the question of the development of a European public, Grimm identifies a discrepancy between a Europeanized elite and the non-Europeanized rank and file. The continuing national context of European decision making, due to the lack of a common language, impedes the development of a European public. Because such a common public does not exist, the development of a collective European identity is, according to Grimm, impossible. This is, however, desirable in order to ensure the nonviolent resolution of conflicts of interest. Because these structural problems cannot be solved rapidly and a solution cannot be forced, democracy at the European level is, by definition, nonexistent, and a constitution as a higher order is therefore not possible. He therefore advocates, in place of a constitution, a core treaty that simply leaves out detailed specifications, and in so doing provides a necessary degree of symbolism. In this way, one could institutionally anticipate societal development and would simultaneously avoid harm caused by the European Union's competence to the member states' sovereignty (cf. Hurrelmann 2005: 15–20). Otherwise, the EU would have the capacity to allocate itself competencies and resources, and the Community law would no longer be the result of the executive order issued by the member states, but rather the result of the constitutional contract.

Grimm's (1995) considerations on a European constitution laid down the guidelines for his later assessment of the factual elaboration of a European constitutional contract. Grimm emphatically stresses that the literal sense of a constitution is not the issue, but rather a constitutional contract is the issue. This is because the EU may not take competencies itself, but rather it receives them from member states following national regulations. Because the EU's aforementioned structural deficits cannot be eliminated, even by means of treaties, the functional hope that is connected to the elaboration of the constitutional contract must, from his point of view, end in disappointment. In his perspective, the constitutional contract cannot represent the focal point of a European identity and cannot promote integration.

In Grimm's eyes, the European constitutional contract lacks a constitutional moment and the broad backing by the public that would allow it to promote sustainable integration. As a supposed 'constitutional moment', the expansion towards the east in 2004 and 2007 is regarded more with concern than euphoria. Instead of a system bestowed by the people, they would have a constitutional contract whose formation would have to be described as gubernatorial, administrative and judicative (Grimm 2005). He identifies as further problems the now implicit reality of peace within the European Union and the difficulty of calling upon genuine European values. Because Europe shares its values primarily with the USA, Grimm draws the conclusion that it would be a contradiction in itself to, like Habermas, define Europe by a nonexclusive European foundation of values and to simultaneously comprehend European identity as an alternative to transatlantic partnership. His sceptical attitude towards a European constitution culminates in doubts as to whether or not national states can, with help from the supranational European Union, reclaim freedom of action lost to globalization. Despite Grimm's fundamental concerns about a European constitution, the failure of the constitutional contract is, from his point of view, undesirable because many institutional reforms would then fall by the wayside, even though these could be carried out by treaties. However, because the fine line between state and confederation runs along the axis between foreign rule and self-determination, the European constitution by no means has a genuinely constitutive character. It logically takes the form of a treaty (cf. Grimm 2003, 2004, 2005).

Jürgen Habermas, in his contribution to the debate, explicitly refers to Dieter Grimm and agrees with his diagnosis of the EU's democratic deficit. According to Grimm, a European constitution would, due to the lack of a European public, possess no legitimacy and would bear with it the EU's tendencies towards an autonomous existence without roots in the people's life. Habermas counters that without a constitution, the EU already leans towards considerable autonomy. According to Grimm's view, the status quo can at least freeze the democratic deficit of the EU (Grimm 1995: 287). For Habermas, however, this deficit grows from day to day, independent of innovations in constitutional law (Habermas 1996: 186). Habermas points out that Grimm himself diagnoses the problem when he argues that democratic decision making resides with the member states whose capacity for decision making is dwindling; this capacity is moving up to the Union where, in turn, decision making can hardly be considered democratic in character. Habermas accuses the Euro-sceptics of passively accepting the erosion of democratic substance in the face of this development.

Habermas attributes a deeply integrative function directly to a European constitution due to his concept of constitutional patriotism. The modern nation of citizens differs from the people's nation by not presupposing a commonly shared history or the fiction of common roots. Instead, it is based on legally-generated and abstract social integration. However, he identifies the lessons of the First and Second World Wars resulting in the recognition of the necessity of a stable European order as a common European experience. The increase of communication density and economic linkage of interests also serve as integrative moments. Habermas places the core of democratic political will in the formation of a European public embedded in a common political culture. The latter is born by civil society; on this basis, parties refer directly to the European Union's decisions and shape themselves into a European party system. A collective identity, according to Habermas, must therefore have a foundation other than ethnicity if the democratic process is to be able to close integration gaps which arise from an increasingly heterogeneous society (Habermas 1996). From his perspective, a European constitution would exert an inducing effect on the emergence of a European public. According to Habermas's logic, a European constitution would have a constitutive character for a collective European identity, whereas, according to Grimm (1995: 290), a collective, if not necessarily ethnically-determined identity, must already exist in order to legitimize a constitution. According to Habermas, a constitution would possess the very power of symbolic solidification that only a political act of foundation can have (Habermas 2001: 225).

For Habermas, the discussion in social science about the necessity of a constitution is a positive sign for the anchoring of a European feeling among the citizens because collective identity is constituted less by discourses in law or philosophy of law than by those in economics and social science, and above all in political science (Habermas 2001: 225). In light of this, it is significant that Habermas himself was the one who, together with other European intellectuals, set off a public debate meant to fulfil precisely this function. The performative act had the goal of proclaiming the birth of a European public and simultaneously offering its own contribution to the formation of such a European public. Constitutional patriotism should, in order to keep citizens of Europe from becoming victims of a rampant neoliberal world economic regime, serve these citizens as an emotional, educational axis.

Habermas recognizes that the global success of European values brings with it the difficulty of defining these very values as genuinely European. He therefore looks for other common historical experiences that could contribute to the configuration of a common European identity. In his opinion, the secular attitude, the European technology scepticism and sensitivity to the paradoxes of progress associated therewith can fulfil this function. According to Habermas, totalitarian experiences, resulting from extreme nationalism, led to the willingness to subordinate national freedom of action to a supranational system. Economic globalization is the result of such international agreements, and it is therefore possible to mitigate its effects by corrective social policies (Habermas 2005). Along these lines of argumentation, he regards Christian social teaching and the labour movement as two cornerstones of European identity. The belief in social justice rooted therein represents a further point of reference for European identity. In his article 'Our Renewal', coauthored with Jacques Derrida, he claims to discover a

European identity as well as a European public. He sees the Letter of the Eight and the mass demonstrations against the war in Iraq as a sign of both a European consciousness and a European public that can create a transatlantic balance in relations with the USA. So, one can note that in Habermas's eyes, supranational identity formation must meet the following functional requirements: (1) the necessity of a European civil society, (2) the construction of a pan-European political public and (3) the creation of a political culture that can be shared by all European citizens.

Habermas (2005: 15) comments on the French and Dutch no-vote on the constitutional contract, saying that the average citizen cannot understand this contract because it reads more like a complicated international treaty and fails to present itself as a transparent framework of basic norms. In his eyes, the draft is unreadable because it lacks a convincing perspective for the future of Europe. The constitution's failure therefore lies more with the failure of a political perspective that, according to Habermas (2005: 15), should be communicated by the constitution. Its failure is less with a nonexistent constitutional moment because in our times, constitutions do not emerge overnight from a revolutionary act, but rather evolve in the course of decades (Habermas 2005: 15). In order to again allow the citizens to dream of Europe, Habermas argues that, most of all, the harmonization of tax, social and economic policies is necessary. They need to regain capacities to act that have vanished from national states.

Habermas, with his radically reason-oriented constitutional interpretation, can be placed in the tradition of Kant. This becomes apparent when he sees Europe to be charged with the development of democratically legitimized capabilities for action belonging to the institutions in Brussels and Strasbourg that must join itself with the goal of realizing cosmopolitan visions for a new and promising international order. This vision is strongly reminiscent of Kant's bold idea of a cosmopolitan order sought by way of practical reason (Habermas 2005).

Habermas interprets the no-vote to the constitutional contract as a rejection of the design of the constitution and not as the denial of the necessity of a constitution. In the previously quoted Article from the Süddeutsche Zeitung, 'Über die Köpfe hinweggerollt' of 6 June 2005, he describes the French no-vote to the EU constitution as a beneficial and necessary corrective for a frozen executive authority that brings the exchange between government and opposition to a standstill (Habermas 2005). For Habermas, the creation of a European constitution is a significant building block in his procedural understanding of European integration. This understanding allows him to ascribe a public-forming function to the constitution, and, in so doing, to circumvent Grimm's logic that only a pre-existing people could create a constitution. Furthermore, he believes that he can, by means of a gradual harmonization of social policies, integrate the demands of the French opponents to the constitution into his concept without having to call into question the need for a constitution itself.

Count Peter von Kielmansegg (1996) predicts a more animated debate about proceeding integration than has yet taken place. The membership of new countries is based primarily on economic interest and therefore lacks the morally charged founder-ethos that von Kielmansegg considers necessary for the long-time uncritical acceptance of the legitimacy of the European Union. He identifies three reasons for a more controversial debate about the progression of the integration process: (1) a larger Union must inevitably grant the majority decision more weight, which, however, can lead to acceptance problems that do not exist under the principle of unanimity; (2) an expansion of EU competencies allows certain strains to emerge more noticeably in citizens' perception and accordingly evokes the issue of legitimacy; and (3) the capacity to act at the level of the member states declines without the same degree of growth of the institutionalized capacity for joint action (Kielmansegg 1996: 49).

Because Europeans' bonds to the Community do not seem to be particularly resistant to pressure (as proven by the failed referendums), these pressures unavoidably lead to legitimacy being called into question. In David Easton's terminology, von Kielmansegg makes a distinction between diffuse and specific support and draws the conclusion that the strategy of specific support pursued by the Union is insufficient as resilient bonds cannot be produced by way of cost-benefit calculations.

For von Kielmansegg, an acceptable constitution represents a necessary, albeit insufficient, condition for the emergence of diffuse support. Due to its legislative capacity, the EU must subordinate itself to the standards of democracy. However, according to von Kielmansegg, the transfer of democratic legitimacy from member states to the EU entails two reasons for a merely limited legitimation potential: (1) European elections take place in the context of the national sphere, and European politics is, for the most part, not a topic of debate; and (2) the transition to majority rule would require that the governments in the Council of Ministers, strictly following the parliamentary model, debate and make decisions publicly. This lack of transparency makes it all but impossible to identify responsibility. In turn, this leads to insufficient democratic control. Increasingly discretionary decision making in a relatively large area of European political competence creates the need for justification in European politics (Kielmansegg 1996: 53).

After diagnosing a democratic deficit, von Kielmansegg raises the question of the EU's democratic ability and identifies the following requirement: A consciousness of belonging must exist. Accordingly, the constitution does not define the people, but rather the people, in an act of constitutional creation, constitute themselves as a political community. Only in this way can a distinction be drawn between unacceptable foreign rule and generally accepted majority rule. He does not deny that a collective identity can be created, but in his opinion, the formation of such an identity requires a great deal of time. According to von Kielmansegg, a collective identity must meet three prerequisites that do not, as such, exist in the European Union: (1) multilingualism prohibits the emergence of a communication community; (2) likewise, the communities of memory are not rooted in a European context, but are, for the most part, bound to national histories; and (3) the communities of experience do indeed represent the category most open to future events, but they, however, require a great deal of time for their formation and are confronted with opposing developments like individualization. These three categories not only bear great significance for the development of a collective identity, but also for the development of democratic participation structures pertaining to a European civil society. Economic interests are the only factors capable of restructuring, though not only through a Europeanization of interests, but also through a Europeanization of member state-aggregated interests (Kielmansegg 1996: 58). According to von Kielmansegg, the result of the absence of these prerequisites is that a European constitution does not necessarily bring with it a functioning democracy. The function of the EU can thus be characterized by a double particularism: the particularism of bonds of loyalty and the particularism of territorial interest aggregation.

This dilemma between democratic deficit and only limited democratic capacity brings with it the question of which kind of bond between federal and democratic principles would be the lesser evil. The idea of federalism is, besides the division of spheres of authority, also familiar with the concept of double representation by a parliament and a senate. This idea is based on the conviction that the democratic state is a republic of citizens and also a republic of states. Admittedly, following the theory of democracy, double representation also entails a problem as the basic principle of equality is often overridden in federal chambers. Whereas individual states are only a weak identification factor on the federal level of the national state, the opposite is true of the European level. According to von Kielmansegg, the principle of federalism must therefore be dominant. Particularly in the constitutional process, the federal principle is of great importance because the national state's bond with its citizens only allows unanimous decisions, whereas federal states can handle such issues with majority decisions. The federal principle therefore clearly has precedence on the constitutional level, whereas on the legislative level, qualified majority decision making applies. The essential principle of the federal idea is the equality of constituent states, to the end that decisions must be made unanimously, whereas a proportional voting weight exists for decisions made by a qualified majority. According to von Kielmansegg, a combination of federal and democratic principles is necessary for the following reasons: (1) European politics must be controlled democratically; (2) the mere application of majority rule would make the transfer of legitimacy from national states to the European level impossible; and (3) European politics is always a compromise between the particularistic interests of member states, but it is the duty of the Commission and the Parliament to pursue a European perspective, as they are, in contrast to the Council of Ministers, obligated to the European common good.

Armin von Bogdandy incorporates elements of both Grimm and Habermas into his analysis. From his point of view, European regulations are pre-existing, seemingly heteronomous forces with which the national legal community must come to terms. National systems of law have become increasingly fragmented because the development of two kinds of constitutional law has occurred, namely national and European. However, member countries also see the EU as a warrantor of their own constituted state of affairs because it understands itself to be an organization of collective order and because it demands uniform standards of democratic rule of law from all public authorities in the European community. It therefore becomes the final authority when all state security mechanisms fail. For von Bogdandy, a common, fundamental European consensus is required as a normative point of reference because otherwise the liberal free market economy, as the sole integration mechanism, endangers societal cohesion (Bogdandy 2000, 2001). Due to lacking common experience, a European constitution, as a text furnished with the strength of validity, could, especially in the European tradition of written constitutions, fulfil an important symbolic function. For him, the constitutional contract's orientation to basic values is a movement in the right direction. The EU as a community of basic rights could be, in contrast to further economic integration, the more convincing vision of the European Union. At the same time, von Bogdandy is clear on the fact that a progressive human rights policy could endanger the balance between member states and the Union. From his judicial point of view however, complete federalization under the banner of common basic rights policies is more appropriate than functional finality based on a common economic policy (Bogdandy 2001). He advocates a three-part standard of basic rights: (1) a standard that can be applied to non-EU countries within the framework of European foreign policy; (2) a standard that serves to monitor the basic rights that are generally to be bestowed by the member states; and (3) a standard that controls the Union and member states in the application of Union law. From his point of view, the development of this standard is an enormous task (Bogdandy 2001: 170).

In his eyes, the value of democracy is exaggerated in the constitutional contract because the EU itself insufficiently represents this value. Although every 'we' requires a counterpart, he argues against the dissociation from the US that, according to his interpretation, shines through the constitution because he assumes that this would more likely divide Europe than unify it (Bogdandy 2004a, 2004b). From his point of view, the dissociation from the US results from both the social model and the words to the strict adherence to and advancement of international law, particularly to the charter of the United Nations. This could foster the formation of an anti-American European identity and could weaken the notion of a common Western world in favour of a multipolar one. Von Bogdandy employs a procedural concept of European integration when he states that the participation of the citizens in the republican tradition represents a significant element of the formation of a collective identity, even though achieving such a goal is laborious. The formation of a collective identity is unnecessary. However, it can be useful for ensuring the stability of a political system (Bogdandy 2004b). It would have a direct identity-forming effect if it were itself a criterion for the significant identity processes; it would be indirectly identity-forming if definite criteria were to be created by the constitution (Bogdandy 2004b: 54–55). In his opinion, the constitution fails in the preamble to answer the question of the collective 'wherefrom' by elaborating on common experience. However, a feeling of belonging could arise from the labelling of the constitutional contract as a 'constitution' because citizens associate this constitution with an established political system to which they belong.

Von Bogdandy answers the question 'Who are we?' with the concept of a modified common destiny by which destiny no longer predetermines the future, but rather initiates its collective formation. Von Bogdandy analyzes the EU under the category of a state, although the constitutional contract rejects the status of statehood for the EU and grants statehood only to member states. In the star symbolism of the flag and the statements in the preamble, which assign the Europeans the role of bearers of civilization, he identifies the concept of treating Europeans as a chosen group. With regard to the notion of a community of values, von Bogdandy states that the emphasis on democracy as a guiding value is not practicable as the EU is, institutionally, decisively characterized by a democratic deficit. From von Bogdandy's point of view, the common values are, like the common 'wherefrom', examined merely diffusely in the preamble. This shortcoming, combined with the constitutional contract's apparently fragile normativity (as the numerous divergences from the EMU's deficit criteria suggest), leads him to derive that it would be wiser to concentrate on an interest-based organizational constitution that allows for successful operations. In this way, citizens' indirect identification with the EU could arise. The constitutional contract's most important contribution to the development of a European identity consists of its potential to effectively and prudently enforce democracy, the rule of law, efficiency and transparency in the operation of European institutions and the fact that it represents the only chance of facing global challenges (Bogdandy 2004b: 61).

An exact determination of the value and usefulness of the constitutional contract is, according to von Bogdandy, only possible by defining the character of the EU more narrowly. It must therefore be taken into account that the concept of the constitution does not refer to the overall political situation, but to its judicial foundations, and that the constitutional contract already conceptually entails an ambivalent statement. However, the public discussion is based more on the term 'constitution', which amounts to a significant entry into the collective dictionary (Bogdandy 2004a, 2004b).

Von Bogdandy releases the notion of the republic from its bond to statehood as such. Because the notion of the republic is a significant part of the discourse about what kind of world we live in and how it should develop (Bogdandy 2005: 24) and because it signifies both a transpersonally understood alliance as well as the goal of its existence (i.e. the common good), von Bogdandy finds it to be suitable as an analytical term. It denotes a polity based on a legitimate constitution that administers the common affairs of its citizens in a democratic form entailing the separation of powers (Bogdandy 2005: 25). The constitutional contract could help to construct a republic that reaches beyond the boundaries of nation states. In his eyes, the constitutional contract would help to better differentiate between competencies of the Union and competencies of the member states and to preserve national autonomy where it is appropriate. Its failing ratification would undermine this improvement compared to the current state of affairs (Bogdandy 2005: 27).

Von Bogdandy tries to resolve the contradiction between the ideas of a confederation and a federal union using the concept of supranational federalism. The concept of supranationality distinguishes itself from a state by way of its lack of instruments of power and its polycentric structure. 'Federalism', as an analytic term, requires that one has to dismiss the concept of a federal state as he takes the transfer of military rights to the EU and a retrenchment of the Council's competences to be unrealistic. In his opinion, the primary functionalist approach to integration has already led to a federalist structure. Hence, a supranational polity with civic participation is only conceivable in a federal form (Bogdandy 1999: 61–66; 2005).

In 2000, the acting German Foreign Minister, Joschka Fischer, gave a speech at the Humboldt University in Berlin. It echoed across Europe and dealt with the finality of Europe, which is, according to Beck and Grande (2004), unattainable. Fischer advocates the concept of dividing sovereignty between national states and the European Union, meaning the establishment of two chambers of parliament; one should be made up of members of national parliaments, while the other, at the European level, should be staffed according to direct elections. This construction is meant to resolve the antagonism between national parliaments and European Parliament and to impute the integrative and identity-promoting function of the national states to the European Union. By means of a constitutional contract, it would be possible to institute clear rules of competences that would determine what should be managed at the European level and what should be done at the national level. The results would be the EU's complete sovereignty in its competence areas and the preservation of self-confident national states. The nation states, with their cultural and democratic traditions, will continue to exist within the framework of the federation (Fischer 2000: 759).

The solution to the democratic deficit and the reforms of horizontal and vertical separation of powers are, according to Fischer, only possible by means of the refounding of Europe based on a constitution and guaranteed civil and human rights. Because of increasing heterogeneity, the differentiation of a core Europe from the entire framework of the EU is unavoidable. Fischer (2000: 760), however, finds it important that such a core Europe establishes an integration magnet open to all. Such a process of differentiation of Europe's various speeds would, according to him, have to proceed in three steps: (1) It would begin with the development of intensified cooperation in order to then (2) construct, using a new contract, a kind of core Europe with its own institutions that would serve as a model for (3) the subsequent complete integration of all into a European federation, whereupon all steps must be voluntary and open to all new members.

Fischer's comments were of course met with criticism. According to Pflüger (2000), Fischer's proposal for the establishment of two chambers of the EU Parliament is a regression with respect to the Europeanization of society. Furthermore, he warns (even though Fischer took this into account in his own considerations) against the disappointment among new member states that could result from the creation of a core Europe. The finality of Europe is, in his view, being postponed to an unforeseeable future by the territorial indecisiveness that includes the possible admission of Turkey and the dilution of admission criteria.

Constitutional patriotism as the embodiment of a European identity?

Kantian and Hegelian positions on the matter of European identity find themselves, in the context of the constitutional debate, at odds with one another. In Hegel's democratically interpreted tradition, the human being is dependent on feelings of collective belonging and on an animated realm of public debate and opinion formation in order to develop an equally animated personal identity which is both devoted to and separate from the collective. Collective identity cannot be formed in an open space without a concentration of public communication. From the point of view of the sceptics, Europe must remain without a collective identity for the foreseeable future because this realm of concentrated public communication is missing. For them, the nation therefore remains the central platform for human identity within the European multilevel system. In contrast, the Kantian tradition considers this notion as an impediment to the development of a more open European identity in the cosmopolitan context. Along these lines, the development of a strong personal identity is dependent on the progressive disengagement from primordial bonds. The Europeanization of public communication is a significant horizon-broadening step which, however, requires reflection in the further context of cosmopolitanism. Even though only the first contours of a European public can be discerned, in the Kantian tradition this is still the only viable path towards a stable and legitimate multilevel organization of multiple identities. From this perspective, the debate about a European constitution is implicitly a debate about the relationship between national and European identity and about the issue of the extent to which personal identity formation should remain bound to the national context or should extend beyond it and adopt European traits in a cosmopolitan context. The following reconstruction of the constitutional debate should be seen in this light.

If one wishes to answer the question of whether or not Europe already possesses a constitution, it is first of all useful to ask which constitutional concept will be taken as a basis. One must distinguish between the pragmatic, functional and integrative, as well as symbolic characters of a constitution. A functional constitutional concept allows for the consideration of a constitution in non-national categories and thus applies the constitutional concept to, for instance, postnational structures (Hirsch 2001). If a constitution should have a merely functional character, then treaties are sufficient. If the Federal Constitutional Court finds that the existing treaties 'effectively [represent] the constitution' (BVerfGE 22, 293) of Europe, then this provides the basis for the line of argument used by legal experts involved in the discourse. This perspective opens a way to applying such a pragmatic constitutional concept to structures that are indeed democratically legitimated and organized, but lack sovereignty and binding jurisdiction. However, the European constitution resulting from treaties differs from other international law treaties in the establishment of a direct relationship between the citizens and the European Union (Beyme 2000).

The ambiguity of the constitutional concept appears in the identification of the constitutional draft as a treaty concerning a European constitution. For Kleger, Karolewski and Munke (2001: 50), the present legal structure of the Union can be described as a 'constitutional alliance' or a 'conglomerate of partial constitutions', but not as a 'constitution'. The drafted contract on a constitution does not really change this situation because the contract is nothing but a treaty.

This assessment makes it clear that varying notions of constitutions are represented, that varying demands are placed on constitutions and that constitutions are subject to varying expectations. Accordingly, Grimm (2005) regards the contract of a European constitution as a treaty based on international law, contracted by the national governments and ratified by the member states according to the specifications of their constitutions.

The intergovernmental formation of the constitutional contract points out the EU's legitimation problem. In order to better analyze the legitimacy deficit, a distinction is drawn between input and output legitimation. With regard to output legitimation, the existing treaties can indeed be placed on the level of a constitution. However, when Fritz Scharpf (2003: 49) argues that, with respect to the constitution, pragmatic solutions to future problems are not the main focus, but rather fundamental matters of the institutional architecture of the community and its legitimation in the light of normative criteria, this reveals a link to the national, normative constitutional concept. This normative loading (Hurrelmann 2005: 13) implies that a constitution, with regard to its content, must meet specific demands.

Democratization is without a doubt one of the most often admonished demands on the structure of the EU. Grimm (1995: 289) assumes, however, that a complete parliamentarization of the European Union following the design of the national constitutional state would more likely worsen than solve the European democracy problem. And von Kielmannsegg assumes that a supranational structure is fundamentally incapable of democracy, that is, the democratic deficit can only be resolved rudimentarily. Democracy taken as sovereignty of the people is inseparably linked to the direct connection between the EU and the citizens. The incorporation of basic rights into the constitution is a significant contribution to this because only by way of actionable rights can it be conveyed to the people that European unification expands civil rights (Leinen 2001: 61). Only on this basis may the emergence of a European identity of the people be expected.

Whereas the Union's structure of due process is considered secure, it is above all the democratic structure of the Union that is intended to be improved by using a constitution as an instrument. Presumptions that such a democratic structure is not feasible at the supranational level (Grimm 1995) are based on Jellinek's theoretical considerations of state and sovereignty (Hurrelmann 2005: 15). If the constitutional concept according to Jellinek's (1900/1966: 394–504) parameters is closely linked to the concept of state-hood, a way out of the European constitutional debate hardly seems possible (Pernice 2001: 149f.). If the constitutional concept is that closely linked to the question of Europe's statehood, it is joined by the question about the member states' remaining sovereignty. The EU's lack of superior competence (cf. Hurrelmann 2005: 15) is in conflict with the complete transfer of sovereignty from the national to the European level. The basis for this position is Jellinek's three-element model, according to which the statehood of a politi-cal unit requires a state territory, a state people and a government whose establishment and organization is sovereign (i.e. not externally dictated). If one dismisses, however, the notion of indivisible sovereignty, then one no longer has to draw a distinction between an intergovernmental constitutional contract and a constitution (Peters 2001: 234ff.). According to the criteria of indivisible sovereignty, any federally organized state would not be sovereign and would therefore be illegitimate. When Habermas (1996) considers German federalism as a possible standard for a European organizational model, he clearly has such a division of sovereignty in mind.

Besides the matter of sovereignty, the role of the people (*demos*) represents another important element of the constitutional debate. Numerous authors assume that the people will take up a constituent role in the formation of the constitution, and that the constitution will have to come about not through heteronomy, but through self-determination. Kirchof stated this idea in the laconic formulation: where no state, there no constitution, where no state-people, there no state (Kirchhof 1994: 59). An important precondition for such a European people would be a European public that conceives itself to be a cohesive community of common experience (Göler 2002: 21). The sig-nificance of the public has its origin in Bentham's theory of democracy and it assumes that the public will take on an important controlling function.

In contrast to such sceptical positions, Habermas even identifies the first signs of the development of a European demos in the discussion about the constitution itself. He assigns the public a controlling and participatory function. However, he does not aim for a superpublic, but rather speaks of inter-translated communication that is so interconnected that relevant contributions are osmotically absorbed from the other respective arenas. In this way, he expects European topics that have hitherto been negotiated without including the public to find their way into the internetworked national arenas (Habermas 2001).

The sceptical position is held by several authors. They show the opinion that the democratic deficit cannot be eliminated because the EU is generally incapable of developing a European public. For lack of a common language and transnational media, a common citizenry, and therefore also a genuine democracy, cannot arise. Nevertheless, creating a European public sphere does not require consensus on matters of European integration. In fact, potential dissent has a polarizing effect and therefore raises the willingness to participate, making the growth of a European public possible (Landfried 2004; Risse 2004). If, however, such dissent exists, this raises the question of whether or not Habermas's concept of constitutional patriotism can still be useful and whether or not a collective prepolitical identity is not, in fact, needed in order to guarantee a sufficient degree of political cohesion among Europeans (Offe 2001).

On the grounds of its uniqueness, the EU is mainly described as an entity *sui generis*. According to the finding of the German Federal Constitutional Court, the EU should be considered a federation because cooperation is closer than in a confederation, but national states maintain considerably more sovereignty than within a federal state (BVerfG 89, 155). The German debate concerning the design of the Union is strongly influenced by the notion of a federal system. Preuß bases his considerations on the idea of a federal system of competition that should, via a kind of first-mover advantage, stimulate participation and therefore has the potential to reduce the democratic deficit (Preuß 1999).

Habermas' concept of Euro-federalism calls for a clearly defined path, but at the same time it also requires a stronger position of national states than is common in classical federal states, such that interstate compromise will continue to be necessary. Habermas's call for a clearly defined path should by no means be understood as the demand for a static final organization. This demand is presented particularly against the background of the eastern expansion of the EU and the accompanying increase in the complexity of voting and decision-making procedures. Given the member states' different levels of development, he advocates a Europe of multiple speeds. The principle of subsidiarity should be a central element in accounting for the differences between the respective national states. Like Fischer, he proposes that EU parliamentarians should also be members of national parliaments so that an interlocking of interests is achieved (Habermas 1996). In contrast, Grimm holds the term 'confederation of states' (*Staatenbund*) to be the considerably better formulation as the constitution is of a state-imparted kind (Grimm 1995).

With the help of the concept of supranational federalism, von Bogdandy attempts to resolve the contradiction between confederation and federal state. The concept of supranationality sets itself apart from the state due to its lack of means of enforcement and its polycentric structure. 'Federalism', as an analytical term, requires that one part with the notion of federal statehood, as he deems the transfer of military competencies to the EU and the retrenchment of Council competencies to be unrealistic. In his opinion, the primary functionalist approach to integration has led to a federalist structure. Accordingly, a perspective on a supranational polity with civil participation can only be gained federally (Bogdandy 1999: 61–66; 2005). Because the EU exhibits both federal and confederate elements and defines itself as a Union of citizens and states, its character will persist *sui generis* even longer, and possibly perpetually (Hänsch 2005: 94). This means that the people will in fact remain primarily committed to their national identity and will only secondarily acquire a European identity.

In Germany, the intellectual discourse concerning the European integration project is characterized by the language of legal experts. Questions of identity are cast in legal categories. This means that conceptual answers to substantial questions and formal solutions to problems of content are sought. First of all, it is a matter of the question of whether or not the European Union needs a constitution. On the one hand, a no-vote corresponds to Dieter Grimm's (1995) line of argumentation. On the other hand, a yes-vote refers to Habermas's (1996) line. The answer to this question depends on whether or not an existing or emerging European people with the constituent precondition of a European public is available as a legitimating foundation for a European constitution (Grimm) or whether or not a constitutional contract, arranged by the states, itself constitutes a necessary impulse for the development of a European community of citizens with a European public (Habermas). Those on Grimm's side predominantly see the EU as a community of states. Those on Habermas's side trust that this community of states will, to an increasing degree, be supplemented by a community of citizens. The European constitution is seen as a precursor to this community. The typically legal handling of this conflict is von Bogdandy's (2005) dialectic resolution of the contradiction between confederation and federal state in terms of the supranational and federal republic. According to this position, the EU is a political structure *sui generis* between a confederation of states and a federal state with divided sovereignty. Unlike in France and Great Britain, sufficient reasons for the legitimation of this model, for which there is no equivalent in those countries, can be found in Germany's federal tradition. Thereby, however, the balance of divided sovereignty, compared to the federal republic, must, to a considerably higher degree, be moved to the side of the member states, with their persisting traditions. This means that legal integration based on economic integration dominates the European project, whereas political, social and cultural integration largely remains on the member state level.

The opponents of a European constitution therefore see the EU as merely a legal community whose bonds to a European community are only possible via the national governments and parliaments. For this reason, Fischer's proposal for the establishment of a chamber of states still goes furthest in the direction of the Europeanization of the polity. In the long run however, and along the lines of Habermas, weight would have to be shifted towards the Union and towards the popularly elected representatives in the higher chamber (i.e. European Parliament) in order to regain, at the European level, the governmental capacity for action and integration lost in the process of economic globalization. Constitutional patriotism, as the embodiment of European identity, and promoted by the European constitution, creates the relevant foundation for legitimation in a European community of citizens. In opposition to this civic optimism, the constitutional sceptics argue that the concept of constitutional patriotism is a hollow concept that has no real connection to Europeans' feelings of belonging or their identification with Europe. For this reason, the sceptics regard Europe as incapable of democracy in the long run. The Federal Constitutional Court officially expressed this scepticism in its Maastricht decision (BVerfG 89, 155). In its recent judgement on the Lisbon Treaty of 30 June 2009, the Court strengthened the right of the national parliament (the federal chamber and also the chamber of states, if affected) to be involved in any changes of the EC Treaty (BVerfG, 2 BvE of 30.06.2009). For the Kantian optimists, a European constitution is a necessary step towards the broadening of horizons and the reflection of national identities within the framework of a European identity that, in turn, requires reflection in the context of cosmopolitanism. For the Hegelian pessimists, this is, for the foreseeable future, an empty promise, without real value, that dissolves national identities and securities without creating in their place a stable basis for the formation of identity at the European level.

Concluding remarks

In the German debate concerning the constitution of the European Union, one can recognize immediately the tense relationship between the Kantian and Hegelian traditions. In comparison to France and Britain, the generally greater willingness to further expand the EU as an alliance with shared sovereignty is, in regard to the further transfer of competencies to the European level, also accompanied by scepticism in Germany. The proponents of continuing European integration, even in Germany, have therefore increasingly been confronted with a legitimation problem. They must place their hopes in a project whose feasibility, in the intended sense, is being judged ever more sceptically. In contrast to the situation in France however, this contradiction is not being waged between the extreme positions of liberalism and antiliberalism, federalism and antifederalism and liberal democracy and republicanism. Furthermore, the debate does not centre on the actual problems of taming global capitalism. That goal is only relevant to contributions in the critical theory tradition. This particularly holds true for Habermas and Brunkhorst. However, even these contributions must use the formalized legal language in order to be recognized. Accordingly, the proposed solutions turn out to be more abstract and more conciliatory than in France. Whereas there the differences clash unforgivingly, in Germany they are reconciled with one another by way of conceptual abstraction. According to optimists in the Kantian tradition, this function is fulfilled by the abstract concepts of constitutional patriotism (Habermas), supranational and federal republic (von Bogdandy) or the European federation with shared sovereignty (Fischer). The notion of the creation of a core Europe that is also open to new members is also in line with this.

The same abstraction and conciliation can also be found in the opposite position of the sceptics of the Hegelian tradition. Whereas in Britain the EU is entitled to no more than the role of an economic community and sovereignty remains solely with the national parliament, the sceptics in Germany consider the functional shift of competencies to the EU as a legal community to be far more conceivable. The imparted legitimation of European legal harmonization via national parliaments is no more than an abstract conceptual construction from which the reality of shifting competencies to the European level is already far away (cf. Lepsius 1991; Bach 1999). The Federal Constitutional Court's judgements in *Solange I*, *Solange II* and *Maastricht* really do not hinder the continuing process of integration, but rather serve as legal aids to soothe the legal conscience that everything that happens in Brussels is ultimately legally correct (BVerfG 37, 271; 73, 339; 89, 155). The effect of the legal language on the intellectual discourse is the latter's higher degree of abstraction and its liberation from political conflict. It is tamed legally. In this way, antagonisms can be resolved by conceptual abstraction. The price that must be paid for this legal taming of the intellectual discourse is its unrealistic nature and its corresponding lack of ability to offer concrete solutions to concrete problems. The gap between the pro-European elite and the rattled masses of the population is therefore particularly large. This results in strong tendencies towards the citizens' alienation from politics. In Germany, the discourse on Europe is characterized by the tense relationship between the open Kantian idea of a European cosmopolitanism and the closed, postauthoritarian Hegelian idea of democracy as exercising sovereignty by the people. The continuing economic integration and the transnationalization of the identity discourse support the symbolic power of the Kantian discourse concerning Europe, but without the Hegelian tradition having struck its sails. This conflict will keep the semantic construction of Europe in an ambivalent position for the foreseeable future.

5   The British dilemma
Free trade and domestic
parliamentary sovereignty against
foreign supranational rule

A prominent position of intellectuals in public discourse, similar to that of France, does not exist in Great Britain. Correspondingly, there is also no similar tradition of intellectual dissent with ruling politics like that which prevails in France (Stuchtey 2006: 14). In spite of this, it is possible to identify a British intellectual class. Its members, however, do not appear as representatives of abstract ideas and general social criticism as their thought is largely marked by empiricism. The reluctance of the members of the intellectual class to identify themselves as intellectuals is expressed by their distaste for the prevalent continental tendency towards abstract theorization (Ash 2006). Consequently, intellectual discourse concerning the European project is different in Great Britain than, in particular, in France or Germany. It is concerned not with theories, but facts, and not with abstract questions, but with concrete problems of European integration and their effects on British politics and society. Examples of this are the loss of the national parliament's sovereignty, the accession to the Economic and Monetary Union (EMU), the adoption of the euro and the loss of individual self-determination to European regulations. In questions regarding the design of the European single market, the advantages and disadvantages for the individual country occupy the place of greatest interest in Great Britain. Whereas the advantages of a European free trade area are welcomed, regulations from Brussels which exceed market creation are rejected as they are seen to be too far-reaching interventions into the economy in general, and into national interests specifically. Whereas the dominant position in the French discourse sees in the European single market an opportunity to tame global capitalism, the dominant position in the British intellectual discourse has recognized the European single market to be an opportunity to construct an economy better primed for international competition.

Another distinct characteristic of the British intellectual discourse concerning the European integration project is Britain's hesitant and late entry into the European Community in 1973. The British have, across all classes and political camps, continuously remained at a distance to the European integration project. The extent to which Great Britain will involve itself in this project and the question of how far this integration will be allowed to progress are still being disputed. The initial question was whether or not Great Britain would join at all, but since its entry, every further step towards integration has been a struggle. Bringing Great Britain into line with countries supporting integration must always be accomplished in the face of heavy resistance. Immediately following the entry into the European Community, it was debated whether or not Britain should even be allowed to remain a member. Only the referendum of 1975 – the only one in the history of the country – provided clarity on the issue. Even so, the question of how Great Britain can economically profit from its membership in the European Community without surrendering too much sovereignty to Brussels has continued to be a topic of contention (cf. Knill 1995; Harlow 1995; Gowland and Turner 2000; Wright 2000).

In 1973 Great Britain joined the European Community for solely economic reasons. The design of the European single market is, first and foremost, seen as an issue of intergovernmental negotiation. Every step towards the development of supranational European competencies must be pushed through against resistance from Great Britain. In the context of continuing integration, the British constantly pose the question whether or not to comply or to maintain an exceptional position. This raises questions concerning the design of the single market, political integration and national identity. The intellectual debate is concentrated on these three issues. The significant positions on these three issues will be illustrated in the following sections; first concerning the construction of Europe on the institutional level of economy and politics, then concerning the construction of Europe on the cultural level of identity. The tradition that underlines the British intellectual debate on Europe can be described as semantics of conventional liberalism. This means a preference for liberty that has gradually evolved from conventions starting with the Magna Charta of 1215 and that is deeply entrenched in institutions and everyday life. In contrast to the constitutional liberalism that evolved in the USA, it is not formally guaranteed by a written constitution. Nevertheless, it is as firmly established as any written guarantee of freedom rights.

The institutional construction of Europe

The dominant British view of the Union in the European multilevel system can be summarized in four points: (1) the Union should be no more than a free trade area, (2) European law should not interfere with the sovereignty of British Parliament, (3) the British understanding of democracy cannot be combined with a federal Europe and (4) the democratic deficit of the European Union stems from the extensive shift of political competencies to the Union level and can only be solved by a shift of competencies back to the national level. These four points are deeply rooted in the tradition of conventional liberalism, which, in this case, states that the European single market should expand its citizens' natural sphere of freedom, and that, for this purpose, only a trade law that ensures trust is necessary. All further limitations on the individual freedom of action can only arise from the familiar, historically emerged conventions of common law or from the familiar, legislative competencies of the national parliament, which is directly accountable to the citizens. From this point of view, Union regulation that goes beyond the ease of economic trade can only appear illegitimate. This in fact does arise in the British intellectual discourse which will, in the following, be represented by a number of exemplary statements. The fact that European law already affects the British institutional structure and jurisprudence to a significant degree makes the legitimacy of the current structure of the EU fundamentally questionable from the dominant British point of view.

Economic integration versus free trade area

Great Britain did not join the European Community until 16 years after the Rome Treaty. Since that time, Great Britain has only confirmed the further steps towards integration with reservation and resistance. This applies to the Single European Act (SEA) of 1986, the Maastricht Treaty of 1991 and the EMU. However, Britain did not adopt the euro and the country has also reserved the right to withdraw from the EMU (Holmes 2000).

From the dominant, markedly economically liberal viewpoint of the British intellectual debate, the political economies of continental Europe are too attached to the belief in positive results of a state-controlled economy. The concept of anticyclical control of the economy developed by Lord Keynes has had no relevance since Margaret Thatcher's neoliberal revolution. Until that time, some Labour administrations, together with the unions, had, by nationalizing basic industries and enforcing employment rights, driven back the economic liberalism deeply rooted in Great Britain. After Margaret Thatcher's revival of economic liberalism, not much of that effort was left. Tony Blair, with New Labour's Third Way, had to invent a social democratic version of neoliberalism in order to attain a governing majority for the left. The pillars of British economic liberalism, now common across party lines, are the right to property, freedom of the individual and free competition (Laughland 1996; Heathcoat-Amory 2004). From Conservative as well as New Labour points of view, the political economies of the continent suffer from chronic weakness of growth and unemployment due to the restraint of market forces caused by statism and excessively high taxes. The British therefore fear that continental Europeans, with their majority in the EU, will, to the disadvantage of citizens, too greatly restrain the dynamic forces of the economy when the competencies of the EU are expanded. Minimal EU competencies are seen by the British as protection from excessive economic intervention on the part of continental Europeans. However, this does not mean that Britain is absolutely opposed to the dominant continental economic philosophy and that the country therefore completely takes the side of the liberal model implemented in the USA. There is, for example, the European Movement Group. It advocates the continuing unification of Europe and professes the notion that the British economic paradigm has more in common with the continental European one than with the liberal one of the USA. According to this group, all European economies share common characteristics of state intervention in order to afford everyone equal opportunities and adequate income. They therefore all provide well-developed retirement systems, health care and long-term care, social support for poor and disabled persons and redistribution by way of taxation (European Movement Senior Expert Group 2005: 1; see also Barysch 2005; Gamble 2006). However, the majority perception is that the more protectionist economic policy on the continent cannot be reconciled with British economic liberalism. This will be more fully examined in the following.

Both the left and the right can be divided into pro-European and anti-European camps. This is particularly true concerning the question of the suitable economic system and its advantage for the citizen. Thereby, a considerable continuity of presented arguments has been observed since the referendum concerning British membership in the EC in 1975 (George 1998: 6).

The right wing is primarily made up of members of the Conservative party. The debate was waged so viciously that it even led to a two-camp rift within the party. Conservatives had always equated economic liberalism with nationalism. The debate on Europe drove a wedge between these two cornerstones of Conservative policy. Pro-European right-wingers see the adoption of the euro as an advantage for the British economy. In their opinion, the euro is not only beneficial for economic undertakings, but also for consumers as it reduces costs of foreign trade and resolves fluctuations in exchange rates. This would lead to transparent pricing and allow the single market to become a reality (George 1998: 7). Additionally, a greater stability in prices could be expected. The British economy's competitive disadvantages would be a thing of the past. Moreover, the pro-European right argues that, without the adoption of the euro, Great Britain would lose influence in the EU decision-making process. The single market would be threatened by the danger of a continental European protectionist, state interventionist EU economic policy if Great Britain lacked the means to work against such a development. For this reason, Britain's advanced integration into the EMU, by the adoption of the euro, is seen as the lesser evil when compared with continued absence.

For the considerably larger group of the Euro-sceptical right wing, the differences between individual member countries are too large for the EMU to be able to function with a common currency. This group expects that certain countries will experience economic difficulties if they lack the ability to counter economic fluctuation with flexible exchange rates. If such problems arise, they will be almost impossible to solve as membership in the EMU binds the hands of governments. Even a change of administration would do nothing to change the situation if the new government did not challenge the commitment to a common currency and stability pact. This could lead to the danger that the citizens would react to their lacking possibilities with a regime change based on direct action and support of extremist parties and groups

(George 1998: 9). From this perspective, the euro represents a symbol of the increasingly powerful state of the EU. In this way, the EU not only construes the appearance of statehood, but also appropriates the power related to it. Accordingly, the British freedom of self-determination would be increasingly restricted (George 1998: 9). Therefore, a further weakening of the British parliament caused by membership in the EMU would not be desirable. This sort of European state structure would not be able to achieve stability because it would lack the support of member states. The pro-European argument that a strong EU would guarantee freedom and stability is rebutted by the counter argument that democracy would be the best guarantee for that; however, the European Commission and the European Central Bank would be responsible for the common currency without subordinating themselves to democratic control (George 1998: 10). A parliamentary democracy would not be possible at the EU level because this form of government is only feasible within a national state with a government of the people by the people. The development of a democratically sovereign European people failed due to the vast differences between member states. Therefore Euro-sceptics repeatedly raise the same topic, namely the dangers of a growing supranational state without political control, made inescapable by the monetary union (George 1998: 10). Thus Euro-sceptics, in contrast to their pro-European counterparts, place their main focus on the political consequences of the EMU. Whereas pro-Europeans focus solely on the material benefits of EMU membership, sceptics point to the political disadvantages, namely the loss of control over fundamental economic decisions (George 1998: 10–11). This makes it clear that, even in Great Britain, the debate concerning economic integration is not possible without the consideration of political integration and its resulting problems.

The debate on the left, which primarily takes place among the New Labour ranks, refers, more than that of the right, to the challenges of globalization. In the EMU, the left has found an instrument for keeping global capitalism within the sphere of the EU in check. For the left, the crucial question is whether or not the EMU contributes to the promotion of economic growth, employment, social cohesion, democracy and ecological sustainability (George 1998: 12). The leftist pro-Europeans promise that the EMU will create substantial investments, more trade and greater stability, and they expect increased price stability, to the benefit of consumers. Furthermore, New Labour would be able to better achieve its goals in the context of monetary stability. Fluctuation in exchange rates would not only be an economic problem, but would also undermine the foundations of social cohesion, partnership, solidarity and 'stakeholding' (George 1998: 12). Some left-wing pro-Europeans are even prepared to surrender a part of British sovereignty to the EU in order to better tackle the challenges of globalization. From their perspective, however, this goal requires a democratization of the Union in order to ensure the legitimacy of its decisions. For this group, one channel towards democratization is the extension of the rights of the European parliament. It would require the strengthening of European citizenship, in which the common appreciation of democracy is rooted, and especially the strengthening of European civic commonality, which cannot be derived from ethnic origin or religious beliefs.

In contrast, left-wing Euro-sceptics see the EMU as a singularly dangerous experiment whose outcome and ramifications are unforeseeable. For Great Britain, entry into the EMU would be particularly risky as it has a different economic system than the continental European countries. In this way, they make arguments similar to those made by right-wing Euro-sceptics. Like this conservative group, they believe that the control of currency policy would be withheld from the democratically elected national governments and assigned to the nonelected experts at the European Central Bank (ECB). Furthermore, their options concerning fiscal policy would be greatly limited by the stability pact. Like their conservative counterparts, they recognize, in the combination of deflationary monetary policy and a growing democratic deficit, the potential for increased support of extremely nationalistic parties (George 1998: 16). However, left-wing Euro-sceptics are primarily concerned with social fallback systems. In their eyes, the EMU increases the power of global capital over national governments, making it increasingly difficult to keep social standards at the regularly high level. Additionally, the EMU is, even for left-wing Euro-sceptics, a danger to the centuries-old British democracy (George 1998: 16).

The debate about the EMU, on both the right and the left, is focused on the conflict between two contrary positions: Whereas one side demands the adoption of the euro as a further logical step towards enforcing Great Britain's influence in the EMU, the other pushes for a renegotiation of Britain's relationship to the EU in order to win back more British sovereignty. It becomes clear that the question of Britain's economic integration into the EU cannot be answered without considering the political, legal and cultural implications that will be more closely examined in the following sections.

European law and the sovereignty of British Parliament

The sovereignty of parliament and the rule of law are two fundamental principles of the British concept of state and law. They were definitely described by Albert Venn Dicey (1835–1922) (Dicey 1885/1982: 107). As to the first principle, according to his famous definition, parliamentary sovereignty means that parliament has the right to make any law, and that no person or body may invalidate or override parliamentary legislation (Dicey 1885/1982: 3f.). The parliament's legislative authority is marked by three characteristics. First, it applies unconditionally to all domains of society. Second, there is no other authority with legislative capacity. Third, it is formally subject to three limitations: (1) a law that infringes on the basic principles of morality is invalid, (2) a law must not intervene in the prerogative rights of the Crown, which are exercised without representation of the people and (3) a law must not be binding for successive parliaments, but can be annulled by these (Griffith 2006: 18).

The second basic principle of the British idea of government and law, aside from parliamentary sovereignty, is the rule of law. This can be characterized by three traits. The first trait is legal certainty. Only the violation of law is the justification for stripping a person of his or her property or physical inviolability. This principle was introduced in Britain much earlier than on the feudally-ruled European continent. The first document illustrating this principle is the Magna Carta of 1215. In the seventeenth century, the principle was finally enforced by the Habeas-Corpus Act of 1679 and the Bill of Rights of 1689. The second trait is equal rights. No one is above the law, and everyone is subject to equal laws and the same ordinary courts (Dicey 1885/ 1982: 114). In contrast to the feudal lordships that long ruled the continent, there is no differentiated legal system based on social position. The law applies to all British citizens, irrespective of class or social position. The third trait is the formation of the rule of law and the basic principles of the unwritten constitution. In contrast to the written constitutions of continental Europe and the US, which were established by a formative act, the basic principles of the unwritten British constitution, as the foundation for the rule of law, were created and confirmed over time by individual case law decisions. A further difference concerning the guarantee of individual rights (e.g. the right to personal freedom) between constitutions created by a formative, written act and the unwritten British constitution is that a law laid down in a single written act can, by way of another such act, be overridden or completely annulled, whereas the overriding of laws upheld by an unwritten constitution is impossible without a revolution in the institutions and customs of a country, especially because individual rights are so deeply rooted in the country's common law (Dicey 1885/1982: 119–20).

Both parliamentary sovereignty and the historically evolved rule of law see their unrestricted validity hindered by the primacy and direct effect of European law. Consequently, there is a fundamental contradiction between the two cornerstones of the British concept of government and law and European integration. In the following, this will be further clarified by a number of examples.

For the British, the crucial question is whether or not membership in the European Union truly limits the sovereignty of national legislation in British Parliament. The principle of parliamentary sovereignty bars all forms of division of sovereignty, both upwardly, meaning the supranational level, and downwardly, as represented by the regional and local levels. The undivided concentration of power in parliament is at the core of the British model of representative democracy (Sharpe 1996: 308). However, a division of power does in fact take place within the framework of the EU. Even from an intergovernmental perspective, power must be shared with other governments (Pilkington 1995: 103–4). As the British already have difficulties with this shared sovereignty, it is especially true of the rule of qualified majority decision making concerning the single market in the Council of Ministers, as laid down in the Single European Act of 1986. This act implies that minority groups have no chance to veto majority-enacted European law. A country must accept laws to which it did not agree (Congdon 2002: 5). British legislation is overridden if it conflicts with European law. This means nothing less than the surrender of parliamentary sovereignty as a result of membership in the EU (Pilkington 1995: 107). In view of this consequence, the defenders of parliamentary sovereignty wish to see the EU as nothing more than a free trade area with no further political capacities (Congdon 2002).

The considerably more pro-European position of Tony Blair's New Labour administration (in contrast to that of Margaret Thatcher) its acceptance of the European Human Rights Convention and its reforms concerning decentralization with a step towards greater autonomy for Scotland and Wales, the reinstatement of London's local government, with a directly elected mayor and the further regionalization of administration, seriously put the concept of parliamentary sovereignty in Great Britain to the test (MacCormick 1999). This process can be understood either as diffusionist or sovereignist. According to the diffusionist reading, these changes represent an increasing division of power between the British Parliament and the EU (ascending), as well as regional and local bodies (descending). For the few pro-Europeans in Great Britain, this is the price the country must pay for the benefits of the European single market and the benefits of regional and local activation. For the many anti-Europeans, this is the gateway to an increasing loss of British self-determination. The more positively formulated sovereignist reading does not see these changes as a crucial renunciation of the principle of parliamentary sovereignty because it simultaneously deals with British Parliament's delegation of power to supranational or regional/local institutions. The parliament remains sovereign and can, at any time, take back delegated power. The delegation of power to other institutions is nothing more than an instrument for the optimization of administration in light of the necessity for European cooperation and regional/local activation that takes place within the framework of parliamentary sovereignty. In the case of a clash of British and European law, European law applies. This means, however, that, from this point of view, there is no interference in parliament's sovereignty, because parliament delegated power to the formation of European law. Parliament still has the sovereignty to take back that delegation. From the critical sovereignist point of view, these are procedures that still must be tested in order to truly retract a delegation of power. Although the sovereignist position is deeply rooted in British history, the diffusionist position is gaining more advocates who see this position as a more realistic means of dealing with real-world factors that can no longer, in neither a descending nor ascending manner, be governed by the authority of the national parliament (MacCormick 1999).

Some authors consider the 1990 ECJ judgement concerning *Factortame* (case 213/89) to be a turning point in the relationship between EU and British law. This decision meant the overriding of a 1988 British law by European law. Sir William Wade regards this as a revolutionary process, as this meant for the first time that British Parliament's 1972 European Communities Act limited a later parliament's freedom to act. In his opinion, this decision shows that, by its EU membership, Great Britain subordinated itself to another regime when the parliament adopted EU law that limited the sovereignty of legislation for successive parliaments (Wade 1996: 571; quoted in Allan 1997: 443). This fundamentally contradicts the British understanding of parliamentary sovereignty. However, Allan considers this interpretation to be exaggerated and irrelevant for the formation of governance under the condition that the national parliament, in the context of global interdependencies, can never be the place where relevant decisions are made. What is far more important is the proper design of cooperation between the EU, the national parliament and the national courts. For Allan, EU membership does not necessarily mean the surrender of national sovereignty. For him, it is the British courts' interpretation of EU law that decides to what extent European law subordinates British law, and to what extent the two can be harmonized. This means that there is some leeway that allows, even in a European framework, to carry on in the British legal tradition (Allan 1997: 451).

James Caporaso and Joseph Jupille (2005) show, however, that European law has made considerable marks on the British system of government and has caused a series of changes in the system. According to their research, limitations on sovereignty, in the sense of freedom from external constraint and in the sense of autonomous organization of internal affairs, have been caused by EU membership (Caporaso and Jupille 2005: 1).

According to Caporaso and Jupille's research, European law's penetration of British jurisprudence has caused a significant institutional change that, at the time of Great Britain's entry into the European Community, was neither intended nor anticipated by the British. This change emerged from European jurisdiction and its principles, but it has increasingly entered into the practical exercise of British jurisdiction (Caporaso and Jupille 2005: 29). The cause has been a veritable transformation of the system of government that is pushing the centuries-old principles of understanding the British government and law into the background. This encompasses no less than the foreign and domestic sovereignty of British Parliament and jurisdiction bound to the wording of the law. The limitation of parliamentary sovereignty, caused by European law, the national practice of judicial review of laws, as well as executive and administrative decisions, and jurisdiction based on the principles of intentional interpretation, proportionality and legitimate expectations have taken its place.

European federalism and the British understanding of democracy

The continuing economic, legal and political integration makes the question of the appropriate institutional form of the European Union ever more pressing (McKay 1999). Since the foundation of the European Community, several models of institutional organization have been competing against one another. They range from the free trade area all the way to a federal state. There is, generally, no place for federalism in the British idea of government. The British can therefore, almost without exception, be found among the ranks of the anti-federalists. However, even in Great Britain, the different meanings of 'federalism' allow for differentiations in the question of the federal form of the EU.

Great Britain is a unitary state in which parliament is the only seat of power, and, for this reason, in which the division of power over different levels (i.e. local, regional and national) is a foreign concept. Admittedly, the reforms of 1997 gave the regions of Scotland and Wales and the City of London rights to autonomy that were previously unimaginable. Nevertheless, this is interpreted as a delegation of power from the national parliament and not as a strict federal separation of powers, as paradigmatically defined in the US constitution of 1789. In the federal system of the USA, the central government (i.e. the president and the congress) are not sovereign in all internal affairs. In some matters, the individual states exercise autonomous power that, due to the constitutionally specified division of power, cannot be taken away by the central government (Bailey 1978: 5). Such a written, constitutionally fixed division of power does not exist in Great Britain.

According to Dicey (1885/1982), the federal system of government is tied to preconditions that do not exist in Great Britain. On the one hand, a group of nations must, due to a common history and geographical proximity, perceive a bond that allows the emergence of a feeling of common nationality. On the other hand, the individual nations must have an individual historical identity that is regarded by the citizens as formative. Following this precondition, it is advisable that the nations form a union in which governance is divided between the union government and the governments belonging to the member states. The citizens of such a union, on the one hand, feel a bond between the states, and, on the other hand, identify with their own countries. As well as the desire for unity between the states, there is a desire for the states' autonomy regarding internal affairs (Dicey 1885/1982: 76). According to Dicey, in order to avoid insurmountable conflict in questions of competencies, such a union requires a constitution in which the competencies of the federal government and the individual states' governments are clearly determined. In order to clearly define the separation of power, it is necessary that there be a written constitution, that constitutional law is solidified and unchangeable and that the various legislative institutions only be allowed to act within the framework of specified competencies (Dicey 1885/1982: 78).

Dicey states that, compared to a system of parliamentary sovereignty, the federal system of government entails a number of drawbacks. Federalism allows for only a weak government, one that cannot hold much sway, as power is divided between different levels of legislation that can block each other and that are individually too weak to develop an enduring impact. A further weakness is the conservatism that follows from a solidified constitution. The constitution is held to be holy and untouchable. This results in a generally conservative stance that categorically works against change. Ultimately, federalism leads to an exaggerated legalism. Written laws dominate thought and action and allow only little latitude for the situationally appropriate adaptation of the law in individual circumstances. Devotion to the law is placed above appropriate solutions to problems. Because all levels of jurisdiction are bound to the constitution, there is no latitude for sovereign decisions of politically accountable bodies (Dicey 1885/1982: 78).

David Heathcoat-Amory (2004) explains why, from the dominant British point of view, the model of federalism, as developed in the USA, cannot be applied to the European Union. For this he refers to the debate concerning the European constitutional contract as a starting point. He is concerned with the question of whether or not it is possible to create supranational institutions that can be classified as democratic and that can ensure the support of the citizens (Heathcoat-Amory 2004: 9). As Alexis de Tocqueville (1945) argued, this was possible in the USA because a range of necessary conditions were met there. Among these were, particularly, a common language, the practiced exercise of self-government, a set of common moral values shared by the ruling class and a widely shared appreciation of equality and freedom (Heathcoat-Amory 2004: 9). Accordingly, the American constitution exists not only as a legally binding document, but also as a general commitment of the people to common values that grew from Anglo-Saxon thought. The question is whether or not this school of thought and the corresponding constitutional model can be applied to the European Union. For Heathcoat-Amory (2004: 9), this is out of the question. This would be inhibited by the simple fact that Europe is made up of many different countries with widely varying historical experience. Some are used to thinking in a continental context, whereas others, like Great Britain, look back on a maritime history and therefore instinctively have a wider world view. This has led to differences in legal tradition and differences in attitudes towards the role of the government and the origin of individual rights. In Heathcoat-Amory's eyes, the expansion of the European Union has increased the diversity of these governmental traditions. For this reason, there can be no unified European people and certainly no European *demos* upon which a European federation or supranational democracy could base itself. Such a *demos* also cannot be synthesized using symbols like the European flag. As Tocqueville pointed out, only the citizens' common, living customs and conventions could provide the necessary foundation for a federal democracy. Therefore, for the foreseeable future, the European Union will have to be satisfied with its contract-regulated relationship between states that trade together, cooperate and find common solutions to common problems, but that will not transfer their power to a supranational government under the rule of a constitution (Heathcoat-Amory 2004: 10). Accordingly, a federal form of governance for the European Union not only infringes on the fundamental principles of the British concept of the government, but also fails in the sense that the preconditions that would have to support such a European federation have not come close to being fulfilled.

Besides Helen Wallace (1985), only a few authors in Britain see European federalism as a chance to harmonize a variety of interests. Most, unlike the Germans with their federal tradition, do not see a federation as a frame of reference for handling diversity and for compromise-oriented negotiation. Instead, for the vast majority of British people, European federalism represents a form of government in which Brussels can seize too much power and the Union can meddle in the internal affairs of member states (Wallace 1985: 6).

Included in the British concept of government are the aforementioned principles of parliamentary sovereignty and the rule of law, as well as the principle of self-government. This principle does not tolerate any external intervention into the self-government of the British people. It is therefore fundamentally opposed to British membership in the EU. This is particularly true for the illegitimate influence of the EU on the living conditions in Great Britain. Whereas the intellectual discourse in Germany and France is, in light of this question, based on the questions of democratization of the Union, the dominant view in Britain is that the path to improved democracy can only lead away from the EU and back towards more competencies for national states. This is shown by the following contributions to the debate.

The coexistence of strong, democratically legitimate political institutions and a social structure focused on the individual freedom of citizens and their quest for utility maximization (utilitarianism) have been created, as a British feature, following from the historical process. Society is understood to be an association of free individuals, and the government is seen as an agency that must act on behalf of the needs of these individuals. In order to achieve this end, the government must be directly controlled by freely elected, democratically replaceable representatives of the people. This is the only insurance for the self-government of the people, and subsequently the only insurance that the highest principles of the British idea of government can be satisfied (Johnson 2000: 16). Following this idea of government, the EU can be perceived only as a threat to the British political tradition and the form of democracy rooted therein. The more authority is transferred to the EU, the more dramatic is the harm done to the genuinely British principles of democracy. This argument also includes the complexity and opacity of European decision-making processes that, as a rule, lead to compromises of the lowest common denominator. In this way, no problem-solving decisions can be made and no clear responsibilities can be identified. This characteristic of the EU decision-making process contradicts the British concept of democratically controlled political responsibility by which a government elected by a majority must make clear decisions and take responsibility for them by presenting itself for re-election. Holding governments responsible for their actions using this form of democratically controlled politics cannot be achieved at the EU level. Therefore, from the British perspective, the EU will never be sufficiently legitimate in the democratic sense. According to Johnson, the fundamental dilemma of the EU lies in its inability to harmonize its quest for a tighter union with demands for responsible, democratic self-government. Instead of fighting this dilemma by limiting itself to the logic of a market economy and leaving politics to national states, Brussels would create a democratically uncontrollable bureaucratic apparatus that would increasingly intervene in member states' internal affairs (Johnson 2000: 26).

The British rejection of a European identity

Along the lines of conventional British liberalism, the EU is a single market that broadens the individuals' latitude for action, but it is not an anchor for a collective identity. Only national history dating back centuries can be an anchor point for collective identity, and only this historical identity can provide sufficient cohesion in times of crisis. A strong European identity would actually limit the obtained space for liberty because the corresponding European regulation of life would be less accessible to control by the individual than national regulation. This position of conventional liberalism has placed the dominant British point of view in opposition to every project that aims to strengthen the European identity. Therefore, it is also in opposition to all intentions of a European constitutional contract that pursue the same goal.

The concept of Union citizenship was introduced by the Maastricht Treaty of 1992. This was meant to ease the development of a European identity. Whether or not this measure actually takes a further step towards a European identity is, however, in light of the plurality of national identities, highly debatable. In Great Britain, more than anywhere else, this is considered neither possible nor desirable. Two levels can be distinguished in this issue. The first level is concerned with the overall possibility of multiple identities. The second level is concerned with the possibility of the emergence of a European identity from the European countries' disparities in history, language, culture and concept of the state. Anthony D. Smith (1999) considers multiple identities, in other words, the coexistence of a European and a national identity within one individual, to be possible. But, in contrast, the emergence of a purely European identity seems to him to be unlikely. We deal here with identities that emerge from an individual's membership in a collective; this could be a nation as well as Europe. Smith argues that such collective identities take shape in a historical process, over a long period of time. Three traits characterize a collective identity: (1) the belief in a certain continuity of a population over a longer period of time; (2) shared memories and formative, commonality-strengthening historical events; and, stemming from these, (3) the belief in a collective's common goal. Throughout the course of history, ever larger collectives with such a common identity, all the way up to nations, have been formed. Today the nation is the formative collective unit, and national identity is the norm. In spite of the dominance of national identity, Smith claims that at present it is normal for people to maintain a variety of affiliations. They accordingly have multiple identities (Smith 1999: 229).

In contrast to individual identities, collective identity is characterized by perpetuity and independence of situational change over long periods of time. So Smith's question is whether or not there is, in this sense, a European identity. It would be situated between the national and a global identity. After all, Smith states that, apart from the differences between nations and their cultures, there are numerous overlaps and transfers of elements of neighbouring cultures. Admittedly, these also include elements that have originated from regions beyond European borders. What is lacking, according to Smith, are the three aforementioned formative elements of a collective identity. In the future, Europe will not, to a sufficient degree, be able to rely on continuity, collective memory and common goals. Therefore, the reality of a collective European identity is not possible, according to Smith's British point of view. This makes it clear that, from the British perspective, only national identities are truly effective, and a European identity of equal quality does not exist.

Since the waves of immigration from the colonies in the 1960s, the question of what constitutes a British national identity has been the subject of heated debate. According to Parekh (2000), two competing interpretations of Britain's national identity have taken form in these debates: right-wing and left-wing viewpoints. The right-wing point of view exemplarily held by Enoch Powell consists of four elements: (1) parliamentary sovereignty in representation of the British people, (2) individualism in the sense of the primacy of individual rights over collective association, (3) British ethnic unity as a foundation of the British national identity and (4) the geographic location and history of the country. The fact that Britain is an island separated from the continent, and can therefore retain its uniqueness, is essential to this right-wing point of view. In terms of politics, a range of consequences arise from this interpretation of British identity. The decentralization and the associated transfer of power to the different regions are seen as a breach of parliamentary sovereignty that lead to the destruction of the unity and identity of the country. The welfare state is regarded as incompatible with the appreciation of individualism. Immigration policy should be more restrictive because, according to the right-wing point of view, black and Asian immigrants would be rejected by the British as representatives of foreign cultures. From this perspective, membership in the EU leads to the destruction of British identity and uniqueness. In contrast, other member states' EU membership would be a less serious problem as they cannot, to the same degree, look back on such a long continuity in their history. Because their democratic institutions were created only in the recent past, the citizens of the other member states would not be as profoundly linked to them (Parekh 2000: 9). Moreover, continental Europeans, more than the British, as a group possess common cultural roots and are, in their political and legal structures, more similar to each other (from the British point of view). Particularly the idea of federalism would be much less of a threat for them than for the British. The emphasis on uniqueness and incompatibility with other identities is typical of the right-wing view of British identity. Margaret Thatcher, John Major and William Hague represented a more moderate form of this concept of British identity.

The left-wing view of British identity is primarily held by New Labour. Mark Leonard (1999), following this view, points out the reciprocal correlation between Great Britain's global relationships and its European roots. He also believes that individualism is a characteristic of British identity. However, he sees it as supplemented by the British sense of justice, fairness and the ethic of sharing (Leonard 1999: 12). In contrast to the conservative right-wing point of view, he considers Britain's multicultural character to be an essential attribute of British identity. Tony Blair shares this interpretation of British identity. He supplements this position with the thesis that not parliamentary sovereignty, but parliamentary democracy, of which decentralization of power is an unavoidable factor, forms the core of British identity. Additionally, Blair sees Britain's long tradition of tolerance, cultural plurality, hospitable nature towards different ways of life, social compassion and youthful spirit as being central characteristics (Parekh 2000: 12).

In the place of conservative right-wing uniqueness, the left-wing concept appreciates tolerance as an attribute of British identity. Concerning the issue of the European Union, this means that there are two competing models. The right-wing model, on the basis of uniqueness, wants to conserve an exceptional position for Great Britain. In contrast, the left-wing model imagines Great Britain to be a diverse part of a diverse union. Admittedly, the conservation of Britain's exceptional position in the context of European integration is the dominant position in British discourse. This is illustrated by the following contributions.

Jeremy Rand (2000) defines British identity by the country's history and culture, which, in his opinion, deviate from those of the continent in all significant points. Following this argument, Great Britain is one of the few countries that have had a long-term historical continuity. For a great length of time, the country has existed without occupation and colonization. It has possessed a high degree of political stability and a deeply rooted national identity comprising a stable system of values that has never been challenged. According to Rand, the historical context that formed Great Britain's relationship to Europe was determined by four key points. First, since the rise of the Tudors, Great Britain has not possessed territories on the continent. This has led to Britain distancing itself from Europe. Second, Great Britain's rise as a colonial empire and world power allowed the country to look far beyond Europe and simultaneously aim to prevent the dominance of a continental country that would seriously be able to compete with Britain. Third, the long history of continuity led to the deep rooting of the country's significant institutions, especially parliamentary sovereignty and the rule of law. The fact that both of these identity-forming institutions seem to be challenged in the context of the EU has once more led to the British distancing themselves from

Europe. Fourth, Great Britain was among the victorious powers of the Second World War. In contrast to the continental European countries, with the exception of France, the British maintain an unquestioned association with national pride and patriotism. At the same time, they believe that the continental Europeans should be grateful to them for their liberation of Europe from the barbarism of National Socialism. Because the country did not experience such severe atrocities of war as those on the continent, the British, unlike continental Europeans, do not see the EU as assuming the role of a guarantee of European peace. They therefore consider themselves less obligated to the EU. Additionally, their lack of wartime occupation and their majority voting system make the British less inclined to compromise with other countries in the context of the EU.

All of these distinctive features separate the British from continental Europeans, according to Rand. Instead, there are rather more similarities with the United States. Consequently, it would be reasonable not to draw distinctions between US and European cultures, but between European and Anglo-Saxon cultures. Along these lines, it is understandable that the British should see the EU as a threat to their own culture, and that they perceive parliamentary sovereignty and indeed their entire way of life to be in danger. They wish to maintain their sovereignty because they want to make their own decisions concerning influences to which they expose themselves (Rand 2000: 30; see also Kumar 2003).

Like many others, Timothy Garton Ash (2001) stresses the fact that the British do not see themselves as Europeans. For them, Great Britain is an extraordinary, unique country that is separate from Europe. This attitude results from the parliamentary democracy that the British consider to be unique and the only truly democratic system of government and from the geographic and political position of an outsider that the country occupied for so long. Instead, the relationship to the United States is much more highly developed. The lacking feeling of belonging can clearly be observed in political speeches in which politicians speak about Europeans as if they themselves did not belong to this group. The history of Great Britain is one of continuity and one that contrasts the continent's incessant transformation, caused by constantly changing regimes, borders, monarchs and constitutions. It is a history of the slow, constant organic growth of institutions, common law, parliament and a unique conception of sovereignty that are all securely anchored in the unrestricted power of the parliament (Ash 2001: 6).

Thomas Risse (2000) also confirms the uniqueness of the British. According to his analysis, the attitude of the British people towards the EU, and indeed Europe, has not changed considerably since the Second World War. For them, Europe is still the continent, and they see themselves as the others. The social construction of English as the core of the British national identity is directly connected to particular English institutions, historical memory and symbols (Risse 2000: 9). Risse also locates the core of these identity-forming institutions in a particular understanding of national sovereignty. According to Risse's analysis, this is comprised of two elements. First, since 1066, the crown has symbolized external sovereignty, meaning independence from Rome and the pope, as well as from the European continent. Second, since the Glorious Revolution of 1688, the sovereignty of Parliament has represented the hard-earned victory over the absolutist endeavours of the crown and the implementation of representative democracy (Risse 2000: 9). Accordingly, British pride for foreign and domestic sovereignty is deeply rooted in history and is linked to the development of a liberal and democratic system. As Risse says, it is therefore no wonder that the British have major problems handing over parts of their sovereignty to the EU. Following the British concept of sovereignty, Europe is therefore only conceivable as a consortium of independent nation states.

Concluding remarks

The current crisis in the EU has presented the chance for Great Britain to pro-mote its model of a loose association of states that can always be enlarged. This model has been praised by Tony Blair as being a Europe of the people, a Europe explicitly anchored in the rights of the states and in representative democracy (Gamble 2006: 38). From the British point of view, this is the best way towards an economically strong and democratically legitimate Europe. It is a European course that, along the lines of conventional liberalism, broad-ens the individual's freedom of action and leaves its normative embedding, beyond the realm of trade law, completely to the historically formed and trusted national authorities (i.e. legislature and jurisdiction) which can be controlled by the citizens. Politics beyond national borders is fundamentally at risk of losing the balance between freedom and normative obligation, to the disadvantage of freedom. From the perspective of conventional liberal-ism, this balance is always precarious and can only be maintained within the familiar environment of national politics. With this stance, the British intel-lectual discourse concerning Europe finds itself, by participating in the European integration project, in the dilemma of necessarily supporting the expansion of Union capacities beyond the guarantee of free trade, whereby the growing institutional supranationalism undermines the national sover-eignty of Britain. With Great Britain's increasing economic integration in the European single market and the accompanying transnationalization of the discursive domain, the powers of further European expansion have gained symbolic force, albeit without considerably decreasing the sway of Britain's insistence upon sovereignty and identity.

Conclusion

Constitutional liberalism as a model for the semantic construction of Europe?

Growing European economic integration raises the question of the accompanying social integration of Europe (i.e. the European Union). It is to be assumed that ongoing European economic integration does create a structural change affecting national societies, which entails the increasing superimposing of the mode of individualistic integration on the presently prevalent mode of collectivist integration. The semantics and the institutional form of constitutional liberalism that developed in the USA in a distinctive manner correspond to this mode of individualistic integration. For this reason, the structural conditions and the internal logic of this semantics of constitutional liberalism in the USA should be elaborated in order to gain a better understanding of the developmental trend of European social integration. On this basis, it is demonstrated for what reasons and in which way European economic integration leads to the superimposing of an individualist mode of social integration and its semantic and institutional formation via constitutional liberalism on the collectivist mode.

The character and historical formation of constitutional liberalism

In England, John Locke's (1690/1963) social contract theory provided the theoretical foundation for the semantics and institutional formation of a social order transcending estates and societal segments. Its fundamental tenet is the ethic of possessive individualism within the framework of a polity limited to conflict resolution and external protection and regulated by a separation of powers. This model has, in the historical process, experienced significant changes; at first via the linking of voluntarism and representative government on the basis of a sovereign parliament, later on through the reshaping of possessive individualism by an ethic of collective inclusion of the working-class via voluntary self-organization and representation, and finally through the renewal of possessive individualism by the ethics of human capital individualism.

What is interesting to us is that Locke's teaching can also be seen as a significant source of the semantic and institutional formation of the social order in the United States. Within the North American colonies, a new social order developed. It was based on English law, with its emphasis on equal liberty rights for all individual Englishmen, irrespective of estate or group membership. In England, freedom and equality were already practised, while in Europe this still had to be won. In England, the primacy of common law, pushed through by Edward Coke against royal power and shaped by lawyers and the independent legal practice, provided very early on for the assurance of rights of freedom. The rights of freedom laid down in the Petition of Right (1628) and the Bill of Rights (1689) must be interpreted as contractual affirmation of those rights vis-à-vis the king, but not as basic rights, above parliamentary legislative competence. The sovereign parliament was in fact considered to be both the reliable protector against the king's potential intrusions into the freedom of the citizens and the highest court. The freedom rights against the government originally granted to earls, barons, freemen and merchants in the Magna Carta (1215) became the uniform rights of all Englishmen in the seventeenth century. They were thereby freed from all connotations of estate privileges (Robertson 1993; Weir and Beetham 1999: 29–30, 299–329).

This is the context out of which the North American colonies' war of independence against the motherland (1776–83) is to be understood. The colonies had no representation in English Parliament, but they were nonetheless bound by the laws passed by Parliament. Despite having no representatives, they were considered to be represented by Parliament. This worked as long as there was no exceptional encroachment on the colonies. The extraordinary tax levied against the uninvolved colonies by Parliament because of the financial hardship caused by the Seven Years War was seen as such an unjustified encroachment and provoked resistance under the motto 'no taxation without representation'. For the colonies, this was a matter of the protection of the old freedom rights from the threatening power of Parliament. Within the old order, built upon the sovereignty of Parliament, this was not possible. They therefore chose the path of independence, which led to a new form of protecting freedom via constitutionalization. The society of independent property owners, freed from 'illegitimate' collective pressures, formed an individualistic mode of social integration that considerably differs from the collective mode of the European nation states differentiated into estates, classes and social strata. The legitimation and institutional shape of this mode of social integration can be found in the semantics and institutional form of constitutional liberalism, whose core consists of the institutional order of citizens living together in freedom (Bailyn 1967).

In the North American colonies, particularly the colonies in New England and less so in the plantation economy of the South, a society of free property owners, without the differentiation into estates still prevalent in Europe, had developed. The colonists practised freedom and equality, influenced by English common law, for all property owners without exclusive rights of estates. Because of the practically limitless space, conflicts over possessions and possible shortages could be handled by constantly extending the settlement area further west and displacing the native Indians. The world of the colonies largely resembled the state of natural law of a settlement community of independent property owners, who were all equally interested in and generally respected security of property, freedom and life. The reason for a constitutional guarantee of those universal freedom rights was provided by the illegitimate encroachment of British Parliament into the property of the colonists via extraordinary taxation. It showed that even the parliament of representatives can be a threat to the property owners' rights to freedom. It was therefore necessary for the Founding Fathers to absolutely protect those freedoms via a Bill of Rights as an amendment to the constitution, by placing them, as unalterable higher law, above the legislative powers of congress. It was also no longer sufficient for them to provide for representation of the people in their own parliament. The experience of British Parliament's extraordinary tax taught them to distrust any sovereign power, even the people's sovereignty representatively exercised in parliament. Even if they had had representatives in the London Parliament, these would have easily been outvoted by the majority, and the extraordinary taxes would have been forced on them nonetheless. The tyranny of the majority over the minority is the evil that they sought to avoid no matter what. Thus the constitution is therefore completely geared towards the protection of autonomous property owners' rights to freedom which, under no circumstances, should be encroached upon by any authority, not even by popular sovereignty acting on the votes of the majority.

In Locke's ideal world of independent property owners in North America, no power, neither internal nor external, was to be able to go as far as to damage the freedoms of the property owners. Therefore, in addition to the constitutional guarantee of equal rights to freedom for all, another pillar, the uncompromising realization of Locke's model of separation of powers as a balanced system of reciprocally controlling entities was brought into being. The legislative, executive and judicial branches not only complement each other, but should also keep each other in check by way of overlapping competencies. Here, due to their experience with British Parliament, the Founding Fathers went further than Locke. The legislature (i.e. the Congress) is itself divided into two equally powerful chambers, each monitoring the other: the Senate and the House of Representatives. However, a law also needs to be signed by the President to come into effect. The practice of case law grants the courts a strong position and legitimizes what, according to the German interpretation of the rule of law, would be considered the rule of judges (*Richterrecht*) and would therefore be disqualified as illegally usurped political power. The interpretation of the constitution, and especially of the individual rights guaranteed by it, has given the Supreme Court, as early as the tenure of legendary chief justice John Marshall (Chief Justice from 1801 to 1835), considerable power (Funston 1978). With the constitutional guarantee of equal freedom rights for all as a higher, inviolable right, the Founding Fathers, faced with real threat to those rights by British Parliament, also went beyond Locke (McDonald 1985; Pangle 1988).

What the Founding Fathers created is best described by the term 'constitutional liberalism' (i.e. regulated by a written constitution). It is the work of two closely linked supporting groups: property owners and lawyers, which are, in many cases, the same people. The freedom rights of the property owners had been placed into the hands of a strong judiciary, whose task it was to actually guarantee the constitutionally certified rights. The basis for this arrangement was a society of property owners that was able to organize itself through free association and primarily required a working judiciary system in order to protect the citizens from private and public encroachment on their property and to resolve occurring disputes. It was possible to limit legislative and executive power to the administration of tasks that could not be dealt with through self-organization, and they had to be subject to strict control by counter-authorities so that they could not become a threat to the freedom rights.

Constitutional liberalism was born by an idea of public-spirited individualism exemplified by the elite of the Founding Fathers. It was an individualism of self-discipline and personal responsibility that included the willingness to commitment in the self-organization of society. One exemplary testimony of this communal individualism was given by Benjamin Franklin in his autobiographical writing. The ethic of individualism incorporated a substantial degree of voluntaristic public spirit, as substantiated in many associations of societal self-organization. Constitutional liberalism was correspondingly supplemented by an element of republicanism. However, the Founding Fathers' republicanism has nothing to do with Rousseau. They see republicanism as a counterforce for the assurance of the individual's freedom in the face of the collective rule of the individual states. Madison's 'Federalist No. 10' (Hamilton, Madison and Jay 1787–88/1961) is famous for this understanding of republicanism. The plea for the federal republic in place of a confederation of states is justified with the arguments that, at the federal level, the factionalism within the states and the accompanying possibility of permanent domination of a majority over the minority can thereby be overcome, that the delegates have to represent a larger constituency with more diverging interests than on the level of the single state, and that this in turn means that they must bundle more interests. On the federal level, the factionalisms of the individual states are broken up so that no perpetual one-sided majority reign is possible. The federal republic protects against the dividing force of gridlocked factionalism in the individual states and against tyranny of the majority. In this system, the freedoms of the citizens are better off than in a confederation of individual states. Republicanism is a plea for federal unity in order to protect the individual citizen from the tyranny of majority in individual states.

The federation frees the citizens from the tight bonds of the collective of the individual state. In this respect, federal republicanism does not aim at the unity of citizens in the general will of a strong community, as proposed by Rousseau, but rather at the safeguarding of its citizens' freedom rights against the collective of the individual states. It is the primary instrument of the individualization of the citizens and is their release from the confines and narrow-mindedness of the individual states. The federation did in fact play this role in a significant and increasing manner. That is why it has repeatedly been ascertained that the dual federalism of the United States, with its extensive provision for individual state's legislation and two administrations working side by side, has, over the course of two centuries, nevertheless clearly shifted its weight to the federal level. This is indeed the case because of the decisive role played by the federal enforcement of the constitutionally guaranteed civil rights. Part of the work was carried out by the Supreme Court in the form of adjudication and another part was carried out by Congress in the form of legislation. This was a matter of the inclusion of ever broader and newly immigrated groups of society into the benefits of civil rights. One significant historical position taken along those lines came with the cessation of the Civil War (1861–65) with the victory of the Union (i.e. northern states) over the secessionist Confederate States (i.e. southern states) (Parish 1975). It reinforced the notion of the federal republic over the concept of a confederation and brought, as one of the first results of the Union's active civil rights policy, the abolition of slavery (1868) through the constitution's fourteenth amendment, which made the black slaves into free citizens of the United States (Johannson 1965; Wright 1970; Sigelschiffer 1973). The fifteenth amendment, added in 1870, prohibited the practice of denying citizens the right to vote based on race, colour of skin or having been a slave. The nineteenth amendment prohibited the exclusion from suffrage based on gender. A further milestone of federal legislature meant to cope with the waves of immigrants arriving since the last third of the nineteenth century and the acute social problems caused by the Great Depression following the stock market crash of October 1929 was the social legislation of F. D. Roosevelt's New Deal in the 1930s (Leuchtenburg 1963; Skocpol 1992). The final milestone with long-term effects was the legislation-strengthening civil rights which were brought underway by John F. Kennedy but definitely put into effect by Lyndon B. Johnson in the second half of the 1960s (Burns 1990; Shklar 1991). The program of Affirmative Action was intended to reduce discrimination by systematic mobilization, education, support and advancement of minorities, and later women, and to thereby create equal opportunities and fairness in a great society. The structure of society based on the principle of achievement was to be complemented by systematically ensuring equality of opportunity. A society that places the individual above all else should also create the conditions for everyone to be able to develop his or her individuality for the good of society.

Besides the legislature, the adjudication of the Union, in particular that of the Supreme Court, has paved the way for the elimination of discrimination with trail-blazing verdicts. The fourteenth amendment of 1868 provided the Supreme Court with an instrument to dispel racial discrimination step by step in a logical, almost 100-year long process. It took until 1896 (in *Plessy v.*

Ferguson) to file for separate but equal public services for African and Caucasian Americans, in this case seats on trains (Lofgren 1987). In *Cumming v. Richmond* (1899) blacks were referred to private schools in cases where there was only a white high school in the district. In *Missouri ex rel. Gaines v. Canada* (1938) it was decided that schools could be separated according to colour, but that they had to be equally accessible. Not until *Sweatt v. Painter* in 1950 was it ruled that schools had to have the same quality. The pivotal change was carried out by the liberal court under Earl Warren in the case of *Brown v. Board of Education of Topeka* on 17 May 1954. Segregated schools were declared inherently unequal and therefore inadmissible because they had a discriminatory effect on the black child. This case led to a long period of fierce controversies. Federal troops even had to enforce, against individual southern states' National Guards, the admission of black students to colleges and universities formerly reserved for whites, for instance in 1957 in Little Rock, Arkansas. This instance emphatically demonstrates the liberating role of the Union in the assertion of minority rights against the majority of the individual states, just as envisioned in Madison's plea for federal republicanism (Gunther and Dowling 1970).

In the 1960s and 1970s the civil rights movement placed its trust in this role of the Union and vastly advanced, through legislation and exemplary rulings of the Supreme Court, the inclusion of not only blacks, but also, to an increasing degree, other minorities and women by actively making use of civil rights. Through the controversial school buses, desegregated schools were legally enforced. On 28 June 1978, a kind of turning point was reached with the Supreme Court's ruling in the case of *Regents of the University of California v. Bakke*. Bakke, a white applicant, was denied admission to the medical school at the University of California in Davis even though his grades were better than those of accepted black applicants. He sued for admission on the grounds of reversed discrimination. The California Supreme Court ruled in favour of Bakke, and he had to be admitted. In the University of California's subsequent appeal, the Supreme Court ruled in favour of Bakke with a slight majority of five to four. The majority found the rejection of Bakke's application to be a violation of the Civil Rights Act of 1964, which states that no federally funded institution may deny access based on race, colour of skin or origin. Because the university was a recipient of such funds, it had to admit Bakke. The minority, however, argued that a system of quotas is legal under both the constitution and the Civil Rights Act of 1964 if it helps to alleviate prior discrimination. Further civil rights policies followed both sides of the ruling. Pure quota systems were indeed rejected. However, prior discrimination was to be countervailed with regard to access to public institutions (e.g. applications to university and public spending) and the application of formerly discriminated minorities was to be taken under special consideration (Abernathy 1980).

The radicalization of the civil rights movement through multiculturalism has meanwhile led to a fierce battle between proponents of constitutional liberalism and radical multiculturalists (Young 1990; Schlesinger 1992; Glazer 1997; Schmidt 1997). The former want to stick to the idea of guaranteeing equal freedom rights for all citizens as individuals; the latter plead for a guarantee of group rights in terms of equal opportunities for every group with its own collective identity. Constitutional liberalism has always dealt with conflicts by broadening access to wealth, prestige, power, education and culture via the elimination of discrimination based on ascriptive features, including race, skin colour, ethnicity, nationality, gender and sexual orientation. That this leads to increased competition over scarce goods is inevitable. Thus it became more and more important to cope with scarcity through economic growth. In this way, it has been possible to prevent more serious conflicts concerning the allocation of resources among citizens.

Economic growth and the incorporation of broader parts of society into the partaking of industrially created wealth was the answer to the rising waves of immigration. The US answer to European socialism was mass production via the assembly line and higher wages corresponding to increased productivity and mass consumption. This model was exemplified by Henry Ford's standardized product (i.e. the Ford T) in Ford's automotive factory. This production model, which has gone down in history as 'Fordism', incorporated workers insofar as they produced exactly those products they could afford themselves (Hounshell 1984; Campbell, Hollingsworth and Lindberg 1991). They created mass prosperity, in which they had a direct stake. The effect was a high level of identification with this culture of capitalist mass production. In this way, the ethics of possessive individualism was transformed into an ethics of acquisitive individualism and mass prosperity. The freedom that had to be protected by the civil rights was now primarily the freedom to increase prosperity through well-paid employment and a variety of mass consumer offerings. Acquisitive individualism means that each individual's access to the market, and the improvement of his or her position in the market, is the main focus. This ethics manifests itself in a variety of ways. For the union leadership of the labour movement, it means focusing on the best possible wage compensation for their clientele (Lipset 1979: 170–204; Heckscher 1988). The success of the business of union work is measured more in wage agreements than in employee participation and social reform, especially since there is a deep-seated identification with the culture of capitalist mass production. That is why there was no class struggle akin to that in Europe and no noteworthy socialist movement (Sombart 1906; Lipset 1996; Lipset and Marks 2000). Instead, the racial conflict dominated and was self-evidently waged as a conflict over inclusion in civil rights. Together with the ethics of acquisitive individualism and mass prosperity, this conflict constellation brought about a concentration on market access as the linchpin of employment opportunities and status. Attention was turned to market access barriers caused by discrimination. Because education became an ever more important prerequisite for success in the market, access to higher education grew in importance. In this respect, acquisitive individualism today manifests itself in form of human capital individualism (Becker 1975; Collins 1979; Reich 1991; Hamilton and Hamilton 1997).

This strategy of the black civil rights movement of the 1960s became the blueprint for subsequent conflicts over discrimination based on gender, religion, ethnicity, nationality or sexual orientation. Each is a matter of access to schools, colleges, universities, private and public employment, public funding, positions in parliaments, commissions and administrations and public contracts for larger and smaller companies. Consequently, the struggle for market access has become significantly fiercer. One thing that has made itself especially clear is the fact that the removal of barriers only helps the active; the inactive are marginalized all the more. So the formation of a black middle class that has left the inner-city ghettos has resulted in an even bleaker black underclass that has been left behind in the ghettos with an extremely high unemployment and crime rate (Wilson 1990). According to the ethics of acquisitive individualism, it now was necessary to mobilize the inactive by active public support to promote their access to the market. This was the task set for the Affirmative Action program. Yet it became clear that the screw of competition was further tightened and just those that could be activated were engaged. For the ethics of acquisitive individualism, there is no legitimation basis for a generous inclusion of those unable or unwilling to compete, independent of their market success. An assurance of life above the poverty line, without the individual transformation of effort into market success, seems completely unfair to those who, through their own accomplishments, sustain themselves and contribute to the accumulation of societal wealth. A shift towards the granting of group rights via radical multiculturalism can therefore be explained by the failure of the mobilization strategy of acquisitive individualism, together with the illegitimacy of market-independent social security. The argument that, in a culture traditionally ruled by White Anglo-Saxon Protestants (WASPs), the descendants of other cultures are automatically disadvantaged cannot be so easily dismissed. Disputing the dominance of white, Anglo-Saxon and Protestant culture in a society where the descendants of this culture, in states like Texas and California, in some places comprise less than 50 per cent, is also not completely absurd. After the barriers of discrimination had largely been removed, the collectively shared cultural identity of minorities was left as the last reason for discrimination. Therefore, it inevitably had to become the centre of the conflict because the ethics of acquisitive individualism does not acknowledge any form of inclusion and approval other than market access (Blauner 1989; Farley 1996; Fischer et al. 1997; Smelser and Alexander 1999).

Outward openness and inner differentiation as an inclusion program

In the United States we find a pronounced moral universalism, closely linked with the ethics of possessive individualism. The ethics of possessive individualism has undergone a transformation into the ethics of acquisitive individualism. The link between those two components is constitutional liberalism, which originated in the marriage of juristic thought and property ownership. Constitutional liberalism is expressed in the constitutional guarantee of equal freedom rights for all, and in the realization of this guarantee in the jurisdiction of the Supreme Court. The republican element is subordinate to the legal guarantee of the freedom rights. Madison's republicanism clearly represents this kind of thinking. The Union is, as has been confirmed by history, compared to the individual states, the better refuge for the rights to freedom. This is complemented by understanding the separation of powers as a system of checks and balances, established to prevent the accumulation of power in order to avoid an endangerment of individual freedoms. The godfather of this construction is John Locke (1690/1963). James Harrington's republican ideas, which are closer to Rousseau, did indeed play a role in the constitutional discussion, as proven by John Pocock (1975: 506–52). However, they receded in favour of constitutional liberalism influenced by Locke. Hamilton was by and large a proponent of strong leadership via a government oriented towards public welfare, but in the long run his position was less influential than the interpretation of the federal republic as the guardian of individual freedoms, as advocated by Madison.

Current interpretations of the constitution continue to point out that republicanism is subordinate to constitutional liberalism (Habermas 1992: 324–48). Bruce Ackerman (1984, 1991) sees presidents like Abraham Lincoln, F. D. Roosevelt and John F. Kennedy, who had to govern in difficult times of turmoil, in the republican role of redefining the objectives of the whole polity, while in less turbulent times the liberalism of the struggle for individual rights and latitudes of interest is dominant (Goldstein 1999; Jauß 1999). Frank Michelman (1988: 1529–32; 1989: 450–52) believes it is the business of the court, especially the Supreme Court, to examine whether or not the political process of legislation allowed for a comprehensive deliberation that included all possible arguments or whether or not appropriate corrections are necessary. Adjudication thereby becomes the refuge of the republican idea. Cass R. Sunstein (1985: 58–59; 1990: 163–92) assigns the Supreme Court the role of abating the discrepancy between the republican ideal and actual pressure politics. This should be done by reviewing the compliance of administrative acts and legislation with the constitution, according to a sensible analysis and as part of a deliberative process; something that in reality tends to happen most when reviewing administrative acts and less when reviewing legislation. In reality, however, the role of enforcing an idea of republicanism, interpreted in terms of Rousseau, cannot be ascribed to the Supreme Court. Interpretation of rights to freedom – not the comprehensive definition of the objectives of the polity and the corresponding idea of the good life – is the precept of the court's decisions. Although jurisdiction is orientated towards a given era's prevalent notions of the good life when interpreting freedom rights and determining latitudes, it is nonetheless not republican decision making in the strictest sense. This is also true for the groundbreaking decisions of the court, wherein it itself pioneers a redefinition of the good life. As far as assuming a republican role, the Supreme Court lacks the power to involve the citizens in a common volition. This is something more likely to be achieved by strong presidents during times of social upheaval. Even Congress, with its division of powers between the Senate and the House of Representatives, cannot assume this duty. It is, because of its predominant practice of working in a multitude of committees and subcommittees, more a platform for coordinating interests.

The role of the Supreme Court is rather deliberative (Habermas 1992: 340–48). As the highest institution of juristic deliberation, it mediates between the moral universalism legally realized in the freedom rights and the prevalent court-influenced ethics of individualism of the respective era. In a negative respect, it can determine what cannot be generalized with regard to the freedom rights, but it cannot articulate positive models for the good life. At the most, such models exist as a given background of the interpretation of rights. They are formed and changed by that interpretation, but they remain unarticulated in the background. They can only come to the foreground as part of a president's direct communication with the nation as a community. In the Supreme Court, we recognize a strong deliberate component in which the discursive juristic assessment of social practices, according to their compatibility with the basic rights, is the main focus. This component places the focus on the unrestricted rights of the individual, independent of the collective of the nation and its ideas of the good life. Only because of its independence from voters was the Supreme Court able to play the role of a moral pioneer in the judicial discourse and provide for a realization of the rights of individuals against the narrow-mindedness of the national collective and the collectives of individual states. The abolition of discrimination in making use of individual rights is, in large part, due to the adjudication of the federal courts, with the Supreme Court leading the way. At the same time, the granting of the freedom rights has, to a great extent, been disassociated from membership in the national collective. This is true for a series of judgements that made legal and illegal aliens without US citizen status equal to US citizens (Joppke 1999: 23–61, 147–85). It can clearly be seen that the judicial discourse regarding the granting of constitutionally guaranteed rights surpasses the particularism of national solidarity and further leverages moral universalism. A republican role would instead bind the courts to the will of the national collective and would hinder their ability to overcome national narrow-mindedness in the interest of moral universalism.

A republican component exists mainly in a president's communication with the nation (e.g. in the form of the yearly report on the state of the nation), whereas Congress serves as a platform for the liberal negotiation of compromises of interest (Greenstein 1990; Neustadt 1990). Here we see the realization of a direct link of the morally inspired universalism of equal freedom for all with the liberalism of the open coordination of interests in negotiation processes, whereas integration of both components into a republicanism characterized by national belonging and the binding, legally substantiated definition of the good life is only weakly developed. For this very reason, a comparatively large latitude for the expansive construction of the right to freedom, even beyond the members of the collective, and the development of individual freedoms in societal self-organization is achieved. However, this commitment to rights to freedom is itself rooted in the republican spirit. The republican consent on common goals has itself confirmed the great openness regarding immigrants and the broad scope of self-organization, respectively. Outward inclusiveness with regard to immigrants is internally coupled with the focus on market access as an individualized form of inclusion. The collectively shared notion of the good life that stands behind this is embodied by the ethic of individualism. In the historical development, this ethic transformed from an ethic of possessive individualism to an ethic of acquisitive individualism. Constitutional liberalism is the link between moral universalism and the contemporary ethic of acquisitive individualism. This complex of ideas bridges the space of communication beyond segmentary differentiation, by way of a concept of order that supports the individual and the individual's rights to freedom, to the point that all particular solidarities, even national solidarity, retreat to the background. For Madison, the federation is the guarantor of the individual's freedom from factionalism and potential tyranny of the majority in the individual states (Hamilton, Madison and Jay 1787–88/1961). Conflicts are overcome by means of the expansion of scopes of action via economic growth and by the removal of barriers to market access, particularly the elimination of discrimination. At the same time, the interplay between moral universalism and the ethic of acquisitive individualism has intensified the competition for access to scarce resources and, after exhausting all means of eliminating barriers to market access, has left discrimination (due to ascriptive identity traits) as the final obstacle of market access. Consequently, the politics of inclusion via the creation of equal opportunity for individuals within white, Anglo-Saxon Protestant culture has come under suspicion of privileging one specific culture among many. It must defend itself against demands for the equal recognition of a multiplicity of other cultural identities. Constitutional liberalism therefore finds itself at a crossroads. The question is whether or not it should be replaced by a kind of constitutional multiculturalism that does not protect individuals' rights to freedom, but rather the cultural identities of groups (Schlesinger 1992; Glazer 1997).

The semantics of constitutional liberalism has proved to be an organizational concept that is suited to offering a society that is outwardly very open and internally very pluralistically composed of a widely shared concept of the good life. This is undoubtedly in line with a concept which emerged from the material situation of the first immigrants, in interaction with their Puritan ethos of self-discipline and personal responsibility, and which the Founding Fathers of the United States placed upon a secular foundation. Later groups of immigrants consistently brought the will to get by in their chosen land. Therefore, they were easily committed to the adoption of the established concept. The specific attribute thereof is the high capacity for the assimilation of immigrants and their inclusion – with or without citizenship – in the rights to freedom, coupled with the simultaneous individualization of the success of inclusion via the elimination of barriers to market access. This individualization of the success of inclusion implicates a broader income spectrum than in the European welfare states, which have coupled a greater degree of collectivization of the success of inclusion in terms of equal living conditions for all, independent from market success, with a more limited outward openness and willingness to include immigrants in full citizenship (Esping-Andersen 1990, 1999; Goodin, Headey, Muffels and Dirven 1999).

Europe: towards a semantics and institutional form of constitutional liberalism?

With regard to the future of the European welfare states, the question arises as to whether or not their involvement in the economic integration of Europe and, in addition, their openness to immigrants from outside Europe create similar structural conditions to those in the United States and whether or not constitutional liberalism could therefore be a model for the semantic and institutional formation of the European social order. Via the single market, European nations open themselves to the mutual exchange of goods, services, people and capital that is supplemented by the intensified exchange of information, knowledge, consumption and lifestyles, as well as art, literature, film and television production. The pioneers of the pan-European exchange are forming a network of transnational social relationships that is becoming the breeding ground of European thought and action, free from national narrow-mindedness. The supporters of this network are active and mobile people with a world view that places greater emphasis on individual self-responsibility and self-development than on group loyalty. They do not owe their mobility to economic ownership, but primarily to human capital gained through education. Equipped with these capacities, they are making the ethic of human capital individualism the model of a converging European culture. According to Eurobarometer surveys, support for European integration and self-identification as European increase relative to the level of education, occupational status and income (European Commission 1998: B21, B40, B42). This cultural model of the European elite obtains a corresponding material base via the fact of single market integration by means of the elimination of barriers to market access and via the corresponding acceleration of transnational division of labour. The precedence of negative integration by way of the elimination of obstacles to transnational economic trade creates a dynamic of expanding freedom of action that comes into conflict with the national welfare states' well-developed positive integration and works towards its erosion (Scharpf 1996, 1998). In the member states – and not only at the European level – the logic of positive integration is encountering narrower boundaries than those that existed prior to accelerated single market integration. This leads to new conflicts of legitimation. The outcome of these is still uncertain, but the model of human capital individualism is already offering a solution. Because it is the model of European integration's mobile elite, there are many signs that this model will prevail and push back the standard of positive integration, even in the individual member states. Intensified competition in the European single market displays the same effect. Free competition in the single market, which is monitored by the competition commissioner, allows fewer competition-reducing subsidies and protective measures for endangered industries than before, as long as one disregards the Brussels subsidy apparatus for agriculture. It is therefore becoming ever more difficult to guarantee job security. As a result, the adoption of the promotion of employability via empowerment as a labour market policy is very apparent. Meanwhile, in the wake of the Lisbon strategy, this has in fact become the member states' common programme. The success of this programme, through the exchange of information and mutual monitoring, is made visible to all in the Open Method of Coordination (OMC). The outcome of this development is a considerable boost towards an ethic of human capital individualism (Crouch, Finegold and Sako 1999).

The model of human capital individualism is further supported by the fact that the level of education has risen, and continues to rise, in every country (Müller, Steinmann and Schneider 1997). In connection with the level of education, the ability to consciously organize one's own life also increases. The better people are educated, the less support they require from collective solidarity. What they need are opportunities for self-realization and a large number of open networks that can be used for coping with problems in different situations. A plurality of counselling agencies and self-help groups is more useful to them than the collective organization of their lives in the custody of the state and the unions. It is therefore a development in which the Europeanization of law and the individualization of lifestyle go hand in hand when we consider, for example, that an empirical study has found that, following entry into the European Union, Ireland's restrictive enforcement of the abortion ban and Sweden's restrictive regulation of alcohol consumption have come under the pressure of liberalization (Kurzer 2001: 73–96, 143–69).

The adjudication of the ECJ works towards the same end (Dehousse 1998; Maduro 1998). It pursues the program of single market integration through the elimination of barriers to market access. The adjudication aims to eliminate the discrimination that disadvantages certain market participants more than others. It deals with the expansion of the freedom of action for the purpose of making use of individual rights. In this way, the legal discourse is attuned to the assurance of individual rights. The ECJ thereby orients itself towards both the Union treaties and the European Convention concerning human rights. It de facto recognizes the protection of Union citizens' fundamental rights to freedom. In this way, the ECJ makes a significant contribution to the enforcement of the ethic of human capital individualism. It has increasingly grown into the role of the legal medium between moral universalism and the ethic of human capital individualism via an evolving quasi-constitutional liberalism without an explicitly established constitution. Union treaties and the cited European Convention on Human Rights have, in the practice of adjudication of the ECJ, attained a quasi-constitutional character (Weiler 1999).

In the institutional arrangement of the European Union, the ECJ, compared to adjudication in the national states, assumes an exceedingly powerful and influential position in the semantic construction of Europe. Because European legislation is, compared with that of the national states, subject to narrower limits, the ECJ has a more sizeable share in the semantic construction of the European social order. Its jurisdiction, which is drawn from the spirit of the Union treaties, is essentially geared towards the protection of Union citizens' individual rights. It forms the centre of an evolving, specifically European semantics of constitutional liberalism that greatly influences the member states.

As early as the 1960s, the ECJ enforced the direct effect (*van Gend en Loos* 26/62) and the precedence of European law over national law (*Costa v. ENEL* 6/64). It cleared the way for the removal of all market access barriers not serving the public interest (*Dassonville* 8/74; *Cassis de Dijon* 120/78). It also made member states liable for citizens' disadvantages due to delayed implementation of European law (*Frankovich* 6/90, *Factortame III* 48/93). In regard to social law, the ECJ had the effect that Union citizens are able to take their social security claims from one member state to another (i.e. being able to continue with a voluntary pension insurance while residing in another member state and being able to claim it as an expense on the income tax assessment in that member state). Gender equality has also been advanced to a greater extent by ECJ jurisdiction than in national adjudication (*Bilka* 170/84). According to ECJ judgement, stipends granted to natives must also be available to Union citizens in every member state (*Casagrande* 9/74). Member states' limits on the freedom of competition and professional service hold no sway before the ECJ (*Bosman v. Royal Club Liègeois* 415/93). However, the ECJ has not scrapped member states' regulations when these have not resulted in foreigners' disadvantages compared to natives (*Keck and Mithouard* 267/91 and 268/91). It has, to the disadvantage of trade, given precedence to member states' protection of the individual from technical risks and environmental pollution when it is a question of scientifically verifiable damage to the health of individual persons. The guideline for this adjudication is not merely the elimination of market access barriers and the assurance of transborder free trade, but also the protection of each individual's rights from restrictions not in agreement with European law. The individual is freed from restrictions to his or her scope of action resulting from national law. By this practice of adjudication, the ECJ created, to a considerable degree, a specifically European semantics of constitutional liberalism long before the thus far failed attempts at concluding a member state agreement on a European constitutional contract.

The contract concerning a European constitution elaborated by the *Convention on the Future of Europe* substantiates, in Part I, the commitment to the respect of human dignity, freedom, democracy, equality, due process, justice, solidarity and nondiscrimination. Aside from the assurance of all relevant freedoms (Article II, 20–26), the charter of basic laws included in Part II also pledges equality and solidarity (Article II, 27–38) (European Union 2003, 2005). Which character equality and solidarity will have in the integrated Europe cannot, however, be derived from these constitutional articles. In order to make statements about this, we must consider the subsidiary division of labour between the Union and the member states, the impact of the Open Method of Coordination (OMC) on social policy, the effect of transborder division of labour and the effects of education policy, emanating from the member states themselves, aimed at ever broader access to higher education.

The demand that the development of a European Social Union follow the single market and the EMU has been made again and again (Habermas 1998). However, the European Union has taken only a few steps in this direction. So far, it has only had a function that is complementary to member states' social policies concerning agrarian policy (i.e. a social program for farmers with the effect of strengthening large agrarian companies), the promotion of undeveloped regions (i.e. regional funding) and member states (i.e cohesion funds), labour protection (i.e. technical safety) and gender equality. All attempts at creating a Social Union have failed so far. As Wolfgang Streeck (1999: 85–93) has demonstrated, spillover from the single market may occur in fields that are located in the immediate neighbourhood of market creation, but not in fields that are farther away such as social policy. The largest part of social policy remains in the hands of the member states due to reasons of differing capacities, institutional regulations and cultural traditions. However, the increased use of the OMC provides a monitoring and benchmarking process that works towards a certain harmonization of social security modes and benefit levels (Bernhard 2005; Schäfer 2005). Everything indicates that this subsidiary, socio-political division of labour between the Union and the member states will remain (cf. Tömmel 2000). From the subsidiarity perspective, the Union's socio-political task is not the replacement of the national welfare state with a European welfare state, but rather, first and foremost, the enhancement of economic potential for all member states. In this way, the less developed member states can also attain a higher level of social benefits. The underlying principle is not postmarket redistribution, but the premarket promotion of the performance of those that have so far been less productive.

Along the lines of this performance promotion, the national traditions of postmarket collective inclusion are overlaid with a European model of individualist inclusion. This overlay does not eliminate individual member states' historically formed collectivist traditions. It does, however, have an impact on the member states. A significant gateway for the European-induced trend towards individualist inclusion is the OMC that aims at the efficiency of social policy in the sense of maximum results with minimal effort and the compatibility of socio-political regulations with economic competitiveness. This trend does not necessarily imply a socio-political race to the bottom for the simple reason that a high level of all population classes' access to prosperity is also a defined goal and because enhanced efficiency is meant to ensure a high level of socio-political benefit. However, the preference for practices of each individual's premarket activation and the guarantee of equal opportunity instead of postmarket redistribution with the aim of approaching an equality of results is unmistakably given.

Meanwhile, member states by no means take this European-induced trend towards the individualization of inclusion to be an externally imposed foreign concept. In fact, it merely strengthens the member states' long-standing trend towards individualization of inclusion. Its most powerful engine is the inclusion of ever broader parts of the population in higher education. By way of this policy, which has been pushed since the 1960s, each individual's access to prosperity has been sustainably shifted from collective to individual inclusion. To the degree to which equal opportunity to educational access has been achieved, educational achievement has become a decisive condition for occupational achievement and its connected access to wealth. Thus, the collective assurance of access to work and wealth has been subjected to narrower limitations. On the one hand, this is apparent in the dwindling numbers of labour union members. On the other hand, it can be seen in the high unemployment rate among those with no skills. European integration not only accelerates this process by way of the practice of socio-political monitoring and benchmarking in the OMC, but also by way of the growing transborder division of labour that relocates production labour requiring little skills to the periphery. Due to the development of global free trade, this process now reaches far beyond the borders of the European Union.

Together with the inclusion of ever broader classes in higher education, growing cross-border division of labour deprives conservative and social democratic semantics of collectivist integration of the material basis for nationally defined economic value creation chains and the socio-structural basis of the collectively organized class society. Transnational economic value creation chains and a society of autonomous individuals removed from collective organization make any semantics of collectivist inclusion appear obsolete and rob them of their validity and efficacy. They are, however, fertile ground for the semantics of individualistic inclusion. The increasing overlay of collectivistic traditions by a new semantics of constitutional liberalism is therefore not sufficiently understood if one only traces it back to the financial bottlenecks of exhausted welfare states and neoliberalism's propaganda campaigns. These two elements are, if anything, superficial aspects of a much deeper-seated transformation of solidarity in the processes of transnational-ization and the channelling of inclusion into the paths of higher education.

Thus far, we can see that a string of factors promote the development of the semantics of constitutional liberalism as a semantic order of Europe. Nevertheless, there are considerable opposing forces that countervail an approximation to the American model: the collectivistic tradition of European welfare states, the still distinctly larger legislative competency of the European Union's member states compared to the individual American states and the existing measure of segmentary differentiation into nations. In the foreseeable future, these opposing forces will see to it that, in Europe, the semantics of constitutional liberalism, in terms of efficacy, will be limited more by the collectivist traditions of the individual member states than is the case in the United States (Leggewie 2000; Hall and Soskice 2001; Offe 2003). The form of collective belonging and identity that is embodied in the United States by the president's leadership role and the patriotism that he represents will not develop at the Union level in Europe. The historical forces of national integration are too strong and the forces of European identity formation are too weak. There will also be no European equivalent to the radicalization of US patriotism into fundamentalist nationalism. For European supranational-ism, the historical experiences and opportunities required for a collective unit are lacking. Feelings of belonging will remain primarily at the national and subnational level. At this level, they will be weakened by the Europeanization of economy, law and policy in order to make room for a pronounced individ-ualization of identities without, at the European level, the emergence of a European collective identity comparable in strength to the old national iden-tities. Nationalist backlashes against the processes of opening and the plural-ization of belonging will therefore continue to be articulated not at the European level, but at the national level (Münch 1993b: 15–104; 1998: 267–324).

These opposing forces cannot, however, keep the semantics of constitu-tional liberalism from gaining ground. We definitely see that the reorienta-tion of social policy from national provision to the activation of personal responsibility and societal self-organization is in full swing in all European Union member states (Streeck and Höpner 2003; Leibfried and Zürn 2006; Hurrelmann et al. 2007). The Europeanization of the economy, law and policy spurs on the individualization process and national disintegration, without the European-level emergence of strong collective supranational integration corresponding to national integration. The guarantee and use of individual rights is coming to the fore. The handling of conflicts in the exer-cise of individual rights is, similar to the situation in the USA, shifting a bit from legislation to adjudication. In this process, the ECJ is assuming a central position.

The processes of national disintegration accompanying increased transna-tional European integration mobilize countermovements of renationaliza-tion to the extent of considerable election successes of right-wing extremist and right-wing populist parties. Continuing transnational integration splits the society into an elite of modernization winners, a mass of modernization tolerators and a marginalized group of modernization losers, to which particularly the group of the less skilled, in a society geared towards constant rise in educational and occupational qualification, belong. The national state accrues new challenges for the inclusion of marginalized groups, whereas the comprehensive accommodation of the entire population loses relevance. If these new integration problems are not solved, the new semantics of constitutional liberalism will lack sufficient legitimacy. Only with difficulty will it then be able to replace the old semantics of collectivism. Whereas the national state has to concentrate on the inclusion of the new marginalized groups, it is the European Union's duty to, with the help of regional promotion programs, reduce the inequality between the regions. Only if this labour division or subsidiary method succeeds in reducing inequality will the semantics of constitutional liberalism gain broad-based legitimacy that reaches beyond the transnational level down to the nation states, inclusive of all classes of society. Lastly, the assertion of the semantics of constitutional liberalism also depends on the fulfillment of this functional requirement of legitimate validity in all classes of society, not only in the class of the transnational elite. Therefore, no final judgement can be made concerning the extent of the assertion of a new European semantics of constitutional liberalism because it depends on contingent requirements. We cannot make reliable predictions on the fulfillment of these requirements (Meyer 2004; Vobruba 2005; Bach, Lahusen and Vobruba 2006).

Admittedly, a lingering tension between the advancing European division of labour and the legal and semantic structures of constitutional liberalism, on the one hand, and the still-effective national traditions of collectivism, on the other hand, can be anticipated for the foreseeable future. The European Union's expansion to 27 countries further accentuated this tension (Heidenreich 2003; Bach 2006; Nissen 2006). The tense relationship between European constitutional liberalism's elite project and the existing traditions of collectivism in the member states confronts the EU with a unique challenge, solution to which cannot yet be foreseen (Kohli 2000; Haller 2008).

Starting with the Rome Treaty, European integration, however, set in motion a liberalization program that can be regarded as a hegemonic project (Gramsci 1971; Laclau and Mouffe 2001). The content of the Rome Treaty and its later expansions aim for the free movement of goods, services, capital and persons and the removal of all regulatory limitations of free competition not justified under Art. 30 (ex 36) of the EC Treaty, as well as the elimination of all forms of discrimination. The European Commission and the ECJ are the authoritative agents of this program, which, far beyond the economy, affects all functional areas of society – civil society and culture just as much as politics. Therefore, culture, civil society and politics can no longer be seen as structures in opposition to the economy. They can no longer be seen as structures that must be Europeanized in order to again work towards the embedding of the economy. Culture, civil society and politics are subordinate to the same hegemonic liberalization project as the economy. Together, all of these form an organic whole. This new hegemonic project of European liberalization is increasingly replacing the old hegemonic project of welfare democracy which has, in the course of transnationalization of societal conditions, been driven into crisis by its internal contradictions. This old project geared all of its economic activities towards the growth of national welfare and broad participation therein. In contrast, the new system places everything at the service of active individuals' self-assertion in a market that permeates all spheres of life, from the market for commodities to markets for services, social welfare, association, intimate partnerships, marriage, electoral votes, etc. across all national borders. It is part of the world culture that is represented by international governmental and nongovernmental organizations (Meyer et al. 1997; Koenig 2005). According to the logic of the new liberal paradigm, national social partnership is an expression of moral particularism, and in contrast, CSR, which cuts jobs in wealthy industrial centres and creates new jobs in developing, emerging and transition countries and, following the Global Compact, champions compliance with basic workers' rights in those places is an expression of moral universalism. In this regard, transnational corporations, stepping beyond the narrow national social partnership are, in the dialogue with an increased number of international humanitarian organizations, the moral pioneers of our time. A hegemonic project gains its stability particularly by way of creating the concepts with which social reality is constructed, interests are articulated and rights are legitimated, just as much by the elites as by the masses and by the winners just as much as by the losers. This organic integration of positions accounts for the efficacy of the hegemonic liberalization project of European integration.

The kind of democracy most feasible in the multilevel system of governance is the liberal type. There is a liberal drift in multilevel governance. The multiplication of levels and arenas of governance implies a greater number of checks and balances so that this kind of controlling government comes along in a natural way with the Europeanization of governance. This does not, however, mean that representational republican and deliberative elements of democratic governance would disappear completely. They rather continue to exist within the overall structure of liberal multilevel governance. National parliaments, in their limited sovereignty, and European Parliament, with its limited power, stand for representational elements of democracy in the multilevel system. In as much as decision making has to be justified before a more or less comprehensive public, there is a place for deliberative democracy. A republican spirit survives as long as there is a place for reflecting on solutions that serve the common good, from the local level through to the global level. The local common good might, however, be at odds with the national, European or global common good. Such conflicts have to be resolved in the multilevel and multiarena system of checks and balances, that is, in a liberal way. Global deliberation might help to convince the people to give the global common good some preference over the European, national or local good (e.g. in matters of global ecological balance). The emerging multilevel system of governance leaves space for such representational, republican or deliberative elements. Special attention to chances of realization helps to strengthen them. Nevertheless, they do not change the overall liberal structure of multilevel governance.

Externally, the new nation state is a mediator of internally articulated interests in intergovernmental negotiation and supranational decision making. Internally, it is a mediator of external constraints. In this way, the intervention state is replaced with the competition state that is focused on training its population for international competition by activating every single individual. In the same process, the coordination and bundling of interests in the neocorporatist collaboration of industrial federations, trade unions and government gives way to the pluralist mode of local-level coordination that can be called 'neo-voluntarism' (Streeck 1999: 103–11). The new emphasis on subsidiarity in the system of European multilevel governance fits with this kind of coordinating interests. It means market creation on the European level and adaptation to market constraints on the national and local levels.

Government within the sovereign nation state was founded on the congruent monopolization of various forms of capital. The monopolization of legitimate force was accompanied by the state's monopoly on legislation, jurisdiction, administration, health, education, statistical information and levying taxes. Legislation, jurisdiction and education in the hands of the state implied the construction of a coherent culture, spirit and view of the world. In this way, the state monopolized the representation of the general as against the particular, of the common good as against particular interests. That means that the state holds the monopoly on symbolic capital, the legitimate power to define the situation in its hands. In a long, historical process, the particular usurpation of the monopoly on legitimate force by a successful ruler against competitors, according to Norbert Elias's (2005) monopoly mechanism, becomes generalized by way of constitutionalization and the construction of legitimacy in symbolic struggles (Bourdieu 1994: Ch. 4). The differentiation of society into relatively autonomous fields, such as the economy, science, arts, sports, etc., was made coherent by their subordination to symbolic power concentrated in the state. Within the new system of multilevel governance, this concentration of symbolic power on the state gives way to its splitting across levels and fields that gain autonomy from state domination. This splitting of symbolic power gives rise to the dominant position of the economic field, both in the material sense of economic constraints and in the symbolic sense of economics being the core discipline of governance. Within the nation state, the political capital of parties and representative associations dominated the field of governance. In the system of multilevel governance, they are increasingly subordinated to the rule of transnational experts. The state no longer controls scientific and informational capital. Scientific capital is concentrated in international, leading research centres.

Information capital is no longer in national statistical bureaus, but in international bureaus such as Eurostat and the Organization for Economic Cooperation and Development (OECD). Think tanks are also major players in the field. This means that the classification of the social world, the identification of problems and the provision of solutions is less in the hands of the nation state, political parties and associations and more in the hands of international statistical agencies, think tanks and transnational networks of experts. This is, for example, one reason why the traditional German way of education for occupations and professions is being displaced by the globally dominant way of laying greater emphasis on general secondary and tertiary education for a more open, less occupationally structured market.

Governance in the European – or even global – multilevel system resides much less in state monopoly of power, rule over a delimited territory or disciplinary power over the individual than governance in the nation state (Foucault 2007, 2008). Its power is much more limited, but it reaches far beyond governmental power over state territories. Lacking the instruments of power monopoly, territorial rule and disciplinary power, it is far more compelled than national governments to respect the freedom of individual action and the economic laws of allocating goods to preferences of actors, production, consumption and distribution of scarce goods. Therefore, multilevel governance is checked by two complementary standards: the freedom rights of the individual embodied in the law and the laws of the market. The law and the market intersect in constituting the liberal market society for which liberal governance has to provide the appropriate frame of reference so that it advances the freedom and wealth of the individuals who are engaged in pursuing their happiness. Governance that meets these critieria attains the quality of liberal governmentality (Lemke 1997; Power 1997; Rose 1999; Miller and Rose 2008). This is the art of optimizing conflicting goals so as to coordinate as much individual freedom of action as possible and to allocate as many scarce resources as possible to articulated preferences. Improving this art of liberal governance is the mission of European governmentality.

Appendix

Judgements of the European Court of Justice

The ECJ's judgements represent the juridical construction of a European societal order. Based on these judgements, what type of societal order is constructed by European jurisdiction, and how it differs from national traditions, is shown. The judgements listed below should be read as follows: 26/62 = number of receipt of the case in 1962; van Gend en Loos = name of the plaintiff; [1963] = year of judgement; ECR 1 = European Court Reports Nr. 1.

26/62	*van Gend en Loos* [1963] ECR 1
6/64	*Costa v. E.N.E.L.* [1964] ECR 585
15/69	*Salvatore Uglioa* [1969] ECR 363
11/70	*Internationale Handelsgesellschaft* [1970] ECR 1125
22/70	*Commission v. Council (ERTA)* [1971] ECR 263
80/70	*Defrenne I* [1971] ECR 445
6/72	*Europemballage und Continental Can v. Commission* [1973] ECR 215
4/73	*Nold* [1974] ECR 491
2/74	*Reyners* [1974] ECR 631
8/74	*Dassonville* [1974] ECR 837
9/74	*Casagrande* [1974] ECR 773
36/74	*Walrave and Koch* [1974] ECR 1405
36/75	*Rutili* [1975] ECR 1219
43/75	*Defrenne II* [1976] ECR 455
106/77	*Simmenthal* [1978] ECR 629
149/77	*Defrenne III* [1978] ECR 1365
120/78	*Cassis de Dijon* [1979] ECR 649
207/78	*Ministère Publique v. Even* [1979] ECR 2019
44/79	*Hauer* [1979] ECR 3727
138/79	*Roquette v. Council* [1980] ECR 3333
53/80	*Kaasfabriek Eyssen* [1981] ECR 409
96/80	*Jenkins v. Kingsgate* [1981] ECR 911
155/80	*Oebel* [1981] ECR 1993

53/81	*Levin vs. Staatssecretaris van Justitie* [1982] ECR 1035
283/81	*CILFIT* [1982] ECR 3415
152/82	*Forcheri v. Belgium* [1983] ECR 2323
13/83	*Parliament v. Council* [1985] ECR 1513
294/83	*Les Verts* [1986] ECR 1339
60/84 and 61/84	*Cinéthèque et al./FNCF* [1985] ECR 2605
142/84 and 156/84	*British American Tobacco und Reynolds v. Kommission* [1987] ECR 4487
170/84	*Bilka-Kaufhaus v. Weber von Hartz* [1986] ECR 1607
205/84	*Commission v. Federal Republic of Germany* [1986] ECR 3755
66/85	*Lawrie-Blum* [1986] ECR 2121
39/86	*Lair v. University of Hanover* [1988] ECR 3161
197/86	*Brown v. Secretary of State for Scotland* [1988] ECR 3205
302/86	*Commision v. Denmark* [1988] ECR 4607
143/87	*Stanton versus INASTI* [1988] ECR 3877
186/87	*Cowan* [1989] ECR 195
302/87	*Parliament v. Council (comitology)* [1988] ECR 5615
305/87	*Commission v. Greece* [1989] ECR 1461
70/88	*Parliament v. Council (Chernobyl)* [1990] ECR I–2041
171/88	*Rinner-Kühn* [1989] ECR 2743
145/88	*Torfaen BC/B*Q* [1989] ECR 3851
262/88	*Barber* [1990] ECR I–1889
213/89	*Factortame* [1990] ECR I–2433
2/90	*Commission v. Belgium* [1992] ECR I–4431
6/90 and 9/90	*Francovich and Bonifaci v. Italian Republic* [1991] ECR I–5357
208/90	*Theresa Emmott v. Minister of Social Welfare and Attorney General* [1991] ECR I–4269
126/91	*Schutzverband gegen Unwesen in der Wirtschaft e.V. v. Yves Rocher GmbH* [1993] ECR I–2361
168/91	*Konstandinidis* [1993] ECR I–1191
267/91 and 268/91	*Keck and Mithouard* [1993] ECR I–6097
292/92	*Huenermund* [1993] ECR I–6787
46/93 and 48/93	*Brasserie du Pêcheur v. Federal Republic of Germany and Factortame III* [1996] ECR I–1029
412/93	*Leclerc-Siplec* [1995] ECR I–179
415/93	*Bosman v. Royal Club Liègeois* [1995] ECR I–4921
470/93	*Mars* [1995] ECR I–1923
2/94	*ENU v. Commission* [1995] ECR I–2767
120/95	*Decker* [1998] ECR I–1831

85/96	*Martinez Sala* [1998] ECR I–2691
158/96	*Kohll* [1998] ECR I–1931
210/96	*Gut Springenheide* [1998] ECR I–4657
274/96	*Bickel and Franz* [1998] ECR I–7637
10–22/97	*IN.CO.GE. '90* [1998] ECR I–6307
303/97	*Verbraucherschutzverein e. V. v. Sektkellerei Kessler* [1999] ECR I–513
342/97	*Lloyd v. Klijsen* [1999] ECR I–3819
220/98	*Estée Lauder v. Lancaster* [2000] ECR I–117
303/98	*Sindicato de Médicos de Asistencia Pública* [2000] ECR I–7963
135/99	*Ursula Elsen* [2000] ECR I–10409
184/99	*Grzelczyk* [2001] ECR I–6193
224/98	*D'Hoop* [2002] ECR I–6191
413/99	*Baumbast* [2002] ECR I–7091
44/01	*Pippig v. Hartlauer* [2003] ECR I–3095
99/01	*Linhart v. Biffl* [2002] ECR I–9375
151/02	*Jaeger* [2003] ECR I–8389
200/02	*Chen* [2004] ECR I–9925
239/02	*Douwe Egberts v. Westrom Pharma* [2004] ECR I–7007
209/03	*Bidar* [2005] ECR I–2119
144/04	*Mangold* [2005] ECR I–9981
341/05	*Lavall* [2007]
438/05	*Viking* [2008]
319/06	*Luxembourg* [2008]
346/06	*Rüffert* [2008]

Judgements of the German Federal Constitutional Court

The judgements made by the German Federal Constitutional Court represent a specific national legal interpretation of European legislation and jurisdiction and the resulting European societal order.

- BVerfG 7, 198. Entscheidungen des Bundesverfassungsgerichts, Bd. 7, 198 – Lüth (15.01.1958).
- BVerfG 22, 293. Entscheidungen des Bundesverfassungsgerichts, Bd. 22, 293 – EWG Verordnungen (18.10.1967).
- BVerfG 37, 271. Entscheidungen des Bundesverfassungsgerichts, Bd. 37, 271 – Solange I (29.05.1974).
- BVerfG 73, 339. Entscheidungen des Bundesverfassungsgerichts, Bd. 73, 339 – Solange II (22.10.1986).
- BVerfG 89, 155. Entscheidungen des Bundesverfassungsgerichts, Bd. 89 – Maastricht (12.10.1993).
- BVerfG, 2 BvE – Lisbon (30.06.2009).

Bibliography

Primary literature

The asterisked (*) references represent the juridical and/or intellectual construction of societal order in general and of political constitution in particular, either with regard to national orders or with regard to the emerging European order. This literature demonstrates in an exemplary way how societal order is conceived in the context of national traditions and what problems result from their particular perspective in the process of Europeanization of the societal order.

Secondary literature

The secondary literature supports the interpretation of primary literature and the judgements of the ECJ and the German Federal Constitutional Court. There is a reflexive relationship between primary and secondary literature, just as there is a reflexive relationship between the semantic construction and the practice of social order. The boundary between primary and secondary literature is, therefore, not determined once and for all. The primary literature entails reflection on the construction of societal order, while the secondary literature takes part in the construction of that order. The labelling of texts as primary or secondary literature therefore only means that they are perceived in this investigation in the respective functions. On the one hand, the investigation presented here is a sociological contribution to reflecting on the construction of a European societal order. On the other hand, it is itself part of this work of construction.

Abernathy, C. F. (1980) *Civil Rights. Cases and Materials*, St. Paul, Minnesota: West Publishing Co.
Ackerman, B. (1984) 'The Storrs Lectures: Discovering the Constitution', *Yale Law Review*, 93 (6): 1013–72.
—— (1991) *We the People*, ed. 1, Cambridge, MA: Harvard University Press.
Allan, T. S. (1997) 'Parliamentary Sovereignty: Law, Politics and Revolution', *The Law Quarterly Review*, 113 (3): 433–52.
Alter, K. J. (1998) 'Who are the Masters of the Treaty? European Governments and the European Court of Justice', *International Organization*, 52 (1): 121–47.
—— (2000) 'The European Union's Legal System and Domestic Policy: Spillover or Backlash?', *International Organization*, 54 (3): 498–518.

—— (2001) *Establishing the Supremacy of European Law: The Making of an International Rule of Law in Europe*, Oxford: Oxford University Press.

Alter, K. J. and Meunier-Aitsahalia, S. (1994) 'Judicial Politics in the European Community: European Integration and the Pathbreaking Cassis de Dijon Decision', *Comparative Political Studies*, 26 (4): 535–61.

Ansell, C. K. and Vogel, D. (2006) *What's the Beef? The Contested Governance of European Food Safety*, Cambridge, MA: MIT Press.

Anweiler, J. (1997) *Die Auslegungsmethoden des Europäischen Gerichtshofs der Europäischen Gemeinschaften*, Frankfurt/New York: Peter Lang.

Arnull, A. (1993) 'Owning up to Fallibility: Precedent and the Court of Justice', *Common Market Law Review*, 20 (2): 247–66.

—— (1999) *The European Union and its Court of Justice*, Oxford: Oxford University Press.

—— (2002) 'The Rule of Law in the European Union', in A. Arnull and D. Wincott (eds) *Accountability and Legitimacy in the European Union*, Oxford: Oxford University Press: 239–58.

*Ash, T. G. (2001) 'Is Britain European?', *International Affairs*, 77 (1): 1–13.

*—— (2006) 'Are there British intellectuals? Yes, and they've never had it so good', *The Guardian*, 27 April 2006. Online. Available HTTP: <http://www.guardian.co.uk/print/0,329466051–103390,00.html> (accessed July 2007).

Axford, B. and Huggins, R. (1999) 'Towards a Post-national Polity: The Emergence of the Network Society in Europe', in D. Smith and S. Wright (eds) *Whose Europe? The Turn Towards Democracy*, Oxford: Blackwell, 121–47.

Bach, M. (1992) 'Eine leise Revolution durch Verwaltungsverfahren: Bürokratische Integrationsprozesse in der Europäischen Gemeinschaft', *Zeitschrift für Soziologie* 21 (1): 16–30.

—— (1999) *Die Bürokratisierung Europas*, Frankfurt/New York: Campus.

—— (2006) 'The Enlargement of the European Union: From Political Integration to Social Disintegration?', in M. Bach, C. Lahusen and G. Vobruba (eds) *Europe in Motion. Social Dynamics and Political Institutions in an Enlarging Europe*, Berlin: sigma, 59–77.

—— (2008) *Europa ohne Gesellschaft. Politische Soziologie der europäischen Integration*, Wiesbaden: VS Verlag für Sozialwissenschaften.

Bach, M., Lahusen, C. and Vobruba, G. (eds) (2006) *Europe in Motion*, Berlin: edition sigma.

Bache, I. and Flinders, M. V. (2004) *Multilevel Governance*, Oxford: Oxford University Press.

Bailey, S. D. (1978) *British Parliamentary Democracy*, Westport, CT: Greenwood Press Publishers.

Bailyn, B. (1967) *The Ideological Origins of the American Revolution*, Cambridge: Belknap Press.

Barysch, K. (2005) 'Liberals versus Social Europe', *Centre for European Reform Bulletin*, 48, August/September. Online. Available HTTP: <http://www.cer.org.uk/articles/43_barysch.html> (accessed July 2007).

Beach, D. (2001) *Between Law and Politics: The Relationship between the European Court of Justice and the EU Member States*, Copenhagen: DJØF Publishing.

Beck, U. (1986) *Risikogesellschaft. Auf dem Weg in eine andere Moderne*, Frankfurt a.M: Suhrkamp.

*Beck, U. and Grande, E. (2004) *Das kosmopolitische Europa*, Frankfurt a.M: Suhrkamp.

*Becker, G. S. (1975) *Human Capital*, Washington, D.C.: National Bureau of Economic Research.

Bell, M. and Waddington, L. (2003) 'Reflecting on Inequalities in European Equality Law', *European Law Review*, 28: 349–69.

*Benda, J. (1927) *La trahison des clercs*, Paris: Grasset.

Bengoetxea, J. (1993) *The Legal Reasoning of the European Court of Justice: Toward a European Jurisprudence*, Oxford: Clarendon Press.

Bernhard, S. (2005) *Sozialpolitik im Mehrebenensystem. Die Bekämpfung von Armut und sozialer Ausgrenzung im Rahmen der offenen Methode der Koordinierung*, Berlin: Wissenschaftlicher Verlag Berlin.

*von Beyme, K. (2000) 'Fischers Griff nach einer europäischen Verfassung', *Jean Monnet Working Paper*, July 2000 – Responses to Joschka Fischer. Online. Available HTTP: <http://www.jeanmonnetprogram.org/papers/00/00f0201.html> (accessed July 2007)

Bieling, H-J. and Deppe, F. (1996) 'Internationalisierung, Integration und politische Regulierung', in M. Jachtenfuchs and B. Kohler-Koch (eds) *Europäische Integration*, Opladen: Leske + Budrich: 481–511.

Blauner, B. (1989) *Black Lives, White Lives. Three Decades of Race Relations in America*, Berkeley/Los Angeles: University of California Press.

Blomeyer, W. (1995) 'Europäischer Gerichtshof und deutsche Arbeitsgerichtsbarkeit im judiziellen Dialog', in W. Blomeyer and K. A. Schachtschneider (eds) *Die Europäische Union als Rechtsgemeinschaft*, Berlin: Duncker & Humblot, 37–73.

*Bodin, J. (1994) 'Four Chapters from the Six Books of the Commonwealth', in J. H. Franklin (ed.), *On Sovereignty*. Cambridge: Cambridge University Press.

*von Bogdandy, A. (1999) *Supranationaler Föderalismus als Wirklichkeit und Idee einer neuen Herrschaftsform*, Baden-Baden: Nomos.

*—— (2000) 'Zweierlei Verfassungsrecht', *Der Staat*, 39 (2): pp. 163–84.

—— (2001) 'Grundrechtsgemeinschaft als Integrationsziel. Grundrechte und das Wesen der Europäischen Union', *Juristen Zeitung*, 56 (3): pp. 157–71.

—— (2004a) 'Wir Europäer', *Frankfurter Allgemeine Zeitung*, 27 April: 8.

—— (2004b) 'Europäische Verfassung und Europäische Identität', *Juristen Zeitung*, 59 (2): 54–62.

—— (2005) 'Die europäische Republik', *Aus Politik und Zeitgeschichte*, 36: 21–27.

Bourdieu, P. (1986) 'La force du droit: Éléments pour une sociologie du champ juridique', *Actes de la recherche en sciences sociales*, 12 (64): 3–19.

—— (1991a) *Language and Symbolic Power*, Cambridge, Mass.: Harvard University Press.

—— (1991b) 'Les juristes, gardiens de l'hypocrisie collective', in F. Chazel and J. Commaille (eds), *Normes juridiques et régulation sociale*, Paris, E.J.A., S. 95–99.

—— (1994) *Raisons pratiques. Sur la théorie de l'action*, Paris: Edition du Seuil.

Boyer, R. (1990) *The Regulation School: A Critical Introduction*, New York: Columbia University Press.

Brickmann, R., Jasanoff, S. and Ilgen, T. (1985) *Controlling Chemicals: The Politics of Regulation in Europe and the United States*. Ithaca, NY: Cornell University Press.

Brown, L. N. and Kennedy, T. (1995) *The Court of Justice of the European Communities*, London: Sweet & Maxwell.

De Búrca, G. (2005) 'Rethinking Law in Neofunctionalist Theory', *Journal of European Public Policy*, 12 (2): 310–26.

De Búrca, G. and Weiler, J. H. H. (eds) (2001) *The European Court of Justice*, Oxford: Oxford University Press.

Burke, E. (1790/1993) *Reflections on the Revolution in France*, Oxford: Oxford University Press.

Burley, A-M. and Mattli, W. (1993) 'Europe before the Court: A Political Theory of Legal Integration', *International Organization*, 47 (1): 41–76.

Burns, S. (1990) *Social Movements of the 1960s: Searching for Democracy*, Boston: Twayne Publishers.

Campbell, J. L., Hollingsworth, J. R. and Lindberg, L. N. (eds) (1991) *The Governance of the American Economy*, Cambridge: Cambridge University Press.

Caporaso, J. A. (2003) 'Democracy, Accountability, and Rights in Supranational Governance', in M. Kahler and D. A. Lake (eds) *Governance in a Global Economy*, Princeton: Princeton University Press, 361–85.

Caporaso, J. A. and Jupille, J. (2005) 'The Second Image Overruled: European Law, Domestic Institutions, and State Sovereignty', 23 January 2005. Online. Available HTTP: <http://www.sobek.colorado.edu/~jupille/research/20051223-SIO.pdf> (accessed July 2007).

Cappelletti, M., Seccombe, M. and Weiler, J. (eds) (1986) *Integration Through Law*, Berlin/New York: Walter de Gruyter.

Checkel, J. T. (1999) *Why Comply? Constructivism, Social Norms and the Study of International Institutions*, Oslo: ARENA Working Paper 99/24.

Christiansen, T., Jørgensen, K. E and Wiener, A. (1999) 'The Social Construction of Europe', *Journal of European Public Policy*, 6 (4): 528–44.

Coenen, R. and Jörissen, J. (1989) *Umweltverträglichkeitsprüfung in der Europäischen Gemeinschaft*, Berlin: Erich Schmidt Verlag.

Collins, R. (1979) *The Credential Society*, New York: Academic Press.

*Congdon, T. (2002) 'It's the people, stupid: Tim Congdon says that demographics show that the Eurozone is heading for crisis: that's why we won't join the new currency', *The Spectator*, 20 (2), 26 January 2002.

Craig, P. (1992) 'Once Upon a Time in the West: Direct Effect and the Federalization of EEC Law', *Oxford Journal of Legal Studies*, 12: 453–79.

Craig, P. and de Búrca, G. (eds) (2003) *EU Law: Text, Cases, and Materials*, Oxford: Oxford University Press.

Crouch, C. (1999) *Social Change in Western Europe*, Oxford: Oxford University Press.

Crouch, C., Finegold, D. and Sako, M. (1999) *Are Skills the Answer? The Political Economy of Skill Creation in Advanced Industrial Countries*, Oxford: Oxford University Press.

Curtin, D. (1993) 'The Constitutional Structure of the Union: A Europe of Bits and Pieces', *Common Market Law Review*, 30 (1): 17–69.

Dashwood, A. and O'Leary, S. (1997) *The Principle of Equal Treatment in EC Law*, London: Sweet & Maxwell.

Dauses, M. (1995) *Das Vorabentscheidungsverfahren der Europäischen Union*, Baden-Baden: Nomos.

Davies, G. (2002) 'Welfare as a Service', *Legal Issues of European Integration*, 29: 27–40.

—— (2003) *Nationality Discrimination in the European Internal Market*, Boston: Kluwer Law International.

*Debray, R. (1992) *Contretemps*, Paris: Gallimard.

Dehousse, R. (1998) *The European Court of Justice*, Houndmills, Basingstoke: Macmillan.

Delanty, G. (1995), *Inventing Europe. Idea, Identity, Reality*, New York: St. Martin's Press.

Delanty, G. and Rumford, C. (2005) *Rethinking Europe: Social Theory and the Implications of Europeanization*, London: Routledge.

*Dicey, A. V. (1885/1982) *Introduction to the Study of the Law of the Constitution*, Indianapolis: Liberty Fund.

Diedrichs, U. and Wessels, W. (2005) *Die Europäische Union in der Verfassungsfalle? Analysen, Entwicklungen und Optionen*, integration, 28(4): 287–306.

Dupuy, R. J. (1963) *Le droit international*, Paris: PUF.

Durkheim, E. (1964) *The Division of Labor in Society*, New York: The Free Press.

Eberlein, B. and Grande, E. (2005) 'Beyond Delegation: Transnational Regulatory Regimes and the EU Regulatory State', *Journal of European Public Policy* 12 (1): 89–112.

Eder, K. and Kantner, C. (2000) 'Transnationale Resonanzstrukturen in Europa. Eine Kritik der Rede vom Öffentlichkeitsdefizit', in M. Bach (ed.) *Die Europäisierung nationaler Gesellschaften*, Kölner Zeitschrift für Soziologie und Sozialpsychologie, special issue 40, Opladen: Westdeutscher Verlag, 306–31.

Eder, K., Hellmann, K-U. and Trenz, H-J. (1998) 'Regieren in Europa jenseits öffentlicher Legitimation? Eine Untersuchung zur Rolle von politischer Öffentlichkeit in Europa', In B. Kohler-Koch (ed.) *Regieren in entgrenzten Räumen. Politische Vierteljahresschrift. Sonderheft* 29. Opladen: Westdeutscher Verlag, 321–344.

Egan, M. P. (2001) *Constructing a European Market. Standards, Regulation, and Governance*, Oxford: Oxford University Press.

Eichener, V. (1996) *Die Rückwirkungen der europäische Integration auf nationale Politikmuster*, Opladen: Leske + Budrich.

—— (1997) 'Effective European Problem Solving: Lessons from the Regulation of Occupational Safety and Environmental Protection', *Journal of European Public Policy* 4 (4): 591–609.

Elias, N. (2005) *The Civilizing Process*, Oxford: Blackwell.

Ellis, E. (2000) 'The Recent Jurisprudence of the Court of Justice in the Field of Sex Equality', *Common Market Law Review*, 37 (6): 1403–26.

Eriksen, E. O. and Fossum, J. E. (2000) *Democracy in the European Union: Integration Through Deliberation?* London: Routledge.

Esping-Andersen, G. (1990) *The Three Worlds of Welfare Capitalism*, Cambridge: Polity Press.

—— (1999) *Social Foundations of Postindustrial Economies*, Oxford: Oxford University Press.

European Commission (1985) *Vollendung des Binnenmarktes. Weißbuch der Kommission an den Europäischen Rat*, Luxembourg: Amt für Amtliche Veröffentlichungen der Europäischen Gemeinschaften.

—— (1990) *Grünbuch der EG-Kommission zur Entwicklung der Europäischen Normung: Maßnahmen für eine schnellere technologische Integration in Europa*, Brussels.

—— (1998) *Eurobarometer* No. 50. Brussels.

—— (2003) *Eurobarometer* No. 60. Brussels.

European Union (2003) 'Entwurf eines Vertrages über eine Verfassung für Europa', *Amtsblatt der Europäischen Union* (189), 18 July 2003, Luxembourg: Amt für amtliche Veröffentlichungen der Europäischen Gemeinschaften.

—— (2005) *Vertrag über eine Verfassung für Europa*, Luxembourg: Amt für amtliche Veröffentlichungen der Europäischen Gemeinschaften.

European Movement Senior Expert Group (2005) 'Anglo-Saxon versus European Social Models of European Economies – Argument by Caricature?', *European Movement*. Online. Available HTTP: <www.euromove.org.uk/publications/expert/ecmodels> (accessed July 2007).

Falkner, G., Treib, O., Hartlapp, M. and Leiber, S. (2005) *Complying with Europe: EU Harmonisation and Soft Law in the Member States*, Cambridge: Cambridge University Press.

Farley, R. (1996) *The New American Reality*, New York: Russel Sage Foundation.

*Ferry, J-M. (2000) *La question de l'état européen*, Paris: Gallimard.

*—— (2002) 'La référence républicaine au défi de l'Europe', *Pouvoirs*, 100: 137–52.

*Fischer, J. (2000) 'Vom Staatenbund zur Föderation – Gedanken über die Finalität der europäischen Integration', Joschka Fischer at the Humboldt–University Berlin, 12 May 2000. Online. Availabe HTTP: <http://www.zeit.de/reden/europapolitik /200106_20000512_fischer?page = 1> (accessed July 2007).

Fischer, W. C., Gerber, D. A., Guitart, J. M. and Seller, M. S. (eds) (1997) *Identity, Community and Pluralism in American Life*, New York: Oxford University Press.

Fligstein, N. (2001) *The Architecture of Markets*, Princeton: Princeton University Press.

—— (2008) *Euroclash. The EU, European Identity, and the Future of Europe*, Oxford: Oxford University Press.

Fligstein, N. and McNichol, J. (1998) 'The Institutional Terrain of the European Union', in W. Sandholtz and A. Stone Sweet (eds), *European Integration and Supranational Governance*, Oxford: Oxford University Press: 59–91.

Fligstein, N. and Stone Sweet, A. (2002) 'Constructing Polities and Markets: An Institutionalist Account of European Integration', *American Journal of Sociology*, 107 (5): 1206–43.

Foucault, M. (2007) *Security, Territory, Population. Lectures at the Collège de France 1977–1978*, Houndmills, Basingstoke: Palgrave Macmillan.

—— (2008) *The Birth of Biopolitics. Lectures at the Collège de France 1978–1979*, Houndmills, Basingstoke: Palgrave Macmillan.

Frerichs, S. (2008), *Judicial Governance in der europäischen Rechtsgemeinschaft. Integration durch Recht jenseits des Staates*, Baden-Baden: Nomos.

Fries, S. A. and Shaw, J. (1998) 'Citizenship of the Union: First Steps in the European Court of Justice', *European Public Law*, 4 (4): 533–59.

Funston, R. (1978) *A Vital National Seminar: The Supreme Court in American Political Life*, Palo Alto, CA: Mayfield.

*Gamble, A. (2006) 'The European Disunion', *The British Journal of Politics & International Relations*, 8 (1): 34–49.

Garrett, G. (1992) 'International Cooperation and Institutional Choice: The European Community's Internal Market', *International Organization*, 46 (2): 533–60.

—— (1995) 'The Politics of Legal Integration in the European Union', *International Organization*, 49 (1): 171–81.

Garrett, G., Kelemen, D. R. and Schultz, H. (1998) 'The European Court of Justice, National Governments and Legal Integration in the European Union', *International Organization*, 52 (1): 149–76.

Gehring, T. (1997) 'Governing in Nested Institutions: Environmental Policy in the European Union and the Case of Packaging Waste', *Journal of European Public Policy*, 4 (3): 337–54.

—— (1998) 'Die Politik des koordinierten Alleingangs. Schengen und die Abschaffung der Personalkontrollen an den Binnengrenzen der Europäischen Union', *Zeitschrift für Internationale Beziehungen*, 5 (1): 43–78.

—— (2002) *Die Europäische Union als komplexe internationale Institution. Wie durch Kommunikation und Entscheidung soziale Ordnung entsteht*, Baden-Baden: Nomos.

Gehring, T. and Krapohl, S. (2007) 'Supranational Regulatory Agencies between Independence and Control. The EMEA and the Authorisation of Pharmaceuticals in the European Single Market', *Journal of European Public Policy*, 14 (2): 208–26.

George, S. (1991), *Britain and European Integration since 1945*, Oxford: Blackwell.

—— (1998) 'The Intellectual Debate in Britain on the European Union', *Groupement d'études et des recherches notre Europe*, Research and Policy Paper, 5 October. Online. Available HTTP: <http://www.notre-europe.eu/uploads/tx_publication/Etud5-en_01.pdf> (accessed July 2007).

Gerhards, J. (1993) 'Westeuropäische Integration und die Schwierigkeiten der Entstehung einer europäischen Öffentlichkeit', *Zeitschrift für Soziologie*, 22 (2): 96–110.

—— (2000) 'Europäisierung von Ökonomie und Politik und die Trägheit der Entstehung einer europäischen Öffentlichkeit', in M. Bach (ed.) *Die Europäisierung nationaler Gesellschaften*, Kölner Zeitschrift für Soziologie und Sozialpsychologie, special issue 40, Opladen: Westdeutscher Verlag: 277–305.

Gerhards, J. with the collaboration of Hölscher, M. (2005) *Kulturelle Unterschiede in der Europäischen Union*, Wiesbaden: VS Verlag für Sozialwissenschaften.

Gessner, V. (1994) 'Global Legal Interaction and Legal Cultures', *Ratio Juris*, 7: 132–45.

*Giddens, A. (1984) *The Constitution of Society: Outline of the Theory of Structuration*, Cambridge: Polity Press.

*Glazer, N. (1997) *We are All Multiculturalists Now*, Cambridge, MA: Harvard University Press.

Goldstein, K. M. (1999) *Interest Groups, Lobbying and Participation in America*, Cambridge: Cambridge University Press.

Göler, D. (2002) *Die neue europäische Verfassungsdebatte*, Bonn: Europa Union Verlag.

Goodin, R. E., Headey, B., Muffels, R. and Dirven, H. J. (1999) *The Real Worlds of Welfare Capitalism*, Cambridge: Cambridge University Press.

Gowland, D. A. and Turner, A. (2000) *Reluctant Europeans: Britain and European Integration, 1945–1998*, Harlow/New York: Longman.

*Goyard-Fabre, S. (1991) 'Y a-t-il une crise de la souveraineté?', *Revue internationale de philosophie*, 45 (4): 480–81.

Gramsci, A. (1971) *Selections from the Prison Notebooks*, London: Lawrence & Wishart.

Granger, M-P.F. (2004) 'When Governments go to Luxembourg: The Influence of Governments on the Court of Justice', *European Law Journal*, 10: 3–31.

Greenstein, F. I. (1990) *Leadership in the Modern Presidency*, Cambridge, MA: Harvard University Press.

Greer, S. L. (2006) 'Uninvited Europeanization: Neofunctionalism and the EU in Health Policy', *Journal of European Public Policy*, 13 (1): 134–52.

Griffith, N. D. (2006) 'Déjà-Vu All Over Again: Constitutional Economics and European Legal Integration', *Constitutional Political Economy*, 17 (1): 15–29.

*Grimm, D. (1995) 'Does Europe Need a Constitution?', *European Law Journal*, 1 (3): 282–302.

*—— (2003) 'Die größte Erfindung unserer Zeit', *Frankfurter Allgemeine Zeitung*, 16 June: 35.

—— (2004) 'Auf ewig unverfasst? Europas Weg, juristisch und symbolisch', *Süddeutsche Zeitung*, 7 January: 11.

—— (2005) 'Der Vertrag', *Frankfurter Allgemeine Zeitung*, 12 May: 6.

Guéhenno, J-M. (1995) *The End of the Nation State*, Minneapolis: University of Minnesota Press.

Gunther, G. and Dowling, N. T. (1970) *Cases and Materials on Individual Rights in Constitutional Law*, Mineola, N.Y.: The Foundation Press.

Haas, E. B. (1958) *The Uniting of Europe. Political, Social and Economic Forces, 1950–1957*, Stanford: Stanford University Press.

*Habermas, J. (1992) *Faktizität und Geltung*, Frankfurt a.M: Suhrkamp.

*—— (1996) 'Braucht Europa eine Verfassung? Eine Bemerkung zu Dieter Grimm', in J. Habermas, *Die Einbeziehung des Anderen*, Frankfurt a.M: Suhrkamp, 185–91.

—— (1998) *Die postnationale Konstellation*, Frankfurt a.M: Suhrkamp.

—— (2001) 'Warum braucht Europa eine Verfassung?' Lecture at the eighth *Hamburg Lecture*, 26 June 2001. Online. Availabe HTTP: <http://www.zeit.de/2001/27/ Warum_braucht_Europa_eine_Verfassung_> (accessed July 2007).

—— (2005) 'Nach den Abstimmungs-Debakeln. Europa ist uns über die Köpfe hinweggerollt', *Süddeutsche Zeitung*, 6 June 2005: 15.

Hailbronner, K. (2004) 'Die Unionsbürgerschaft und das Ende rationaler Jurisprudenz', *Neue Juristische Wochenschrift*, 57 (31): 2185–89.

Hall, P. A. and Soskice, D. (2001) *Varieties of Capitalism. Institutional Foundations of Comparative Advantage*, Oxford: Oxford University Press.

Haller, M. (2008) *European Integration as an Elite Process. The Failure of a Dream*, London/New York: Routledge.

*Hamilton, A., Madison, J. and Jay, J. (1787–88/1961) *The Federalist Papers*, Cambridge, MA: Belknap Press.

Hamilton, M. A. and Hamilton, S.F. (1997) *Learning Well at Work: Choices for Quality*, Washington, D.C.: National School-to-Work Office.

*Hänsch, K. (2005) 'Europa in Form bringen – Innenansichten eines beispiellosen konstitutionellen Prozesses', in C. Gaitanides (ed.) *Europa und seine Verfassung*, Baden-Baden: Nomos: 92–108.

Harlow, C. (1995) 'The National Legal Order and the Court of Justice: Some Reflections on the case of the United Kingdom', *Rivista italiana di diritto pubblico comunitario*, V: 929–45.

Harlow, C. and Rawling, R. (1992) *Pressure through Law*, London: Routledge.

*Heathcoat-Amory, D. (2004) 'The European Constitution and what it means for Britain', *Centre for Policy Studies*, May. Online. Available HTTP: <http://www.cps.org.uk/pdf /pub/2.pdf> (accessed June 2006).

Heckscher, C. C. (1988) *The New Unionism. Employee Involvement in the Changing Corporation*, New York: Basic Books.

*Hegel, G. W. F. (1821/1995), 'Grundlinien der Philosophie des Rechts', in E. Moldenhauer and K. M. Michel (eds), *Werke in 20 Bänden, vol. 7.* Frankfurt a.M: Suhrkamp.

Heidenreich, M. (2003) 'Territoriale Ungleichheiten in der erweiterten EU', *Kölner Zeitschrift für Soziologie und Sozialpsychologie* 55: 1–28.

Héritier, A. (2003) 'New Modes of Governance in Europe: Increasing Political Capacity and Policy Effectiveness', in T.A. Börzel and R.A. Chichowski (eds), *The State of the European Union*, vol. 6, *Law, Politics, and Society*, Oxford: Oxford University Press: 105–26.

Hirsch, G. (2001) 'Nizza. Ende einer Etappe oder Beginn einer Epoche?', *Neue Juristische Wochenschrift*, 54 (37): 2677–78.

Höland, A. (1993) 'Die Rechtssoziologie und der unbekannte Kontinent Europa', *Zeitschrift für Rechtssoziologie*, 14 (2): 177–89.

*Holmes, M. (2000) 'The Single Currency: Evaluating Europe's Monetary Experiment', in V. N. Koutrakou and L. A. Emerson (eds), *The European Union and Britain*, Basingstoke: Macmillan, 180–89.

Hooghe, L. and Marks, G. (2001) *Multilevel Governance and European Integration*, Lanham: Rowman & Littlefield.

Höpner, M. (2008) 'Usurpation statt Delegation. Wie der EuGH die Binnenmarktintegration radikalisiert und warum er politischer Kontrolle bedarf', MPIfG Discussion Paper 08/12.

Hoskyns, C. (1996) *Integrating Gender: Women, Law, and Politics in the European Union*, London: Verso.

Hounshell, D. A. (1984) *From the American System to Mass Production, 1800–1932: The Development of Manufacturing Technology in the United States*, Baltimore, MD: Johns Hopkins University Press.

Hurrelmann, A. (2005) *Verfassung und Integration in Europa – Wege zu einer supra-nationalen Demokratie*, Frankfurt/New York: Campus.

Hurrelmann, A., Leibfried, S., Martens, K. and Mayer, P.(eds) (2007) *Transforming the Golden Age Nation State*, Basingstoke: Palgrave.

Jachtenfuchs, M. (2001) 'The Governance Approach to European Integration', *Journal of Common Market Studies* 39 (2): 245–64.

—— (2002) *Die Konstruktion Europas. Verfassungsideen und institutionelle Entwicklung*, Baden-Baden: Nomos.

Jacqueson, C. (2002) 'Union Citizenship and the Court of Justice: Something New under the Sun?', *European Law Review*, 27 (6): 260–81.

Jaeckel, L. (2003) 'The Duty to Protect Fundamental Rights in the European Community', *European Law Review*, 28 (8): 508–27.

Jauß, C. (1999) *Politik als Verhandlungsmarathon. Immissionsschutz in der amerikanischen Wettbewerbsdemokratie*, Baden-Baden: Nomos.

*Jellinek, G. (1900/1966) *Allgemeine Staatslehre*, Bad Homburg v.d.H.: Gehlen.

Joerges, C. (1991) 'Markt ohne Staat? Die Wirtschaftsverfassung der Gemeinschaft und die regulative Politik', in R. Wildenmann (ed.), *Staatswerdung Europas? Optionen für eine Europäische Union*, Baden-Baden: Nomos: 225–68.

—— (1993) 'European Economic Law, the Nation-State and the Maastricht Treaty', in R. Dehousse (ed.) *Europe after Maastricht: An Ever Closer Union*, Munich: C.H. Beck: 29–62.

—— (2003), 'The Challenges of Europeanization in the Realm of Private Law: A Plea for a New Legal Discipline', *Duke Journal of Comparative and International Law* 24: 149–96.

Joerges, C. and Neyer, J. (1997) 'From Intergovernmental Bargaining to Deliberative Political Processes: The Constitutionalisation of Comitology', *European Law Journal*: 3 (3): 272–99.

—— (2006) 'Deliberative Supranationalism Revisited', *EUI Working Paper-LAW* 2006/20.

Joerges, C. and Vos, E. (eds) (1999) *EU-Committees: Social Regulation, Law and Politics*, Oxford: Hart.

Johannson, R. W. (ed.) (1965) *The Lincoln-Douglas Debates of 1858*, New York: Oxford University Press.

*Johnson, N. (2000) *Can self-government survive? Britain and the European Union*, London: Centre for Policy Studies.

Joliet, R. (1995) 'The Free Circulation of Goods: The Keck and Mithouard Decision and the New Directions in the Case Law', *Columbia Journal of European Law*, 1 (3): 437–51.

Joppke, C. (1999) *Immigration and the Nation State. The United States, Germany and Great Britain*, Oxford: Oxford University Press.

*Kant, I. (1793/1964) 'Zum ewigen Frieden', in I. Kant, *Werke in sechs Bänden*, vol. VI, ed. by Wilhelm Weischedel. Frankfurt a.M: Insel Verlag: 195–251.

*—— (1797/1968) 'Die Metaphysik der Sitten' in I. Kant, *Werke in 12 Bänden*, ed. by Wilhelm Weischedel, Frankfurt a.M: Insel-Verlag.

Kelemen, R. D. (2003) 'The EU Rights Revolution: Adversarial Legalism and European Integration', in T. A. Börzel and R. A. Cichowski (eds), *The State of the European Union*, vol. 6: *Law, Politics, and Society*, Oxford/New York: Oxford University Press: 221–34.

*von Kielmansegg, P. G. (1996) 'Integration und Demokratie', in M. Jachtenfuchs and B. Kohler-Koch (eds), *Europäische Integration*, Opladen: Leske + Budrich: 47–71.

*Kirchhof, P. (1994) 'Kompetenzaufteilung zwischen den Mitgliedstaaten und der EU', in Vertretung der Kommission in der Bundesrepublik Deutschland (ed.) *Europäische Gespräche. Die künftige Verfassungsordnung der EU*, Bonn: 59.

Kleger, H., Karolewski, I. and Munke, M. (2001) *Europäische Verfassung. Zum Stand der europäischen Demokratie im Zuge der Osterweiterung*, Münster: LIT.

Knill, C. (1995) *Staatlichkeit im Wandel. Großbritannien im Spannungsfeld innenpolitischer Reformen und europäischer Integration*, Wiesbaden: Deutscher Universitätsverlag.

Koenig, M. (2005) 'Weltgesellschaft, Menschenrechte und der Formwandel des Nationalstaats', in B. Heintz, R. Münch and H. Tyrell (eds), *Weltgesellschaft. Theoretische Perspektiven und empirische Problemlagen, Sonderheft der Zeitschrift für Soziologie*, Stuttgart: Lucius & Lucius: 374–93.

—— (2007) 'Europäisierung von Religionspolitik – zur institutionellen Umwelt von Anerkennungskämpfen muslimischer Migranten', *Soziale Welt*, Sonderheft Islam: 345–67.

Kohler-Koch, B. (ed.) (1998) *Regieren in entgrenzten Räumen*, Politische Vierteljahresschrift, special issue 29, Opladen: Westdeutscher Verlag.

—— (2000) 'Framing the Bottleneck of Constructing Legitimate Institutions', *Journal of European Public Policy* 7 (4): 513–31.

Kohli, M. (2000) 'The Battlegrounds of European Identity', *European Societies*, 2 (2): 113–37.

Kotzian, P. (2003) *Verhandlungen im europäischen Arzneimittelsektor. Initiierung – Institutionalisierung – Ergebnisse*, Baden-Baden: Nomos.

Krapohl, S. (2004) 'Credible Commitment in Non-Independent Regulatory Agencies: A Comparative Analysis of the European Agencies for Pharmaceuticals and Foodstuffs', *European Law Journal* 10 (5): 518–38.

—— (2007) 'Thalidomide, BSE and the Single Market: A Historical-Institutionalist Approach to Regulatory Regimes in the European Union', *European Journal of Political Research* 46 (1): 25–46.

Krislov, S., Ehlermann, C-D. and Weiler, J. (1985) 'Community Policy-Making and Implementation-Process', in M. Cappelletti, M. Seccombe and J. Weiler (eds), *Integration Through Law. Europe and the American Federal Experience*, Berlin/New York: Walter de Gruyter: 3–110.

Kumar, K. (2003) 'Britain, England and Europe. Cultures in Contraflow', *European Journal of Social Theory*, 6 (1): 5–23.

Kumm, M. (1999) 'Who is the final Arbiter of Constitutionality in Europe?', *Common Market Law Review*, 36: 251–72.

Kurzer, P. (2001) *Markets and Moral Regulation. Cultural Change in the European Union*, Cambridge: Cambridge University Press.

Laclau, E. and Mouffe, C. (2001) *Hegemony and Socialist Strategy. Towards a Radical Democratic Politics*, London: Verso.

Lahusen, C. and Jauß, C. (2001) *Lobbying als Beruf: Interessengruppen in der Europäischen Union*, Baden-Baden: Nomos.

*Landfried, C. (2004) 'Das Entstehen einer europäischen Öffentlichkeit', in C. Franzius and U. K. Preuß (eds) *Europäische Öffentlichkeit*, Baden-Baden: Nomos: 123–39.

Leggewie, C. (2000) *Amerikas Welt. Die USA in unseren Köpfen*, Hamburg: Hoffmann und Campe.

Leibfried, S. and Zürn, M. (eds) (2006) *Transformationen des Staates?* Frankfurt a.M: Suhrkamp.

*Leinen, J. (2001) 'Eine europäische Verfassung – Grundlagen einer föderalen und demokratischen Verfassung', in H. Timmermann (ed.), *Eine Verfassung für die Europäische Union. Beiträge zu einer grundsätzlichen und aktuellen Diskussion*, Opladen: Leske + Budrich: 64–74.

Lemke, T. (1997) *Eine Kritik der politischen Vernunft. Foucaults Analyse der modernen Gouvernementalität*, Berlin: Argument Verlag.

*Leonard, M. (1999) *Network Europe: The New Case for Europe*, London: The Foreign Policy Centre.

Lepsius, M. R. (1991) 'Nationalstaat oder Nationalitätenstaat als Modell für die Weiterentwicklung der Europäischen Gemeinschaft?', in R. Wildenmann (ed.), *Staatswerdung Europas? Optionen für eine Europäische Union*, Baden-Baden: Nomos Verlagsgesellschaft: 19–40.

Leuchtenburg, W. E. (1963) *Franklin D. Roosevelt and the New Deal*, New York: Harper & Row.

*Levy, B. H. (1987) *Eloge des intellectuels*, Paris: Biblio essais, le livre de poche.

Liebert, U. (2005) 'Der Verfassungsvertrag. Ein Fortschritt für die demokratische Legitimität in der Europäischen Union?', in M. Jopp and S. Matl (ed.), *Der Vertrag über eine Verfassung für Europa. Analysen zur Konstitutionalisierung der EU*, Baden-Baden: Nomos: 383–410.

Lipset, S. M. (1979) *The First New Nation*, New York/London: Norton.

—— (1996) *American Exceptionalism. A Double-Edged Sword*, New York/London: Norton.

Lipset, S. M. and Marks, G. (2000) *It Didn't Happen Here. Why Socialism Failed in the United States*, New York/London: Norton.

*Locke, J. (1690/1963) 'Two Treaties on Government', in *The Works*, 20 vols. Aalen: Scientia.

Lofgren, C. A. (1987) *The Plessy Case: A Legal-Historical Interpretation*, New York: Oxford University Press.

Luhmann, N. (1983) *Legitimation durch Verfahren*, Frankfurt a.M: Suhrkamp.

*MacCormick, N. (1999) *Questioning Sovereignty*, Oxford: Oxford University Press.

McDonald, F. (1985) *Novus Ordo Seclorum: The Intellectual Origins of the Constitution*, Lawrence: University Press of Kansas.

McKay, D. (1999) *Federalism and European Union. A Political Economy Perspective*, Oxford: Oxford University Press.

Maduro, M. P. (1998) *We, the Court. The European Court of Justice and the European Economic Constitution*, Oxford: Oxford University Press.

Majone, G. (1996) *Regulating Europe*, London: Routledge.

—— (2001) 'Two Logics of Delegation. Agency and Fiduciary Relations in EU Governance', *European Union Politics* 2 (1): 103–22.

—— (2005) *Dilemmas of European Integration: The Ambiguities and Pitfalls of Integration by Stealth*, Oxford: Oxford University Press.

Mancini G. F. and Keeling, D. T. (1991) 'From CILFIT to ERT: the Constitutional Challenge Facing the European Court', *Yearbook of European Law*, 11: 1–13.

—— (1995) 'Language, Culture and Politics in the Life of the European Court of Justice', *Columbia Journal of European Law*, 1 (3): 397–413.

van Marrewijk, C. (2002) *International Trade and the World Economy*, Oxford: Oxford University Press.

Marshall, T. H. (1964/1976) *Class, Citizenship, and Social Development*, Westport, CT: Greenwood Press.

Mattli, W. (1999) *The Logic of Regional Integration. Europe and Beyond*, Cambridge: Cambridge University Press.

Mattli, W. and Slaughter, A-M. (1995) 'Law and Politics in The European Union: A Reply to Garrett', *International Organization*, 49 (1): 183–90.

Meyer, J. W., Boli, J., Thomas, G.M. and Ramirez, F. O. (1997) 'World Society and the Nation State', *American Journal of Sociology* 103: 144–81.

Meyer, T. (2004) *Die Identität Europas: der EU eine Seele?*, Frankfurt a.M: Suhrkamp.

*Michelman, F. I. (1988) 'Law's Republic', *The Yale Law Journal*, 97 (8): 1493–1537.

*—— (1989), 'Conceptions of Democracy in American Constitutional Argument: Voting Rights', *Florida Law Review* 41 (3): 443–90.

Micklitz, H-W. (2005) *The Politics of Judicial Co-operation in the EU*, Cambridge: Cambridge University Press.

Miller, P. and Rose, N. (2008) *Governing the Present. Administering Economic, Social and Personal Life*, Cambridge: Polity Press.

*Minc, A. (1997) *La mondialisation heureuse*, Paris: Plon.

Moravcsik, A. (1991) 'Negotiating the Single European Act: National Interests and Conventional Statecraft in the European Community', *International Organization*, 45 (1): 19–56.

—— (1993) 'Preferences and Power in the European Community: A Liberal Intergovernmental Approach', *Journal of Common Market Studies*, 31 (4): 473–524.

—— (1998) *The Choice for Europe: Social Purpose and State Power from Messina to Maastricht*, Ithaca, NY: Cornell University Press.

—— (1999), 'Liberal Intergovernmentalism and Integration: A Rejoinder', *Journal of Common Market Studies* 33 (4): 611–28.

*Morin, E. (1987) *Penser l'Europe*, Paris: Gallimard.

Müller, H-P. (2007) 'Auf dem Weg in eine europäische Gesellschaft? Begriffsproblematik und theoretische Perspektiven', *Berliner Journal für Soziologie* 17 (1): 7–31.

Müller, W., Steinmann, S. and Schneider, R. (1997) 'Bildung in Europa', in S. Hradil and S. Immerfall (eds), *Die westeuropäischen Gesellschaften im Vergleich*, Opladen: Leske + Budrich: 177–245.

Münch, R. (1992) 'The Law as a Medium of Communication', *Cardozo Law Review* 13 (5): 1655–80.

——. (1986/1993a), *Die Kultur der Moderne*, 2 vols, Frankfurt a. M.: Suhrkamp.

—— (1993b) *Das Projekt Europa*, Frankfurt a.M: Suhrkamp.

—— (1998) *Globale Dynamik, lokale Lebenswelten*, Frankfurt a.M: Suhrkamp.

—— (2001a) *The Ethics of Modernity*, Lanham, MD: Rowman and Littlefield.

—— (2001b) *Nation and Citizenship in the Global Age*, Basingstoke: Palgrave.

—— (2008) *Die Konstruktion der europäischen Gesellschaft. Zur Dialektik von transnationaler Integration und nationaler Desintegration.* Frankfurt/New York: Campus.

Münch, R., Lahusen, C., Kurth, M., Borgards, C., Stark, C. and Jauß, C. (2001) *Democracy at Work: A Comparative Sociology of Environmental Regulation in the United Kingdom, France, Germany and The United States*, Westport, London: Praeger.

Neustadt, R. E. (1990) *Presidential Power and the Modern Presidents*, New York: Free Press.

Neyer, J. (2000) 'Justifying Comitology: The Promise of Deliberation', in K. Neunreither and A. Wiener (eds), *European Integration After Amsterdam*, Oxford: Oxford University Press: 112–28.

Nissen, S. (2006) 'European Identity and the Future of Europe', in M. Bach, C. Lahusen and G. Vobruba (eds), *Europe in Motion. Social Dynamics and Political Institutions in an Enlarging Europe*, Berlin: sigma: 155–74.

O'Leary, S. (1996) *The Evolving Concept of Community Citizenship*, The Hague: Kluwer International.

Offe, C. (2001) 'Gibt es eine europäische Gesellschaft? Kann es sie geben?', *Blätter für deutsche und internationale Politik*, 46 (4): 423–35.

—— (2003) *Herausforderungen der Demokratie*, Frankfurt/New York: Campus.

Ory, P. and Sirinelli, J-F. (1986/1992) *Les intellectuels en France, une histoire*, Paris: Armand Colin.

Outhwaite, W. (2008) *European Society*, Cambridge: Polity.

Padoa-Schioppa, T., Emerson, M., King, M., Milleron, J-C., Paelink, J., Papademos, L., Pastor, A., and Scharpf, F. (1988) *Effizienz, Stabilität und Verteilungsgerechtigkeit. Eine Entwicklungsstrategie für das Wirtschaftssystem der Europäischen Gemeinschaft*, Wiesbaden: Gabler.

Pangle, T. L. (1988) *The Spirit of Modern Republicanism: The Moral Vision of the American Founders and the Philosophy of Locke*, Chicago: University of Chicago Press.

Parekh, B. (2000) 'Defining British National Identity', *The Political Quarterly*, 71 (1): 4–14.

Parish, P. (1975) *The American Civil War*, London: Methuen.

Parsons, T. and White, W. (1964) 'The Link between Character and Society', in T. Parsons (ed.), *Social Structure and Personality*, New York: Free Press: 183–235.

Pernice, I. (2001) 'Europäisches und nationales Verfassungsrecht', *Report VVDStRL* 60/2001: 148–93.

Peters, A. (2001) *Elemente einer Theorie der Verfassung Europas*, Berlin: Duncker und Humblot.

*Pflüger, F. (2000) 'Fischers Europa – Für den Pragmatismus der Vetragsmechaniker', *Blätter für deutsche und internationale Politik*, 45 (8): 954–60.

Pierson, P. (1996) 'The Path to European Integration: A Historical Institutionalist Analysis', *Comparative Political Studies*, 29 (2): 123–63.

*Pilkington, C. (1995) *Britain in the European Union Today*, Manchester: Manchester University Press.

Pocock, J. and Greville, A. (1975) *The Machiavellian Moment. Florentine Political Thought und the Atlantic Republican Tradition. Princeton*, N.J.: Princeton University Press.

Polanyi, K. (1944) *The Great Transformation. The political and economic origins of our time*, Boston: Beacon Press.

Pollack, M. A. (2003) *The Engines of European Integration: Delegation, Agency, and Agenda Setting in the EU*, Oxford: Oxford University Press.

Power, M. (1997) *The Audit Society: Rituals of Verification*, Oxford: Oxford University Press.

*Preuß, U. K. (1999) 'Auf der Suche nach Europas Verfassung', *Transit – Europäische Revue*, 17 (19): 154–99.

Quermonne, J-L. (1994) *Les régimes politiques occidentaux*, 3. ed., Paris: Seuil.

*Rand, J. (2000) 'British Identity and European Integration', in V.N. Koutrakou and L.A. Emerson (eds), *The European Union and Britain*, Basingstoke: Macmillan: 24–43.

Rasmussen, H. (1984) 'The European Court's Acte Clair Strategy in CILFIT', *European Law Review*, 9: 242–59.

—— (1998) *The European Court of Justice*, Copenhagen: Gad Jura.

Rawls, J. (1972) *A Theory of Justice*, Oxford: Clarendon Press.

Reich, N. (1999) *Bürgerrechte in der Europäischen Union*, Baden-Baden: Nomos: 212–32.

—— (2003) *Understanding EU Law: Objectives, Principles and Methods of Community Law*, Antwerp: Intersentia.

Reich, R. B. (1991), *The Work of Nations*, New York: Alfred A. Knopf.

*Renan, E. (1947) 'Qu'est-ce qu'une nation? Conférence faite en Sorbonne, le 11 Mars 1882', in E. Renan *Oeuvres complètes*, vol. 1, Paris: Calmann-Levy: 887–906.

Ricardo, D. (1817/1977) *On the Principles of Political Economy and Taxation*, Hildesheim: Olms.

Risse, T. (2000) 'Nationalism and Collective Identities: Europe versus the Nation-State?', in P. Heywood, E. Jones and M. Rhoades (eds), *Developments in West European Politics*, Basingstoke: Palgrave.

—— (2004) 'Auf dem Weg zu einer europäischen Kommunikationsgemeinschaft: Theoretische Überlegungen und empirische Evidenz', in C. Franzius and U. K. Preuß (eds), *Europäische Öffentlichkeit*, Baden-Baden: Nomos: 139–53.

Robertson, G. (1993) *Freedom, the Individual and the Law*, Harmondsworth: Penguin Books.

Rosamond, B. (2000) *Theories of European Integration*, Basingstoke: Palgrave.

Rose, N. (1999) *Powers of Freedom. Reframing Political Thought*, Cambridge: Cambridge University Press.

*Rousseau, J.-J. (1762/1964) 'Du contrat social', in B. Gagnebin and M. Raymond (eds), *Œuvres complète*, vol. III, Paris: Gallimard.

Rueschemeyer, D. (1982) 'On Durkheim's Explanation of Division of Labor', *American Journal of Sociology* 88: 579–89.

Sacco, R. (2003) 'Concepts juridiques et création du droit communautaire par le juge', in R. Schule and U. Seif (eds), *Richterrecht und Rechtsfortbildung in der Europäischen Rechtsgemeinschaft*, Tübingen: Mohr Siebeck: 81–88.

*Sadoun, M. (2002) 'République et Démocratie', *Pouvoirs*, 100: 5–19.

Sandholtz, W. and Stone Sweet, A. (eds) (1998) *European Integration and Supranational Governance*, Oxford: Oxford University Press.

*Sapir, J. (2006) *La fin de l'eurolibéralisme*, Paris: Seuil.

Schäfer, A. (2005) *Die neue Unverbindlichkeit. Wirtschaftspolitische Koordinierung in Europa*, Frankfurt/New York: Campus.

Scharpf, F. W. (1990) 'Regionalisierung des europäischen Raums. Die Zukunft der Bundesländer im Spannungsfeld zwischen EG, Bund und Kommunen', in U. von Aleman, R. G. Heinze and B. Hombach (eds). *Die Kraft der Region: Nordrhein-Westfalen in Europa*. Bonn: Verlag J. H. W. Dietz Nachf: 32–46.

—— (1996) 'Negative and Positive Integration in the Political Economy of European Welfare States', in G. Marks, F. W. Scharpf, P. C. Schmitter and W. Streeck (eds) *Governance in the European Union*, London: Sage: 15–39.

*—— (1998) 'Jenseits der Regime-Debatte: Ökonomische Integration, Demokratie und Wohlfahrtsstaat in Europa', in S. Lessenich and I. Ostner (eds), *Welten des Wohlfahrtskapitalismus. Der Sozialstaat in vergleichender Perspektive*, Frankfurt/New York: Campus: 321–49.

—— (1999) *Governing in Europe. Effective and Democratic?* Oxford: Oxford University Press.

—— (2003) 'Was man von einer europäischen Verfassung erwarten sollte und was nicht', *Blätter für deutsche und internationale Politik*, 48 (1): 49–59.

—— (2009) 'Legitimacy in the Multilevel European Polity', *MPIfG Working Paper 09/1*.

Schepel, H. and Wesseling, R. (1997) 'The Legal Community: Judges, Lawyers, Officials and Clerks in the Writing of Europe', *European Law Journal*, 3 (2): 165–88.

*Schlesinger, A. M. (1992) *The Disuniting of America: Reflections on a Multicultural Society*, New York: Norton.

*Schmidt, A. J. (1997) *The Menace of Multiculturalism: Trojan Horse in America*, Westport, CT: Praeger.

*Schnapper, D. (1994) *La communauté des citoyens: sur l'idée moderne de nation*, Paris: Gallimard.

Schneider, V. (1985) 'Coporatist and Pluralist Patterns of Policy-Making for Chemicals Control: A Comparison between West Germany and the USA', in A. Cawson (ed.), *Organized Interests and the State*, London: Sage: 174–91.

Schwarze, J. (ed.), (1999) *Werbung und Werbeverbote im Lichte des europäischen Gemeinschaftsrechts*, Baden-Baden: Nomos.

Sciarra, S. (2001) 'Integration Through Courts: Article 177 as a Pre-Federal Device', in S. Sciarra (ed.), *Labour Law in the Courts: National Judges and the European Court of Justice*, Oxford: Hart Publishing.

Shapiro, M. (2001), 'The Institutionalization of European Administrative Space', in A. Stone Sweet, W. Sandholtz and N. Fligstein (eds), *The Institutionalization of Europe*, Oxford: Oxford University Press: 94–112.

—— (1992), 'The European Court of Justice', in A.M. Sbragia (ed.), *Euro-Politics. Institutions and Policymaking in the 'New' European Community*, Washington D.C.: Brookings Institution: 123–56.

*Sharpe, L. J. (1996) 'British Scepticism and the European Union: A Guide for Foreigners', in M. Holmes (ed.), *The Eurosceptical Reader*, London: Macmillan: 303–22.

Shklar, J. N. (1991) *American Citizenship: The Quest for Inclusion*, Cambridge: Harvard University Press.

Shuibhne, N. N. (2002) 'The Free Movement of Goods and Article 28 EC: An Evolving Framework', *European Law Review*, 27 (8): 408–44.

Sigelschiffer, S. (1973) *The American Conscience. The Drama of the Lincoln-Douglas Debates*, New York: Horizon.

Skocpol, T. (1992) *Protecting Soldiers and Mothers: The Political Origins of Social Policy in the United States*, Cambridge: Harvard University Press.

Slaughter, A.-M., Stone Sweet, A. and Weiler, J. H. H. (eds) (1998) *The European Court and National Courts – Doctrine and Jurisprudence: Legal Change in its Social Context*, Oxford: Hart Publishing.

Smelser, N. J. and Alexander, J. C. (eds) (1999) *Diversity and Its Discontents. Cultural Conflict and Common Ground in Contemporary American Society*, Princeton: Princeton University Press.

*Smith, A. (1776/1952) *An Inquiry into the Nature and Causes of the Wealth of Nations*, Chicago: University of Chicago Great Books.

*Smith, A. D. (1999) *Myths and Memories of the Nation*, Oxford: Oxford University Press.

Snyder, F. (1993) 'The Effectiveness of European Community Law: Institutions, Processes, Tools and Techniques', *Modern Law Review* 56 (1): 19–54.

*Soin, R. (2005) *L'Europe politique*, Paris: Armand Colin.

Sombart, W. (1906) *Warum gibt es in den Vereinigten Staaten keinen Sozialismus?* Tübingen: Mohr.

Stone Sweet, A. (2000) *Governing with Judges. Constitutional Politics in Europe*, Oxford: Oxford University Press.

—— (2004) *The Judicial Construction of Europe*, Oxford: Oxford University Press.

Stone Sweet, A. and Caporaso, J. A. (1998). 'From Free Trade to Supranational Polity: The European Court and Integration', in W. Sandtholtz and A. Stone Sweet (eds),

European Integration and Supranational Governance, Oxford: Oxford University Press: 92–133.

Stone Sweet, A., Sandholtz, W. and Fligstein, N. (eds) (2001) *The Institutionalisation of Europe*, Oxford: Oxford University Press.

Streeck, W. (1999) *Korporatismus in Deutschland*, Frankfurt/New York: Campus.

Streeck, W. and Höpner, M. (eds) (2003) *Alle Macht dem Markt? Fallstudien zur Abwicklung der Deutschland AG*, Frankfurt/New York: Campus.

Stuchtey, B. (2006) 'Sartre und ein warmes Bier', *Süddeutsche Zeitung*, 12 July: 14.

Sunstein, C. R. (1985) 'Interest Groups in American Public Law', *Stanford Law Review*, 38 (1): 29–87.

—— (1990), *After the Rights Revolution. Reconceiving the Regulatory State*, Cambridge, Mass.: Harvard University Press.

Swedberg, R. (1994), 'The Idea of 'Europe' and the Origin of the European Union – A Sociological Approach', *Zeitschrift für Soziologie* 23 (5): 378–87.

Theodossiou, M. A. (2002) 'An Analysis of the Recent Response of the Community to Non-Compliance with Court of Justice Judgements: Article 228 (2) E.C.', *European Law Review*, 27 (1): 25–46.

Therborn, G. (1995) *European Modernity and Beyond: The Trajectory of European Societies 1945–2000*, London: Sage.

De Tocqueville, A. (1945) *Democracy in America*, 2 vols, New York: Alfred A. Knopf.

Tömmel, I. (2000) 'Jenseits von regulativ und distributiv: Policy-Making der EU und die Transformation von Staatlichkeit', in E. Grande and M. Jachtenfuchs (eds), *Wie problemlösungsfähig ist die EU? Regieren im europäischen Mehrebenensystem*, Baden-Baden: Nomos: 165–87.

Trenz, H.-J. (2005) *Europa in den Medien*, Frankfurt/New York: Campus.

Tsebelis, G. (2002) *Veto Players. How Political Institutions Work*, Princeton, N.J.: Princeton University Press.

Tsebelis, G. and Garrett, G. (2001) 'The Institutional Foundations of Intergovernmentalism and Supranationalism in the European Union', *International Organization*, 55 (2): 357–90.

*Védrine H. (2005) 'Pour l'Europe: repartir du réel', *Le débat*, 136, September–October, Paris: Gallimard.

Vesterdorf, B. (2003) 'The Community Court System ten Years from now and beyond: Challenges and Possibilities', *European Law Review*, 28 (3): 303–23.

Vobruba, G. (2005) *Die Dynamik Europas*, Wiesbaden: VS Verlag für Sozialwissenschaften.

*Wade, W. (1996) 'Sovereignty – Revolution or Evolution?', *Law Quarterly Review*, 112: 568–75.

*Wallace, H. (1985) *Europe: The Challenge of Diversity. The Royal Institute of International Affairs*, London: Routledge and Kegan Paul.

Weatherill, S.(1996) 'After Keck: Some Thoughts on How to Clarify the Clarification', *Common Market Law Review*, 33 (5): 886–906.

Weatherill, S. and Micklitz, H.-W. (1997) *European Economic Law*, Dartmouth: Ashgate.

Weber, M. (1922/1972) *Wirtschaft und Gesellschaft*, Tübingen: Mohr Siebeck.

Weiler, J. H. H. (1999) *The Constitution of Europe*, Cambridge: Cambridge University Press.

Weir, S. and Beetham, D. (1999) *Political Power and Democratic Control in Britain*, London: Routledge.

Weiss, F. and Wooldridge, F. (2002) *Free Movement of Persons within the European Community*, Boston: Kluwer Law International.

Wiener, A. (1998) *European Citizenship Practice – Building Institutions of a Non-State*, Oxford: Westview Press.

Wiener, A. and Diez, T. (eds) (2004) *European Integration Theory*, Oxford: Oxford University Press.

Wilson, W. J. (1990) *The Truly Disadvantaged. The Inner City, the Underclass, and Public Policy*, Chicago, Ill.: University of Chicago Press.

Wincott, D. (2000) 'A Community of Law? 'European' Law and Judicial Politics: The Court of Justice and Beyond', *Government & Opposition*, 35 (1): 3–27.

Wind, M. (2001) *Sovereignty and European Integration: Towards a Post-Hobbesian Order*, Basingstoke: Palgrave.

Windolf, P. (2000) 'Wer ist Schiedsrichter in der Europäischen Union?', in M. Bach (ed.), *Die Europäisierung nationaler Gesellschaften*, Kölner Zeitschrift für Soziologie und Sozialpsychologie, special issue 40, Wiesbaden: Westdeutscher Verlag: 39–67.

Wobbe, T. (2003), 'From Protecting to Promoting: Evolving EU Sex Equality Norms in an Organizational Field', *European Law Journal* 9: 88–108.

Wolf, R. (1991) 'Zur Antiquiertheit des Rechts in der Risikogesellschaft', in U. Beck (ed.), *Politik in der Risikogesellschaft*, Frankfurt a.M: Suhrkamp: 378–423.

Wright, J. S. (1970) *Lincoln and the Politics of Slavery*, Reno, NE: University of Nevada Press.

Wright, T. (2000) *The British Political Process*, London: Routledge.

*Young, I. M. (1990) *Justice and the Politics of Difference*, Princeton: Princeton University Press.

Zuleeg, M. (1995) 'Der rechtliche Zusammenhalt der Europäischen Gemeinschaft', in W. Blomeyer and K. A. Schachtschneider (eds), *Die Europäische Union als Rechtsgemeinschaft*, Berlin: Duncker und Humblot: 9–36.

Index